Shopping for Meaningful Lives

Shopping for Meaningful Lives

The Religious Motive of Consumerism

BRUCE P. RITTENHOUSE

CASCADE *Books* • Eugene, Oregon

SHOPPING FOR MEANINGFUL LIVES
The Religious Motive of Consumerism

Copyright © 2013 Bruce P. Rittenhouse. All rights reserved. Except for brief quotations in critical publications or reviews, no part of this book may be reproduced in any manner without prior written permission from the publisher. Write: Permissions, Wipf and Stock Publishers, 199 W. 8th Ave., Suite 3, Eugene, OR 97401.

Cascade Books
An Imprint of Wipf and Stock Publishers
199 W. 8th Ave., Suite 3
Eugene, OR 97401

www.wipfandstock.com

ISBN 13: 978-1-62032-114-0

Cataloging-in-Publication data:

Rittenhouse, Bruce P.

Shopping for meaningful lives : the religious motive of consumerism / Bruce P. Rittenhouse.

xii + 212 pp. ; 23 cm. Includes bibliographical references and index.

ISBN 13: 978-1-62032-114-0

1. Consumption (Economics)—Religious aspects—Christianity. 2. Christianity and culture. I. Title.

BR115.C67 R10 2013

Manufactured in the U.S.A.

The Scripture quotations contained herein are from the New Revised Standard Version Bible, copyright © 1989 by the Division of Christian Education of the National Council of the Churches of Christ in the U.S.A., and are used by permission. All rights reserved.

Soli Deo gloria.

Contents

List of Figures / ix

Acknowledgments / xi

Abbreviations / xii

1. Introduction / 1
2. The Religious Significance of Recent Developments in Western Culture / 17
3. Types of Consumerism Theories / 47
4. An Empirical Evaluation of Current Consumerism Theories / 92
5. The Religious Motive of Consumerism and How It May Be Redirected / 132
6. Conclusion / 172

APPENDIX 1: Regression model for U.S. real annual household housing expenditures, 1984–2006 / 179

APPENDIX 2: Regression models for U.S. real annual household housing expenses, 1984–2006, for a) households without minor children, and b) households with minor children / 181

APPENDIX 3: Regression models for U.S. real annual household housing expenses, 1984–2006, for a) bottom household income quintile, b) second household income quintile, c) middle household income quintile, d) fourth household income quintile, and e) top household income quintile / 184

Bibliography / 191

Index / 203

Figures

Figure 1:   U.S. labor force participation rate, 1948–2007   /   98

Figure 2:   U.S. employment by full- or part-time classifications, 1956–2007   /   99

Figure 3:   U.S. real family income by income percentile, 1948–2006   /   100

Figure 4:   U.S. personal savings rate vs. real per capita disposable personal income, 1952–2007   /   101

Figure 5:   U.S. real total household debt by income quintile, 1989–2004   /   104

Figure 6:   U.S. real total household debt for upper-income households, 1989–2004   /   104

Figure 7:   U.S. household debt-to-income ratio by income quintile, 1989–2004   /   105

Figure 8:   U.S. household debt-to-income ratio for upper-income households, 1989–2004   /   106

Figure 9:   U.S. household debt-to-assets ratio by income quintile, 1989–2004   /   107

Figure 10:   U.S. household debt-to-assets ratio for upper-income households, 1989–2004   /   107

Figure 11:   U.S. real total household assets by income quintile, 1989–2004   /   108

Figure 12:   U.S. real total household assets for upper-income households, 1989–2004   /   109

Figure 13:   U.S. real per capita personal consumption expenditures, 1945–2007   /   111

Figures

Figure 14: U.S. subjective happiness in the non-institutionalized English-speaking population age eighteen and older, 1972–2006 / 112

Figure 15: U.S. real annual household housing expenses by household type, 1984–2006 / 126

Figure 16: U.S. real annual household housing expenditures by household income quintile, 1984–2006 / 128

Figure 17: U.S. real household mortgage and home equity loan debt by income quintile, 1989–2004 / 129

Figure 18: U.S. real household mortgage and home equity loan debt for upper-income households, 1989–2004 / 130

Acknowledgments

I would like to thank those who took the time to read early manuscripts of this work and give me detailed critiques: Jean Bethke Elshtain, Robert Frank, Eric Grush, Robert Nelson, Michael Palmer, Steve Prodanich, and especially William Schweiker. Their feedback helped me to sharpen my arguments, to make them accessible to a broader audience, and to realize the full potential of this project. I am also grateful to a number of colleagues who offered me feedback on early draft chapters. These include Elizabeth Sweeny Block, Joe Blosser, Elizabeth Bucar, Aimee Burant Chor, David Clairmont, Josh Daniel, Sandra Sullivan Dunbar, Courtney Fitzsimmons, Hillel Gray, Joel Harter, Michael Hogue, Michael Johnson, Peder Jothen, Jung Lee, Santiago Piñon, Daniel Shin, Joyce Shin, Michael Sohn, Garry Sparks, Michael Turner, Andrea White, and Roger Willer.

I wish to acknowledge with gratitude the grant support I received from the Louisville Institute for the initial research upon which this project is based.

I am grateful to my editors at Cascade Books, Rodney Clapp and Christian Amondson, for their efforts in bringing this book to publication.

Finally, I am profoundly thankful to my wife, Denise, and the rest of my family for their patience, understanding, and sacrifices on my behalf, which have enabled me to enjoy the privilege of writing.

Abbreviations

adj	adjusted
CES	Consumer Expenditures Survey
Coef	coefficient
COMECON	Council for Mutual Economic Assistance
CPI	Consumer Price Index
CPS	Current Population Survey
DF	degrees of freedom
EU	European Union
F	f statistic
GATT	General Agreement on Tariffs and Trade
GSS	General Social Survey
ln	natural logarithm
MS	mean squares
NAFTA	North American Free Trade Agreement
NIPA	National Income and Product Accounts
NORC	National Opinion Research Center
P	p statistic
PCE	personal consumption expenditures
PUMA	Public Use Microdata Area
R-Sq	R-squared
SCF	Survey of Consumer Finances
SE	standard error
SS	sum of squares
T	t statistic
VIF	variance inflation factor
WTO	World Trade Organization

1

Introduction

CONSUMERISM IS A MORAL problem that has broad negative consequences for society. On this much, nearly all Christian theologians and ethicists agree. So, too, do many sociologists, economists, psychologists, social theorists, and cultural critics. Even in the aftermath of the worst recession since the Great Depression, consumerism persists. One sign of this is that, since the beginning of the recession in December 2007, the savings rate for U.S. households has remained lower than at any time during the 1950s, 1960s, 1970s, or 1980s.[1]

When scholars attempt to describe what consumerism is, beyond a moral problem, they reach widely divergent answers. There is no consensus on what consumerism is, and far less agreement on what personal motives or cultural forces drive it. I show in this book that, despite the attention that it has received as a moral issue, consumerism has been misunderstood. Without understanding what drives consumerism, the many proposals that have been offered by Christian theologians, ethicists, and other thinkers to lessen its influence have been ineffective or impossible to implement. A great deal has been said about consumerism, but, because it remains misunderstood, little has been done that could effectively change it. The key question regarding consumerism, if one wishes to change it, is the question of consumerism's motivation. This is the question I answer in this book.

---

1. U.S. Department of Commerce, National Income and Product Accounts.

Few of the thinkers who have engaged the question of consumerism's motivation are fully and fairly engaged in conversation with those who interpret consumerism differently than themselves. For example, among the thinkers whose theories I describe in detail in Chapter 3, neither John Paul II nor Thorstein Veblen acknowledges the existence of other consumerism theories. John Kenneth Galbraith and Colin Campbell acknowledge Veblen's theory but fail to address its full complexity and nuance. Galbraith and Campbell's most meaningful empirical evaluations are limited to their critiques of rival theories. These critiques, of course, do not validate their own claims.

I draw the existing consumerism theories into conversation by constructing a typology of theories and evaluating them according to a consistent set of empirical criteria. This empirical analysis validates which theoretical positions, if any, have practical and not merely speculative significance. Following my empirical critique of the existing theories, I propose a new theory of consumerism's motivation, and show that my proposed theory is consistent with the empirical evidence and with the anthropological and theological understandings of the Protestant Christian theological tradition, particularly as it is represented in the thought of Paul Tillich.

Introduction to the Argument

Let us begin by specifying a broad definition of consumerism that is consistent with the thinking of most theorists who have addressed it. According to this broad definition, consumerism can be understood as a form of life that is characterized by:

1. an insatiable desire to consume economic goods and services,
2. the rejection of any objective standard of economic sufficiency, and
3. the sacrifice of other consciously-valued goods and norms for the sake of increased economic consumption.

Given this definition, it is not consumerism to have a rising standard of economic consumption if, for example, the society's objective standard of sufficiency rises due to other persons' adoption of technologies that increase the level of consumption necessary for full social participation. An example of this would be the need to own an automobile to participate fully in a society in which automobile ownership is sufficiently widespread to foster low-density development and poor-quality public transportation.[2] Nor is it consumerism to exceed a minimally-sufficient level of consumption if consumption in excess of the level of sufficiency is not obtained at the expense of other consciously-valued goods and norms. The consumeristic individual whose behavior is fully determined by this definition is an ideal type. This type is only approximated in the behavior of concrete individuals and populations.

Consumerism can exist concretely only in the cultural context of a particular society. Cultural context influences how widespread consumerism is in a particular society and what forms it takes. My investigation is limited to consumerism as it is found in the affluent Western capitalist democracies that share the cultural heritage of the Christian religion and the Enlightenment. I make no claim that consumerism is exclusive to the West or universal within Western societies, but I assume provisionally that Western forms of consumerism are sufficiently similar to treat as a single phenomenon. I also assume provisionally that consumerism has become sufficiently prevalent in Western cultures to generate observable effects on national economic statistics. I address the first of these assumptions more fully in chapter 2 and the second in chapter 4.

Despite the influence of culture, consumerism cannot be understood purely as a matter of socioeconomic structures and institutions, but only through the existential concerns and forms of life of the individual persons who inhabit these structures and institutions. The consumerism theory that I advance in this book is based on the proposition that consumerism is not only a pattern of behavior that characterizes an individual life, but a way in which an individual organizes his or her particular life to seek to give it meaning. In characterizing consumerism as an existential form of life, I am arguing that it should be understood more narrowly than the definition I gave above. My claim is that consumerism is an existential stance in response to the existential threat of meaninglessness. As such, it represents a flawed working solution to a religious question that Christians believe can finally be answered only through Christ. Individuals who live a consumeristic life seek to defend themselves against the existential threat of meaninglessness by displaying purchases that have meanings as signs that are intended to procure recognition from other persons. When successful, such recognition temporarily validates the subjective value that a person places on the meaning of his or her own individual life.

2. This example is from Sen, "Poor, Relatively Speaking," 162.

The existential problem of securing the meaning of one's life lies at the root of every individual's moral motivation. I use *moral motivation* to mean the existential commitment through which an individual adopts a form of life and a direction for his or her particular desires. These existential commitments may be unconscious, fractured, fragmented, or over-determined. The existential commitments adopted before a person grows to self-awareness may never have been re-evaluated. Yet these commitments are revealed through the sum of an individual's words and actions. Every exercise of individual agency has moral significance. Therefore the existential commitment that establishes the motivating force behind the exercise of individual agency is the individual's moral motivation. This definition of moral motivation accepts Augustine's understanding of free will, in which human beings are free to do what they desire to do but what they desire is determined by their most basic religious and existential orientation.[3]

The implication of my claim that consumerism is a form of life rooted in an existential commitment is that it has the power to override or co-opt conscious moral ideals in determining individuals' economic decisions. This accounts for the practical failure of earlier proposals to counteract consumerism. If it is an existential form of life, consumerism cannot be dislodged by rational arguments or moral exhortations towards moderation, benevolence, sustainability, or social justice that do not address the underlying existential threat of meaninglessness. If it is rooted in an existential commitment, consumerism can only be overcome by individual conversion to another existential commitment that offers the individual threatened by meaninglessness a more adequate ground of meaning. An individual cannot desire or choose a life that lacks a ground of meaning. Therefore a change of existential foundations for an individual life must be accomplished by means of a discrete transformation.

I shall argue, using a methodology derived from Tillich, that a more adequate ground of meaning than consumerism can be found in Christian faith, rightly understood. Faith is not merely a self-directed social affiliation, cognitive worldview, or ethical program. Rightly understood, Christian faith is an existential trust and commitment that arises in the experience of "being grasped by" that which transcends the self.[4]

---

3. Augustine, *City of God* 14:13, 14:28.
4. Tillich, *Systematic Theology*, vol. 2, 155.

Introduction

The Ethical Significance of Consumerism

Consumerism morally deforms the lives of individuals and communities, and these deformations lead to widespread negative social and environmental consequences. This can be demonstrated through empirical evidence and reason, without appeal to any particular theological standpoint. Because consumerism is characterized by an infinite and absolute imperative for economic consumption, its demands radically circumscribe an individual's sense of personal responsibility towards other persons, other generations, and other life that are affected by his or her economic activity. Consumerism's imperative of unlimited consumption violates Immanuel Kant's categorical imperative to "act only on that maxim through which you can at the same time will that it should become a universal law."[5] No one could wish *everyone* to engage in unlimited consumption. Consumption produces negative social and environmental externalities, and unlimited consumption produces unlimited externalities. For the same reason, consumerism violates Jürgen Habermas's principle of universalizability, that "all affected can accept the consequences and the side effects . . . [a norm's] general observance can be anticipated to have for the satisfaction of everyone's interests."[6] Consumerism also violates John Rawls's principle of justice as fairness, that "social and economic inequalities . . . are just only if they result in compensating benefits for everyone, and in particular for the least advantaged members of society."[7] If every member of society consumes as much as possible it widens the inequality of economic consumption. The greater the disparity in economic consumption between rich and poor, the more the poorest members of society suffer externalities like the financial neglect of schools in poor communities and dislocation due to urban redevelopment. For persons who recognize no higher moral claim, consumerism fails even to satisfy individual self interest.

In an individual life, the commitment to a consumeristic form of life undermines physical health, psychological health, and subjective happiness. Psychologist Tim Kasser finds that "adults who focused on money, image, and fame reported less self-actualization and vitality, and more depression than those less concerned with these values. What is more, they also reported significantly more experiences of physical symptoms. That

---

5. Kant, *Groundwork of the Metaphysics of Morals*, 88.
6. Habermas, *Moral Consciousness and Communicative Action*, 65.
7. Rawls, *Theory of Justice*, 13.

is, people who believed it is important to strive for possessions, popularity, and good looks also reported more headaches, backaches, sore muscles, and sore throats than individuals less focused on such goals."[8] In addition to these relatively minor symptoms, psychiatrists Patricia Cohen and Jacob Cohen found that consumeristic values were correlated with higher rates of conduct disorder, oppositional/defiant disorder, attention deficit disorder, alcohol abuse, marijuana abuse, separation anxiety, major depression, schizoid, schizotypal, paranoid, histrionic, borderline, narcissistic, passive-aggressive, dependent, avoidant, and obsessive disorder.[9]

With respect to the question of subjective happiness, marketing researchers Marsha Richins and Scott Dawson "developed a scale that assesses how much people think possessions reflect success in life, how central materialism is to their desires, and how much they believe wealth and possessions yield happiness.... Compared with nonmaterialistic respondents, those with a strong materialistic orientation reported less satisfaction with their lives overall, with their family, their income, and their relationships with friends, as well as with how much fun they have."[10] Kasser notes that Richins and Dawson's results have been reproduced by various researchers who surveyed groups of adults, adolescents, business students, and entrepreneurs. Researchers repeated these results for sampled populations in Australia, Canada, China, Denmark, Germany, India, Romania, Russia, Singapore, South Korea, Turkey, and the United Kingdom.[11]

Survey respondents may underreport materialistic values due to a lack of self-awareness or—to the extent that they believe there is a social stigma toward materialistic values—a bias toward socially desirable responses. David Glen Mick finds evidence of socially desirable response bias in surveys of materialistic values, compulsive buying, and impulse buying. He suggests that the practices of self-deception and impression management that result in underreporting of materialistic values and practices are themselves characteristic of symbolic consumer behavior, i.e., consumerism.[12] To the extent that survey studies misidentify a share of consumeristic

---

8. Kasser, *High Price of Materialism*, 11.

9. P. Cohen and J. Cohen, *Life Values and Adolescent Mental Health*.

10. Kasser, *High Price of Materialism*, 18–20; referring to Richins and Dawson, "A Consumer Values Orientation for Materialism," 303–16.

11. Kasser, "Good Life or the Goods Life?," 57; Kasser et al., "Materialistic Values," 19; Kasser, *High Price of Materialism*, 21.

12. Mick, "Dark Side Variables," 115–17.

individuals as non-consumeristic, these studies underestimate the differences in health and subjective well being.

When we consider the positive goods of individual psychological and spiritual well being, and not merely the absence of recognized disorders, these goods are likewise undermined by consumerism. Kasser cites experimental psychological research that confirms that conscious materialistic values are inversely related to personal autonomy, vitality, and self-actualization. According to Kasser and colleagues, the research demonstrates that "people with a strong MVO [materialistic value orientation] are less focused on having choices than they are on obtaining rewards."[13] The moral character of the individual who leads a consumeristic form of life is also negatively affected. Indeed, the transgression of other consciously valued goods and norms is central to the broad definition of consumerism that I presented above. Kasser identifies empirical studies that confirm these moral failings. He notes that materialistic values are correlated with greater narcissism, and that "an MVO tends to conflict with the desire to help the world be a better place and to take care of others."[14] Likewise, "an MVO can also lead people to care less about environmental issues and to engage in more environmentally destructive behaviors and attitudes."[15]

The moral deformation of consumerism harms interpersonal and social goods. These harms are the direct consequence of consumeristic individuals' priorities. Consumerism compromises the quality of marriage and child-rearing, friendships, and civic engagement. Political scientist Robert Lane finds that "revealed preferences favor marginal increments of wealth over increments of affiliation," and that these value preferences are associated with fewer friendships, greater isolation and loneliness, and greater rates of depression.[16] Kasser and colleagues observe that "the love relationships and the friendships of those with a strong MVO [materialistic value orientation] are relatively short and are characterized more by emotional extremes and conflict than by trust and happiness." They attribute this to the fact that their studies show that "people with a strong MVO tend to place less importance on values such as affiliation . . . and benevolence,"

---

13. Kasser et al., "Materialistic Values," 21; Kasser, "Good Life or the Goods Life?," 56; Kasser, *High Price of Materialism*, 7–8.

14. Kasser et al., "Materialistic Values," 20–21.

15. Ibid., 22.

16. Lane, "Road Not Taken," 221, 236–38.

diminishing consumeristic individuals' interest in relationships and leading them to treat others in a less empathetic, more objectifying manner.[17]

The consequences of consumerism go beyond the impoverishment of personal lives. In societies in which consumerism is widespread, it may undermine the educational and moral foundations of a stable and productive economy, and the social trust necessary for functioning democratic political institutions. Kasser and colleagues report that "research shows that people strongly focused on materialistic values are also lower in social interest, pro-social behavior, and social productivity . . . are more likely to engage in anti-social acts . . . have more manipulative tendencies . . . and compete more than cooperate."[18] This research suggests a causal connection between the growing prevalence of consumerism in U.S. society and the erosion of altruism, honesty, social trust, friendship, and civic participation that I discuss in chapter 2 in connection with the research of Robert Putnam.

In an integrated global economy, the moral deformation of consumerism has social and environmental consequences far beyond the lives and communities in which this form of life is practiced. These consequences endanger both present and future generations. For example, the practical indifference to social justice among those who practice a consumeristic form of life in developed nations contributes to destabilizing economic and social disparities in developing nations between those who do and those who do not produce goods and services for customers in richer nations. The prevalence of the consumeristic form of life also drives a collective narcissism in Western nations' exercise of power in international relations that prioritizes the interests of the wealthy classes in the West at the expense of developing nations' interests. Where developing nations' governments cannot, as a result, meet their citizens' aspirations for economic sufficiency and relative equity, these governments are delegitimized and conditions are created for civil unrest, tyranny, civil war, and failed states.[19]

The practical indifference to environmental sustainability among those who practice a consumeristic form of life has the long-term potential to undermine the global civilization that Western economic and political culture has brought into being. As with consumerism's impact on personal and social goods, these environmental harms are directly attributed to the

17. Kasser et al., "Materialistic Values," 20.
18. Ibid., 22.
19. Rittenhouse, "Developing World's Relationship with Global Governance," 45.

priority given to consumeristic values, relative to competing values. Kasser reports that "substantial evidence shows that choices arising from a materialistic value orientation are often unconcerned with, or actively hostile toward, nature."[20] Marketing researcher Russell Belk observes that "how we consume, how we get from one place to another, our travel proclivities, how we read and write, our use, reuse, and disposal of our consumer goods and packaging, how we wash and dry our clothes, how we heat and cool ourselves, how we light our homes, how many electric and electronic appliances we use, and, generally, how much we consume, all have a direct impact on the environment. . . . Consumption in one part of the world impacts the entire planetary ecosystem."[21] The connection between consumption patterns and environmental impacts means that any remediation of the ecological problems that presently threaten the sustainability of the world's ecosystems and the human societies that rely on them would require a substantial reorientation of the consumeristic form of life prevalent today in the Western industrialized nations.

The Religious Significance of Consumerism

By establishing consumerism as a problem rooted in the existential need for meaningful individual life, I intend to draw attention to the failure of Western cultures to establish a less destructive basis for individually meaningful lives for the majority of persons in society. I suggest that it is this failure that lies at the root of the so-called "clash of civilizations" between Western consumer culture and traditional Islamic culture,[22] a clash that should be understood at base as a conflict between competing sources of meaning. In demonstrating that consumerism functions as a religion, I also seek to disclose to Christians the religious-existential contradiction between consumerism and Christian faith, and thus the problematic status of cultural syntheses between the forms of Christian religion and the substance of consumerism.

From the standpoint of Christian theology, Tillich's description of the religious basic experience is useful for illustrating two ways in which consumerism subverts an authentic encounter with the divine ground of

20. Kasser, *High Price of Materialism*, 92.
21. Belk, "Changing Consumer," 155.
22. The term "clash of civilizations" was coined by political scientist Samuel Huntington. See Huntington, *Clash of Civilizations*.

meaning. According to Tillich, true religion is the experience of the unconditioned absolute reality, which is attained through the experience of absolute nothingness—nothingness of entities, values, and personal life.[23] An individual can never attain this condition of absolute nothingness except through involuntary separation from his or her culture's preexisting world of meanings as it is socially defined and given to her or him. In contemporary consumer cultures, this given world is awash in associations between consumer goods, cultural meanings, and social identities. The individual who moves from this world to nothingness and thence to authentic religious experience must experience existential disappointment, the collapse of one's culturally-defined self that Tillich calls the catastrophic "price for idolatrous ecstasy."[24] Therefore the first way in which consumerism subverts the authentic encounter with ultimate meaning is by diverting the individual—through empty promises of existential meaning in preliminary concerns—from accepting the necessity of existential disappointment in order to encounter the divine.

A second way in which consumerism subverts the authentic encounter with ultimate meaning is that the individual whose answer to the existential problem of meaning fails is so anxious to escape the experience of existential disappointment that he or she grasps at the first promise of existential meaning that he or she encounters, without critically assessing whether it is truly capable of securing his or her individual meaning. Since persons in consumer cultures inhabit a world shaped by commercial speech and consumeristic meaning associations, the existential promises of the consumer culture are offered again and again under various guises. The individual who experiences existential disappointment will encounter these promises in one form or another, and will frequently attach himself or herself to one or another form of consumerism again.

In comparison with Tillich, my description of religious experience places greater emphasis on the givenness of the cultural world of meanings into which persons are thrown at birth, the impossibility of attaining the experience of nothingness except through involuntary existential disappointment, and the difficulty for the individual suffering existential disappointment to maintain a critical stance toward competing promises of existential meaning. Theologically, these positions are consistent with the traditionally Protestant Christian doctrines that assert the need for

---

23. Tillich, "On the Idea of a Theology of Culture," 24.
24. Tillich, *Systematic Theology*, vol. 3, 355.

revelation and grace to convert from other existential commitments to existential Christian faith. Through the revelation of law, Protestant theology maintains, the person facing an existential decision is aware of the Christian judgment that other existential commitments contradict existential Christian faith, the one existential commitment that is capable of securing the meaning of an individual life. This is what Martin Luther calls the theological use of the law.[25] Through the revelation of gospel, Protestant theology holds, a person facing an existential decision is aware of the Christian promise that the meaning of her or his life can be secured in relation to God through existential Christian faith. Through grace alone, Protestant theology maintains, a person who experiences existential disappointment in an existential form of life that cannot truly ground individual meaning is able to trust the judgment of revelation upon other existential commitments and the promise of revelation concerning existential Christian faith.

Concepts of a Theology of Culture

In order to understand my interpretation of the present religious situation and my theory of consumerism's existential motivation, it will be useful to review the conceptual world of Tillich's theology of culture. Tillich understands meaning to be present in all cultural creations. *Meaning*, for Tillich, refers to a correspondence between the human spirit and reality. In Tillich's account, meaning is the essential substance of culture, content is what is accidentally expressed in culture, and form is what mediates both meaning and content. Thus, for example, in Pablo Picasso's painting *Guernica*, the medium of painting is form, the specific objects portrayed—dead bodies, body parts, anguished faces, a bull, a horse—are content, and the underlying meanings—the horrors of war, idolatrous nationalism, and human self-destruction—are substance. Tillich uses *substance* as a synonym for meaning. Substance or meaning is grounded in the unconditioned ground of meaning, God, and is therefore an inherently religious concept.[26]

Tillich defines *religion* as "the experience of the unconditioned . . . the experience of absolute reality founded on the experience of absolute nothingness."[27] The "unconditioned" refers to God, understood as ultimate

25. Luther, "Lectures on Galatians," 309.

26. Tillich, "Conversation: Culture and Religion," 14; Tillich, "Idea of a Theology of Culture," 27; Tillich, "On the Boundary," 61.

27. Tillich, "Idea of a Theology of Culture," 24.

meaning.[28] The religious experience is not a feeling but "an activity of spirit in which something practical, something theoretical, and something emotional are joined together."[29] For Tillich, *spirit* is the "dynamic power of creativity in the human personality."[30] The individual human spirit creates meanings, but these individual meanings are always embedded in a meaningful whole. "The system of all possible systems of meaning we call objectively *world*, subjectively *culture*."[31] This system of meanings encompasses all areas of culture. It is not restricted to an explicitly religious sphere of "dogma, cultus, sanctification, community, church" that has an explicitly religious content as well as religious substance.[32]

Tillich also describes an existential sense of meaning—i.e., meaningful personal existence. Meaningful personal existence requires existential trust in the meaningfulness of the world of meanings. "In every meaning . . . lies the silent presupposition of the meaningfulness of the whole, the unity of all possible meanings, i.e., faith in the meaningfulness of life itself."[33] Faith in the meaningfulness of life implies faith in an unconditioned ground of meaning, God. "The basis of meaning is . . . the basis of personality and community . . . not only as they exist (the theoretical aspect), but also insofar as they experience something that they ought to be (the practical aspect)."[34] Thus, Tillich argues that meaningful existence requires personality and community to be integrated in and based upon an unconditional ground of meaning, God.

Because Tillich does not confine religious substance to a particular sphere of culture, the meaning of a particular historical and cultural situation cannot be interpreted solely with reference to a particular sphere of culture. Rather, the *situation* is "the totality of man's creative self-interpretation in a special period," including the scientific, artistic, economic, political, legal, ethical, and ecclesial forms in which this interpretation is expressed.[35] What is relevant to theology and theological ethics in the

---

28. Ibid., 25.
29. Ibid., 23.
30. Palmer, "Tillich's Theology of Culture," 10.
31. Tillich, "Church and Culture," 222.
32. Tillich, "Idea of a Theology of Culture," 35.
33. Tillich, "Church and Culture," 221.
34. Ibid., 223–24.
35. Tillich, *Systematic Theology*, vol. 1, 4.

situation are those cultural phenomena that have existential and religious significance.

Tillich defines *theology* as "the concrete normative science of religion."[36] Theology describes religion as it should be, not as it is. Since Tillich maintains that religious substance or meaning is not restricted to an explicitly religious sphere of culture, *theology of culture* can be understood as the concrete normative science of the religious meanings expressed in a cultural situation. Tillich's theology of culture describes how a culture should express religious-existential questions and answers, not only how it actually does so. Tillich defines three tasks of a theology of culture. It "carries out a . . . religious analysis of all cultural creations, it . . . [classifies] cultural creations from the point of view of the religious substance realized in them, and . . . it fashions the ideal design for a culture religiously fulfilled."[37] In my use of Tillich's theology of culture methods, I limit myself to the tasks of identifying and classifying cultural creations according to their religious significance.

This brief introduction to Tillich's conceptual world forms the basis of my interpretation of the present world situation in chapter 2 and my constructive theological ethical method in chapter 5. I will now situate these elements in the context of my overall argument.

Outline of Subsequent Chapters

I organize the remainder of this book as follows. In chapter 2, I apply Tillich's theology of culture method to evaluate the present religious situation in mainstream Western culture. Instead of attempting to evaluate all cultural spheres for their religious significance, I focus on those spheres in which Tillich identifies the most significant twentieth-century efforts to express and answer the religious-existential question of meaning: the scientific-technical, political, economic, philosophical, and explicitly religious spheres of culture.

In chapter 3, I describe the theories of the most important and most recent thinkers who have developed coherent theories of consumerism, whether or not they identify it by that name. I sort these consumerism theories into a typology according to their explanation of consumerism's

---

36. Tillich, "Idea of a Theology of Culture," 20.
37. Ibid., 27.

motivation. I identify five types of theories. The first type, which I call "greed theories," attributes consumerism to consumers' intemperate materialistic hedonism. The second type, which I call "status signaling theories," attributes consumerism to consumers' desire to communicate superior social status though the meanings signified by their consumption patterns. The third type, the "manipulation theories," attributes consumerism to the domination of consumers' wills through the manipulations of economic producers and their marketing and advertising agents. The fourth type, the "imaginative hedonism theories," attributes consumerism to the motive of seeking emotional pleasure through the imaginative identities signified by consumer goods. The fifth type, the "parental concern theories," attributes consumerism to parents' desire to maximize their children's well-being by acquiring the best possible education, relative to other children, through their housing and college expenditures. For each of these theoretical types I review one or two emblematic thinkers in detail and give more cursory treatment to other representatives of the type. These emblematic thinkers are John Paul II for the greed theories, Thorstein Veblen for the status signaling theories, John Kenneth Galbraith for the manipulation theories, Colin Campbell for the imaginative hedonism theories, and Elizabeth Warren and Amelia Warren Tyagi for the parental concern theories.

In chapter 4, I evaluate each of the five theoretical types empirically to assess their adequacy as descriptions of consumerism as it is found in contemporary Western cultures. Empirical validation has the potential to falsify theological ethical interpretations of concrete historical socioeconomic phenomena if the interpretations predict patterns of human judgment and action other than those that are empirically observed. If, as I propose, consumerism is motivated by an existential strategy to secure personal meaning and the choice of existential strategy is subject in some measure to human freedom and thus variable over time, then my theory of consumerism may explain a number of patterns in the recent historical economic data that are anomalous from the viewpoint of standard economic theory. These anomalies include the lack of growth in subjective happiness, the decline of time devoted to leisure, and the decline of savings rates as real incomes have risen. They also include sustained growth in real housing spending by middle-class and working-class households at the same time as their wages stagnated. These anomalies are the starting point from which I develop empirical criteria by which to evaluate the theoretical types of consumerism theories. The empirical criteria by which I evaluate the theoretical types are:

1. the historical location of consumerism,
2. the social class location of consumerism,
3. whether consumerism is associated with subjective happiness,
4. whether consumerism is associated with social utility as well as personal utility,
5. the extent to which consumer motives are consciously understood,
6. the extent to which consumer choices are determined by advertising,
7. the relationship between housing consumption growth and social class location, and
8. the relationship between housing consumption growth and the presence or absence of minor children in the household.

As econometric markers for the historical and class location of consumerism, I identify which consumers sacrifice leisure and savings for the sake of increasing economic consumption over and above the level of economic sufficiency, as indicated by the official poverty level.

In chapter 5 I present a constructive Christian ethical interpretation of the motivation of consumerism. I advance the argument that, from the standpoint of Protestant theological ethics, consumerism can be understood as a provisional answer to the existential problem of meaning, and that Christian faith, rightly understood, comprises an alternative answer to the problem of meaning that is existentially and morally superior to consumerism. As part of this argument, I use evidence from philosophy, psychology, the social sciences, and business research to show how consumerism functions as an existential meaning strategy. I validate this claim empirically according to the criteria that I used in Chapter 4 to evaluate the competing theories of consumerism's motivation. I then validate my proposal theologically by demonstrating its consistency with traditionally Protestant doctrines such as the noetic effect of sin, the bondage of the will, the theological use of the Law, and the dialectical relationship between conviction of sin and justification.

In chapter 6, I conclude with a discussion of the implications of my analysis. My constructive position suggests the futility of ethical critiques of consumerism that do not at least implicitly acknowledge its religious dimension, and the impossibility of avoiding the religious question of individual meaning which consumerism seeks to answer. I thus seek to sharpen the theoretical problem of consumerism for thinkers who acknowledge the moral problems associated with the consumeristic form of life but seek to exclude the religious dimension from their ethical analysis and constructive proposals. For those thinkers for whom the substance of the Christian message is a matter of ultimate concern, my constructive position points to a different problem: a widespread dominance of consumeristic existential commitments in place of existential faith among self-identified Christians and churches in Western nations, and not only in the broader societies. This is a serious contradiction of Christianity's monotheistic norm as expressed in the First Commandment. In concluding, I identify some of the questions raised by this research, such as how existential consumerism can be said to coexist with Christian cultural content and institutional forms, and how existential Christian faith can be lived and fostered within churches and cultures dominated by consumerism.

2

The Religious Significance of Recent Developments in Western Culture

TO UNDERSTAND WHY CONSUMERISM has become so important in Western cultures in recent decades, we need to examine our present cultural situation in terms of its religious significance. That is, we must explore how Western cultures ask the question of what makes individual life meaningful and what answers they offer to enable individuals to defend themselves against the existential threat of meaninglessness. In this chapter, I explore our "world situation," in the sense that Paul Tillich uses this term. In Tillich's theology of culture, the first two steps are a religious analysis of cultural creations and a classification of these creations according to the religious substance, or existential meaning, realized in them.[1] These steps identify the world situation. So my aim here is to interpret and classify the religious-existential meanings expressed in the most important recent developments in Western cultures.

To speak of the world in which consumerism is embedded is to speak primarily of the dominant culture in the affluent democratic nations of western Europe and North America. These nations are distinct in sharing what Tillich calls a Christian culture, that is, a culture that is historically influenced by an explicitly religious sphere—the sphere of institutional religion—in which existential questions of being and meaning are asked and answered using Christian symbols.[2] Out of their Christian roots, Western cultures developed a distinctly Christian secularism, and distinctly

---

1. Tillich, "Idea of a Theology of Culture," 27.
2. Tillich, "Conversation: Culture and Religion," 8–10.

17

Christian secular ideologies of scientific and economic progress.[3] These Christian secular ideologies provided the values upon which modern economic development is founded.

In a larger sense, the world can be understood as a single cultural system because all of the world's cultures are subject to the influence of the dominant Euro-American culture. The late modern technical and economic integration of the world known as globalization has provided the conditions for Western economic culture to be exported to nations throughout the world, along with the secularized Christian roots upon which it rests. In the process of developing capitalist economies, economist Robert Nelson argues, the adoption of "modern" values—i.e., secularized Judeo-Christian values that originated in Euro-American civilization—has been a criterion of economic success for developing nations.[4] In developing nations, even those who decry the influence of Western culture on their societies generally aspire to some elements of Western affluence. Jared Diamond observes that the Western consumer lifestyle has become the object of aspiration to billions of persons in developing nations who are exposed to Western consumer products and advertising and who may have relatives or acquaintances who have emigrated to the West.[5] To the degree that they succeed in these aspirations either through emigration or through economic advancement in their own society, the citizens of developing nations are participating in a world that is significantly constructed in Western terms. A similar but stronger influence is exercised upon minority and immigrant subcultures within Western nations.

The "world situation" that I describe in this chapter, then, is the situation of the dominant culture in Western nations that also exerts influence on the cultures of other nations and subcultures. It is my intention to treat the situation of the affluent cultures of western Europe and North America that share a history shaped by Christianity, Enlightenment, democracy, and capitalism as a unified whole, while recognizing that cultural difference remain within this world. I will address other nations and cultures only insofar as they are influenced by the dominant Euro-American culture.

---

3. Tillich, "Religious Situation in Germany," 366–67. I am using the term "secular," as Tillich does, to refer to cultures and cultural creations that mainly express religious-existential meanings outside the explicitly religious sphere.

4. Nelson, *Economics as Religion*, 7n.

5. Diamond, *Collapse*, 351, 372, 495.

The Religious Significance of Recent Developments in Western Culture

Writing in the early twentieth century, Tillich identified natural science, technology, and the capitalist economy as the three spiritually most powerful cultural creations in the Western world. He saw the practical economic sphere as the dominant element in this historical situation, a sphere dominated by a spirit of self-sufficient finitude. He characterizes this spirit by the autonomy of economic activity from other social powers, the domination of other functions of life by the economic, a lack of attention to the eternal, and unlimited desire for the finite.[6]

The most significant spiritual force that Tillich identified that was opposed to the spirit of self-sufficient finitude was nationalism. In the explicitly religious sphere, Tillich saw Christianity as largely unable to resist the capitalist spirit. Either churches were co-opted and secularized, or they were marginalized by their failure to engage the modern world. He identified two spiritual protests against the spirit of self-sufficient finitude. The first was the Religious Socialism movement of the 1920s and 1930s, which sought to expose the idolatrous elements of capitalism and nationalism. The second was the existentialist philosophy of the postwar period that expressed the human existential predicament and the failure of industrial capitalist culture to answer that predicament.[7]

While the situation in the dominant Western culture continues to be dominated by the practical economic sphere, there are major differences from the situation that Tillich described. The most important of these differences are:

1. Science and technology have demonstrated greater ambiguity than ever before, and the idea of progress and the authority of its proponents have been further undermined.

2. New information technologies, deregulation, and trade liberalization have enabled the capitalist economy to become fully globalized. The effects of globalization, mass affluence, and television have shifted the ground of personal identity and meaning from the individual's role as a worker to the individual's role as a consumer. This has facilitated the rapid growth of consumerism as an existential phenomenon.

---

6. Tillich, "Religiöse Lage," 15; Tillich, *Religious Situation*, 71, 75; Tillich, "Demonic," 119.

7. Tillich, "Demonic," 119; Tillich, "Religious Situation in Germany," 364–65; Tillich, "On the Boundary," 45, 58; Tillich, "Aspects of a Religious Analysis of Culture," 43–45; Tillich, "Religion and Secular Culture," 60.

3. Marxism has been discredited by its obsolete industrial production-based economic presuppositions and its utopian anthropology. These led to the practical failure of communist nations to meet their citizens' economic aspirations. Nationalism has likewise been marginalized.
4. Environmentalism has replaced nationalism as the principal practical-romantic opposition to capitalism.
5. The explicitly religious sphere of culture has lost much of its remaining power to critique the economic culture because of further secularization and the development of syntheses between consumerism and Christian religious content.
6. The existentialist critique of capitalist culture has been marginalized. The most significant new theoretical movement is postmodernism, which—particularly in its post-structuralist form—reflects rather than critiques the epistemological and anthropological premises of consumerism.

In the remainder of this chapter I explore each of these developments.

Developments in Science and Technology

Science and technology are not religiously significant as such. What Tillich found significant and objectionable in modern technological society was the idolatrous elevation of the human capacities for intellectual objectification and tool-making. Intellectualization leads to the objectification of everything, including the self. If the individual is reduced to a thing alongside other things, then he or she lacks any ultimate purpose. Thus intellectualization contributes to the widespread experience of meaninglessness in modern society. In its practical activity, Tillich observed, modern technological society makes an end out of its means. It lacks any transcendent purpose. Its sole objective is to extend control over the world and over human beings. The modern spirit makes everything including the self into a tool, but it offers no answer to the question, "For what?"[8]

In place of an end, modern technological society offers the individual the idea of progress. This is, at least provisionally, an answer to the existential question of the meaning of personal existence. The idea of progress

---

8. Tillich, "Aspects of a Religious Analysis of Culture," 46; Tillich, "Demonic," 117; Tillich, "Lost Dimension in Religion," 43; Tillich, "How Has Science Changed Man's View?," 79.

The Religious Significance of Recent Developments in Western Culture

unites the ideas of the progressive realization of human moral ideals, the spatial and technological extension of human activity, and the fulfillment of human potentialities. What these ideas share, in Tillich's view, is a belief in the self-sufficiency of the human temporal order. Likewise, they all fail to acknowledge the distinction between what human beings are existentially and what they are in their ideal essence.[9]

The sphere of science and technology can no longer credibly serve as a source of meaning. The world wars, genocides, and economic depressions of the first half of the twentieth century contradicted and undermined the plausibility of the idea of progress. "Progress" failed to explain the reality of human failure, suffering, and evil.[10] More recent history has been equally ambiguous. While in earlier generations, technology produced the heroic symbols of workers buildings dams and skyscrapers or men landing on the moon, these technological feats have come and gone without delivering the utopia promised by the idea of progress. The dams that provided power and water for development depleted fisheries and fostered unsustainable desert agriculture and urbanization. The skyscrapers that symbolized urban vitality proved vulnerable to low-technology terrorists. The lunar missions' failure to yield social or economic benefits destroyed the rationale for public space programs.

Nelson observes that the power of science to explain the physical universe and the power of technology to control it have failed to develop any comparable capacity to understand and control human beings and society. Science cannot explain all issues that matter to human beings, and it is increasingly evident that science should not be given the responsibility to do so. If technological means become self-justifying, then these must include the means of humanity's self-destruction, which now include genetic engineering in addition to nuclear weapons. When faced with the question of meaning, environmental historian Thomas Dunlap argues, scientific positivism fails in its pretensions to explain everything. Physicists and biologists discovered no purpose or hope in the cosmos. Their theories described a world of meaningless struggle and death. What science and technology *have* revealed more clearly than ever before is the ambiguity of using human power to alter the physical world.[11]

---

9. Tillich, "Idea of Progress," 83–87; H. R. Niebuhr, "Preface," xvi; Tillich, "Aspects of a Religious Analysis of Culture," 44.

10. Tillich, "Idea of Progress," 87.

11. Nelson, *Economics as Religion*, 19; Dunlap, *Faith in Nature*, 119.

One example of growing technological ambiguity has been the proliferation of limited-access highways which made possible a massive migration to suburban and exurban areas. In the United States, sociologist Robert Putnam reports that the suburban population grew from 23 to 49 percent of the nation's population between 1950 and 1996. Associated with this shift has been an increase in driving time, traffic congestion, stress, and uncivil driving, and a decline in civic engagement, altruism, honesty, and social trust. The identity of suburban residents is increasingly fragmented geographically between work, home, shopping, and community activities.[12]

A second example of growing technological ambiguity is the cultural impact of television. In the United States, Putnam found that the introduction of television—particularly television viewing during childhood—is correlated with more time spent passively, at home, indoors, and alone, with less social interaction, civic engagement, and social trust, with greater dissatisfaction and malaise, and with poorer academic and vocational achievement. Although television viewership is higher in the United States than in other affluent nations, these adverse effects have been found in studies of many other countries as well.[13]

The development of networked computer technology in the 1980s and 1990s has also had significant and ambiguous cultural impacts. I will discuss the impact of computer networks on the nature of work, economic organization, and identity when I address the religious significance of economic globalization. In social interaction, Putnam observes, the Internet lowers the cost of communication and increases its anonymity. This undermines social control, honesty, and interpersonal trust, increases the volume and incivility of speech, and further prioritizes speaking over listening. Like suburbanization, the Internet contributes to the delocalization of personal identity and community.[14]

Economic Globalization

Tillich's religious analysis of the economic sphere contended that capitalist societies produce self-destructive contradictions and spiritual crises. The contradictions are that capitalism produces structural unemployment, the increasing poverty of the masses, and the loss of individual freedom to the

---

12. Putnam, *Bowling Alone*, 142–43, 205–14.
13. Ibid., 217–41.
14. Ibid., 172–78.

imperatives of economic development. The idolatrous character of capitalist society, in Tillich's view, is revealed in its spirit of unlimited self-assertion, which fosters inequity, class distinction, and class conflict. The effect of this spirit, Tillich contends, is to destroy an individual's personal center and conform her or him to a determinate pattern to meet the demands of the economy. Capitalist society also destroys community, in Tillich's account, because there is nothing left to have in common. The result is a profound existential loneliness.[15]

In the economic sphere, the idea of progress has proved just as flawed as in the scientific-technical sphere. In its economic formulation, Nelson defines the idea of economic progress—which he calls "economic religion"—as the proposition that all of humanity's individual and social ills are due to material deprivation. Thus, rising affluence can produce a moral and spiritual transformation of humanity, and eliminate crime, hatred, and war. Economist John Maynard Keynes exemplified this idea of progress when he predicted that rising affluence would lead people to cease their striving for material goods.[16] Despite the massive rise in Western living standards during the twentieth century, his utopian hopes have not been realized. Our social ills remain, and our desires for material goods remain unsatiated.

As theologian Langdon Gilkey observes, we have learned to be more skeptical about the claim that economic growth is unambiguously good. The belief in endless economic growth was challenged in the 1970s by the publication of the Club of Rome study, *The Limits to Growth*, which used scientific analysis to support Thomas Malthus's hypothesis that the physical world imposes limits on the exponential growth of human population and economic activity.[17] The oil supply shocks of 1973–4 and 1979–80 suggested

---

15. Tillich, "End of the Protestant Era?," 224; Tillich, *Religious Situation*, 75–77; Tillich, "Dämonische," 48–49; Tillich, "Spiritual Problems of Postwar Reconstruction," 264; Tillich, "Storms of Our Times," 246. Tillich only addresses the corporate industrial form of capitalism found in Western Europe and North America in the early twentieth century. His analysis is dependent on Marxian theories which implicitly assume that the laissez-faire monetary and fiscal policies and the mercantilist trade policies practiced by capitalist nations in the late nineteenth and early twentieth centuries are fixed features of capitalist societies.

16. Nelson, *Economics as Religion*, 12–13, 30–31, 322–23; Keynes, "Economic Possibilities for Our Grandchildren," 369–72.

17. Gilkey, "Religious Situation at the End of the Twentieth Century," 15; Dunlap, *Faith in Nature*, 128–30; Meadows et al., *Limits to Growth*; Malthus, *Principle of Population*. The Club of Rome report failed to predict the rate of development and diffusion of new technologies such as the high yielding hybridized grains, fertilizers, and pesticides that

that the world might be closer to the limits of a petroleum-based economy, at least, than nearly everyone had previously believed. In the last decade, several petroleum geologists forecast the peak of global oil production to occur by 2009. According to Diamond, a more inescapable natural limit is implied in human utilization of the potential photosynthetic capacity of the world's plants. In 1986 this utilization was estimated to be fifty percent. By the mid-twenty-first century, with current population and economic growth forecasts, it will approach 100 percent.[18] Even if world population growth could be halted immediately, Diamond argues, to bring just the population of China up to the consumption standards currently enjoyed by the affluent West would roughly double the world's current resource use and environmental impact, which is impossible to sustain.[19]

The most profound change in the economic sphere since Tillich assessed the world situation is globalization. Economist Joseph Stiglitz defines globalization as "the closer integration of the countries and peoples of the world which has been brought about by the enormous reduction of costs of transportation and communication, and the breaking down of artificial barriers to the flows of goods, services, capital, knowledge, and (to a lesser extent) people across borders."[20] As Stiglitz's definition makes clear,

---

enabled many developing nations to become self-sufficient in food production in recent decades. It also failed to predict the rate of declining fertility in developing nations due to reduced infant mortality, growing urbanization, women's education, and access to birth control. However, the primary impact of *The Limits to Growth* was not its predictive power, but its reintroduction of Malthus's hypothesis into the popular consciousness in societies that had, at least since World War II, largely been able to ignore the material resources upon which their prosperity was built.

18. Deffeyes, *Hubbert's Peak*, 148–49; Diamond, *Collapse*, 490–91. This forecast may be overly optimistic because of the impact of global warming upon agricultural productivity. The Intergovernmental Panel on Climate Change estimates that average global temperature will rise 1.4 to 5.8 degrees Celsius during the twenty-first century, which will substantially reduce crop yields and reduce fresh water available for irrigation. Brown, *Plan B 2.0*, 61–68.

19. Diamond, *Collapse*, 372–73. This calculation understates the problem in three ways. First, citizens of other developing nations (besides China) cannot be expected to accept lectures from the affluent nations that they may not aspire to a First World consumer lifestyle. Second, most citizens of affluent nations do not accept the message that they must halt the growth of their material consumption. Ibid., 495–96. Third, it is demographically impossible to halt world population growth immediately. According to its *lowest* forecast in 2004, the United Nations Population Division predicts that world population will grow from 6.5 billion in 2005 to 7.7 billion in 2050. United Nations, *World Population Prospects: 2004 Revision*, 2.

20. Stiglitz, *Globalization and Its Discontents*, 9.

technological and economic factors drive the process of globalization, but they do not comprise the entire cultural process. Nicholas Boyle identifies three consequences of globalization. First, the political sphere is radically diminished. Second, the meaning of an individual life is reduced to the economic roles the individual performs. Third, the concepts of value and truth are restricted to the present moment, so that the questions of permanent values and permanent identity no longer arise. I consider the first and second of these consequences here and the third below when I address the theoretical movement of postmodernism.[21]

As Tillich recognized, economic globalization began with the European empires of the late-nineteenth and early-twentieth centuries and their increasing economic integration, and was accelerated by World War II. Boyle argues that the colonial empires were undermined by global market forces that they initiated but could not control. World War II broke down the political structures that had held the colonial empires together and enforced trade barriers between them. The war destroyed most of Europe and Japan's industrial infrastructure and dissolved the meaning of national identity in the nations that suffered defeat. The postwar political economic order was international. It was rebuilt and governed by institutions created at the July 1944 Bretton Woods conference—the International Monetary Fund and the World Bank—and by the European Economic Community, now the European Union, which was established by the Treaties of Rome in March 1957. For twenty-five years, from 1945 to 1970, these institutions facilitated the rebuilding of technologically-advanced industrial economies in western Europe and Japan and managed the conditions of trade between the industrialized nations.[22]

By 1970, the western European and Japanese economies were exerting growing competitive pressure on the U.S. economy. Deficit spending in the late 1960s to finance the Vietnam War and President Johnson's Great Society social programs created inflationary pressure in the U.S. economy. In 1971 President Nixon responded by suspending the convertibility of the U.S. dollar to gold, and in 1973 he allowed freely-floating currency exchange rates. The significance of these steps, notes Mark C. Taylor, was to create the conditions for markets to exchange Treasury securities and

---

21. Boyle, *Who Are We Now?*, 78–79.

22. Ibid., 73, 142–43; Stiglitz, *Globalization and Its Discontents*, 11; European Union, "History of the European Union: 1957." The Bretton Woods conference also authorized the creation of a World Trade Organization, but this organization was not actually established until 1995. Stiglitz, *Globalization and Its Discontents*, 15–16.

currency futures contracts. A second major step in the elimination of political control over global economic processes occurred in 1979, when U.S. Federal Reserve Board Chairman Paul Volcker abandoned a policy aimed at managing interest rates in favor of a policy directed toward managing the growth of the money supply, thereby allowing capital markets to determine interest rates. This move was followed in the early 1980s by U.S. legislation to deregulate financial institutions. These laws allowed greater integration of financial services companies, greater competition between them, and more widely available consumer credit. Deregulation in the United States was, to a significant extent, followed by deregulation in other affluent nations. Between 1984 and 1996, for example, every major industrialized nation privatized its telecommunications industry.[23]

Stiglitz identifies three events in the late 1980s and 1990s that accelerated the political dimension of globalization. The first event was the collapse of the Soviet Empire between 1989 and 1991. This opened the way for the reunification of Germany and the integration of the eastern European nations and former Soviet republics into a global capitalist economy. I consider the existential significance of this event below in my discussion of Marxism. By 2012, seven formerly communist eastern European nations and three former Soviet republics have joined the European Union, and four additional eastern European nations are candidate countries. The second event was the signing of the North American Free Trade Agreement (NAFTA) in 1992, which eliminated tariffs among Canada, Mexico, and the United States. The third event was the conclusion of the eighth General Agreement on Tariffs and Trade (GATT)—the Uruguay round—which came into effect on January 1, 1995. This agreement created the World Trade Organization and thereby delegated the responsibility to enforce the terms of international trade between member states to an international political entity that lacks democratic accountability.[24]

In the West, the meaningfulness of work has been radically undermined by globalization. Networked computer technology dramatically lowers the value of geographical proximity in coordinating economic activities. It thus creates the technological preconditions for a decentralized network economy in which many jobs can be done virtually anywhere.

---

23. Taylor, *Confidence Games*, 127–28, 135–38, 156–60.

24. European Union, "Member States of the EU"; Stiglitz, *Globalization and its Discontents*, 4, 7n, 21–22. As of May 2012, the WTO includes 154 member states and the European Union. World Trade Organization, "Members and Observers."

The Religious Significance of Recent Developments in Western Culture

Since the political preconditions were established through financial market deregulation and the GATT treaty, this network economy has rapidly come into being. In the network economy, information and capital are more mobile than labor, so the emergence of the global network economy has been accompanied by a shift in power from managers and employees to shareholders. This shift enables shareholders to demand and get short-term rather than long-term profits and capital appreciation. Sociologist Richard Sennett notes that one consequence of this shift is that workers experience the labor market as increasingly unstable, chaotic, and risky. At the same time, the global economy's intensified competition among suppliers and lower cost of information produce a shift in power from producers to consumers. This exacerbates the instability and risk of employment. Increased consumer power and the volatility of consumer demand create demands for more flexible and specialized production, which further adds to workplace volatility.[25]

Tillich's interpretation of industrial capitalism followed the depiction of sociologist Max Weber, who saw the modern workplace as a bureaucratic hierarchy of authority, regulation, and routine, modeled on the German army. This type of workplace rationalization continued to be common in the 1950s and 1960s, as described in William Whyte's 1956 classic, *The Organization Man*. Tillich saw the industrial workplace as meaningless because it eliminated opportunities for craftsmanship and autonomous work, two sources of personal meaning that had characterized the pre-industrial workplace.[26]

What Tillich did not recognize when he described the rationalized industrial workplace as meaningless is that the rationalization of time in bureaucratic institutions creates a means for employees to ground their identities existentially in their work, even though the content of their work is standardized and their individual creativity suppressed. Sennett observes that "rationalized time enabled people to think about their lives as narratives . . . of how things should happen. It became possible, for instance, to define what the stages of a career ought to be like, to correlate long-term

---

25. Taylor, *Confidence Games*, 159; Sennett, *Culture of the New Capitalism*, 37–41; Sennett, *Corrosion of Character*, 51.

26. Sennett, *Culture of the New Capitalism* 20–23, 103–6, 111–12; Whyte, *Organization Man*. Craftsmanship and autonomous work are also difficult to sustain in the workplace of the global network economy, which is characterized by even greater productivity pressures and even greater interdependence than the workplace of industrial capitalism.

service in a firm to specific steps of increased wealth."[27] In mass society, Sennett argues, people feel a sense of meaning in an individual life that stands out from the mass. This sense of meaning is grounded socially through recognition. The linear, cumulative narrative of a rationalized and predictable career gave workers a sense of agency, self-respect, social recognition, and meaning as distinct individuals, even in jobs where the content of the work lacked social prestige.[28] This existential strategy of grounding the meaning of personal existence through a socially-recognized narrative of a rational and predictable career was viable so long as Weber's rationalized workplace existed.

The past three decades of globalization have largely eliminated Weber's rationalized workplace in the West. Global competition, network technology, and impatient investors have both enabled and compelled businesses to radically restructure their operations. Hierarchical organizations have been delayered. The lifetime employment contract has given way to periodic downsizing and restructuring, strategies which managers no longer reserve for economic downturns. The economic value of length of employment has fallen, so employers have less incentive to retain senior employees. Most careers today are spent in multiple institutions, and a growing share of workers have multiple careers. Organizations now change so quickly that the consequences of switching jobs are no longer calculable, depriving employees of a sense of agency to improve their work situation. Businesses and educational institutions increasingly employ casual labor instead of workers with ongoing employment contracts. In the United States, nearly 30 percent of all workers now fall into this category. Business demands for adaptability regularly disrupt work team staffing and erode trust.[29]

For a worker's career narrative to be an effective ground of meaning, it has to be recognized and validated by others. This validation is increasingly absent. To believe that a job is meaningful, a worker has to believe that he or she is needed, but the disposability of the contemporary worker refutes this belief. The contemporary workplace no longer provides a boss whose own career is stable enough to serve as a witness to the worker's career performance. The culture at large no longer grants prestige and recognition

---

27. Sennett, *Culture of the New Capitalism*, 23.

28. Sennett, *Corrosion of Character*, 16, 30, 64.

29. Sennett, *Culture of the New Capitalism*, 24–25, 48, 66–68; Putnam, *Bowling Alone*, 88–90; Sennett, *Corrosion of Character*, 85–86.

in exchange for long service. These trends have greatly reduced the opportunities for Westerners to ground the meaning of their individual lives through their work.[30]

The contemporary workplace shaped by economic globalization is no longer a source of meaning, but a source of insecurity. In the affluent nations, workers experience the workplace as constantly demanding more and providing less. Among full-time workers in the United States, work hours increased by 163 hours per year between 1969 and 1987. These statistics do not fully measure increasing workplace demands. In 1992, sociologist Robert Wuthnow found that "two-thirds of the American labor force claim they are . . . working harder than five years ago; half say they wish they could work fewer hours than they do."[31] In the 1980s and 1990s, Putnam found increasing percentages of Americans who said that they "'work very hard most of the time' and . . . frequently 'stayed late at work.' The groups that feel most harried are full-time workers (especially those with advanced education), women, people aged twenty-five to fifty-four, and parents of younger children, especially single parents."[32] Since the 1970s, self-reported financial anxiety has increased steadily across all economic strata, regardless of macroeconomic conditions.[33]

Growing economic risks are not just in workers' minds. The global network economy systematically produces risk. Markets inherently decentralize control and lack predictability. Regulation has the potential to mitigate this unpredictability, but the global economy has been characterized by greater and greater deregulation. In addition, financial instruments like futures contracts that were designed to minimize financial market risks have had the opposite effect, creating opportunities for speculation and financial leverage which produce unpredictable market disruptions.[34]

---

30. Sennett, *Corrosion of Character*, 146; Sennett, *Culture of the New Capitalism*, 75–8. There are, of course, exceptions to this generalization. Certain jobs in unionized trades, government, and higher education retain sufficient prospects of stability to sustain a lifetime employment narrative. Elite jobs that are visible beyond the boundaries of the workplace also give a relatively small number of persons an opportunity to validate work-centered claims to personal meaning.

31. Schor, *Overworked American*, 29; Wuthnow, *God and Mammon*, 40, 270.

32. Putnam, *Bowling Alone*, 189.

33. Putnam, *Bowling Alone*, 192; Wuthnow, *God and Mammon*, 136, 270.

34. Sennett, *Corrosion of Character*, 80; Beck, *Risk Society*, 19; Taylor, *Confidence Games*, 11, 152–54, 168–75.

The responses of workers to rising employer demands, stagnating wages, and the growing unreliability of employment have tended to exacerbate their existential anxieties. Perhaps the most culturally-significant response was the widespread entry of women into the paid workforce. According to Putnam, in the United States, "on average, women are spending roughly one more hour per day in paid labor in the 1990s than in the 1960s," and "virtually all the increase in full-time employment of American women over the last twenty years is attributable to financial pressures."[35] This has a spillover effect on time that women spend outside the workplace. Traditionally, women in the affluent nations invest more time than men in maintaining families, social relationships, and civil society organizations. Women who work in full-time paid employment are more likely to spend time on personal relaxation and shopping and less time on child-rearing, maintaining social ties, and community involvement. Men who are equally stressed in their work respond in similar ways rather than taking these responsibilities upon themselves.[36] A second response of workers to labor market demands has been a greater willingness on the part of workers to relocate in order to find or to maintain employment.

Don Browning observes that greater household workforce participation, greater job mobility, and greater workplace stress have combined to undermine the institutions of marriage and the nuclear family. Since the 1960s, "the marriage rate in all advanced countries has declined significantly; there are fewer second marriages and more people live longer periods of their lives in the single state." Accompanying the decline in marriage has been an increase in cohabitation, which studies show to be less stable than marriage and more likely to result in divorce when cohabiting couples marry. The share of out-of-wedlock births to cohabiting couples has grown, contributing to an insecure family environment for children. Since the 1960s, the rate of out-of-wedlock births "increased from 5 percent to 33 percent in the U.S., from 4 percent to 31 percent in Canada, from 5 to 38 percent in the United Kingdom, and from 6 to 36 percent in France."[37] With respect to the marriage partners themselves, Putnam finds that divorce is correlated with greater poverty, financial instability, and reduced involvement in church and youth-related activities. The second-generation effects are more significant. Divorce and out-of-wedlock births increase

---

35. Putnam, *Bowling Alone*, 194, 197 (original emphasis removed).
36. Ibid., 194–96.
37. Browning, *Marriage and Modernization*, 9, 15–16.

the distance of fathers from children which reduces children's access to financial resources and social capital, impedes conscience formation, and reduces trust in parents and in the reliability of the world in general. The general decline in trust that results from the untrustworthiness that individuals experience in today's workplaces and families fosters a widespread withdrawal from community and civic life.[38]

The declining social trust produced by unstable workplaces and families increases cynicism towards government, which produces a greater tolerance for laissez-faire governance, and for social and economic inequality. Western secular governments, whose authority is no longer built upon traditional religion or nationalist spirit, have lost legitimacy in their role as the institutional guarantors of the idea of economic progress.[39] This feedback effect has accelerated the loss of influence that governments can exert over the economic sphere.

With diminishing government redistribution, the dynamics of economic globalization tend to produce greater and greater income inequality. First, the supply of capital becomes scarcer relative to the supply of labor, increasing the economic returns to capital and depressing economic returns to labor. Second, the supply of high-skill labor became scarcer relative to the supply of low-skill labor. This increases the wages of high-skill workers and depresses the wages of low-skill workers. Third, among the ranks of high-skill workers, the growth of winner-take-all markets in the global network economy delivers enormous economic rewards to a small number of best-in-market performers, and diminishing rewards to next-best performers.[40] A certain amount of inequality is accepted in a political economic system in which even those disadvantaged by the system feel that they have democratic accountability and ownership.[41] But in the global network economy democratic accountability is greatly diminished. Economic processes are less and less subject to control by national governments, national governments are less willing to regulate them, and existing global governance institutions are not answerable to individuals. Therefore

---

38. Putnam, *Bowling Alone*, 34–37, 60–62, 135–47, 278, 305; Browning, *Marriage and Modernization*, 18; Sennett, *Corrosion of Character*, 141–42.

39. Sennett, *Culture of the New Capitalism*, 173–77; Putnam, *Making Democracy Work*, 101–15.

40. Reich, *Work of Nations*, 174–77; Frank and Cook, *Winner-Take-All Society*, 45–58.

41. Boyle, *Who Are We Now?*, 172–75.

greater inequality produces greater cynicism and greater cynicism produces greater inequality in a vicious cycle.

Increasingly, economic consumption is the center of meaning for persons in affluent Western societies because it is the principal sphere in which they retain some degree of agency. I have already noted how the global network economy shifts market power from producers to consumers. This has the effect of shifting individual agency from production to consumption as well. No matter to what extent decisions in the workplace and the political sphere are determined by others, consumer purchases are almost entirely free, within the constraints of household income, assets, and credit limits. Therefore it is natural for individuals in the affluent Western societies, who have both the means and the opportunity to make purchases in global markets, to relate their sense of personal identity to their purchasing decisions.[42] In a society in which work-centered identity is increasingly untenable and the political sphere reduced to irrelevance, Boyle argues, individual identity becomes defined solely through our economic transactions. "We are at best the series of consumer choices we have made . . . and the series of jobs from which we have been made redundant."[43] While this is hyperbole, since agency and freedom are not *exclusively* confined to the economic sphere, it is true to the degree that individual agency is now concentrated in acts of consumption. Boyle does not acknowledge that the degree to which an individual's agency is concentrated in economic consumption is itself partly determined by human freedom. The typical individual in an affluent culture has the means that she or he may still choose greater freedom in the sphere of work at the expense of purchasing power, and she or he may still choose greater freedom in the spheres of politics, family, or civil society at the expense of work hours and purchasing power.

It is only those persons who commit themselves to the existential strategy of consumerism—i.e., to grounding the meaning of their lives through the interpersonal validation of the meanings signified by their purchases—who sacrifice agency in all other spheres of their existence to maximize their agency in economic consumption. However, consumerism is uniquely attractive as an existential strategy in the contemporary world situation precisely because so many other existential strategies have been marginalized in this context, including those grounded in work, nation,

---

42. Boyle, *Who Are We Now?*, 116; Wuthnow, *God and Mammon*, 31–33.
43. Boyle, *Who Are We Now?*, 79.

heteronomous religion—i.e., religion that demands subjection to clerical authority—and the various ideologies of progress.

The Decline of Nationalism and Marxism

Apart from capitalism, Tillich considered nationalism to be the most significant spiritual force of the modern age. In Tillich's account, the nationalist spirit is characterized by the idolatrous elevation of a sovereign people, which is a counter-movement against capitalism. The unbounded spirit of nationalism leads to totalitarian government, which has a quasi-religious—i.e., existential—as well as a political dimension.[44] As an existential strategy, nationalism answers the question of meaningful personal existence through participation in a collective national meaning that requires the absolute subordination of the individual to the political authority. The weakness of existential nationalism in the modern world is that it demands the sacrifice of "freedom for security, autonomy for certainty, individuality for community, and personality for an absolute symbol."[45] Consumerism is more attractive to the modern spirit than heteronomous nationalism because consumerism emphasizes the significance of the autonomous individual. Tillich foresaw that nationalism would be vulnerable to the growing influence of capitalism, which undermines the distinctiveness of nations and imposes a common economic structure on them.[46]

Even though the nature of capitalism has changed dramatically in the decades since Tillich wrote, his analysis remains valid. Capitalism in its global network form is antithetical to the spirit of nationalism. It has marginalized nationalism as an existential strategy in affluent Western nations—the rhetoric of politicians notwithstanding—and it is weakening nationalism as a force elsewhere in the contemporary world. In democratic nations, declining civil participation is an indicator of the declining significance of national citizenship for personal identity. Legal scholar Sanford Levinson judges that "the 'death of constitutionalism' [faith centered on a national constitution] may be the central event of our time, just as the 'death of God' was that of the past century (and for much the same reason). . . . One ultimately can believe only in that which one can also

---

44. Tillich, "Demonic," 119; Tillich, "Storms of Our Times," 248.
45. Tillich, "Storms of Our Times," 247.
46. Tillich, *Religious Situation*, 86.

respect."⁴⁷ The legitimacy of secular Western nations rests upon their roles as the guarantors of natural morality and economic progress. But the idea of natural morality has been undermined by religious pluralism and the moral relativism of consumerism, and the idea of economic progress has been undermined by growing economic inequality and stagnation. In the United States, Putnam finds that all of the following indicators of civic participation fell sharply between 1973–4 and 1993–4: voting in presidential elections, attending public meetings, attending political rallies or speeches, writing legislators, writing letters to newspapers, signing petitions, belonging to better government groups, working for political parties, and running for public office. While the declines were observed across all age cohorts, they are larger for each succeeding generation, indicating that the decline in the existential significance of national citizenship is likely to continue.[48]

Personality in the global network economy is most commonly constructed upon the individual's identity as consumer, which is inherently atomistic. In making consumer decisions the individual retains a sovereign freedom, and it is in these decisions that he or she most commonly seeks a ground of meaning. But the spirit of existential nationalism demands the surrender of individual identity and freedom for the sake of the group, and in this it is fundamentally pre-modern. This spirit corresponds to personal life under totalitarian government, Boyle observes. "Nationality is . . . essentially a substitute for bourgeois individuality and nationalism is a likely product of the attitudes of those who come from an absolutist state, and would like to attain one of the forms of the modern state, but who are not individuated in the capitalist manner as free economic units."[49] However, totalitarian government itself is undermined by the global network economy. It can only survive today through total suppression of information from the outside world, gross impoverishment of its citizens, and violent repression of their economic aspirations. Therefore, existential nationalism is only viable today through a thorough rejection of the common world and only as a vestige of a previous era. It cannot survive as an existential form of life in the open societies of the affluent West.

Along with nationalism, Tillich saw communism as one of the most significant quasi-religious forces in the postwar era. He described communism as a radicalization and transformation of socialism that, like

47. Levinson, *Constitutional Faith*, 52.
48. Putnam, *Bowling Alone*, 31–34, 45, 252–53.
49. Boyle, *Who Are We Now?*, 109.

nationalism, manifests an idolatrous communal self-affirmation.[50] In its theoretical formulation, Marxism demands ultimate concern and promises a ground of meaning through a this-worldly eschatological narrative. Nelson summarizes this Marxist eschatology as follows:

> Humankind has fallen into evil ways, corrupted by the workings of the forces of the class struggle. The resulting "alienation" for Marx has virtually the same meaning for the human situation as "original sin" in the biblical message. Human beings are today still living in a state of darkness, depravity, and corruption. The prospect of escape from this terrible condition, however, is close at hand. God (now replaced in Marx by the economic laws of history) has promised to deliver the world from sin (alienation). There will be a fierce struggle and a great cataclysm (a final war in history between the capitalist and the working classes), followed by the arrival of the kingdom of God on earth (the triumph of the proletariat and the arrival of pure communism).[51]

Because this narrative is historical, the ability of Marxist theory to ground the meaning of personal existence depends upon historical events.

Marxism no longer exerts a significant influence upon the world situation. The fate of Marxism as a solution to the problem of meaningful personal existence was captive to the ability of communist states to fulfill its eschatological promises in history. This they failed to do. Marxist anthropology could not account for poor worker motivation in collective state-owned enterprises, the material aspirations of workers in communist states, and the corruption and will-to-power exhibited by Communist Party elites. Moreover, the preeminent communist state, the Soviet Union, continued to exhibit the characteristics of a colonial economic empire. As such, Boyle observes, it was subject to the same pressures from the global marketplace to break down political barriers to trade and investment that had earlier undermined the colonial empires of Britain and France.[52]

The Soviet empire did not fall to military and ideological pressures alone, but, more significantly, to the pressure that Western affluence placed upon its captive populations. The vulnerability of the Soviet empire to Western military and ideological pressures was not evident until the 1970s and 1980s, when the unequal abilities of the East and West to

---

50. Tillich, *Encounter of World Religions*, 4–5.
51. Nelson, *Economics as Religion*, 24.
52. Boyle, *Who Are We Now?*, 81.

support the requirements of the emerging information economy dramatically widened the disparity between Eastern and Western economic productivities, state resources, and lifestyles. The Western economies reaped the economic fruits of successfully adapting themselves to the demands of the global economy for decentralization, integration, knowledge use, and competitiveness, which the communist Eastern economies could not do. The failure of the communist nations resulted from their commitment to centralized economic planning and to the industrialism upon which the Marxist theory of work organization was based.[53] The political disintegration of the COMECON trading bloc and of the Soviet Union itself created a decisive historical refutation to the Marxist narrative of history, confirming the counter-narrative of triumphant capitalism suggested by China's embrace of capitalist enterprise, foreign investment, and free trade earlier in the 1980s.

Environmentalism

Environmentalism has emerged since the 1960s as one of the most significant contemporary critiques of Western capitalism and consumerism. Environmentalism functions as an existential strategy whereby persons seek to ground the meaning of their existence through a practical form of life organized around their relationship to the natural world. Understood in this way, Dunlap contends, "environmentalism addresses the alienation in modern society in a modern context, finding the sacred in a material world and a way of personal knowledge and engagement with the world on the basis of objective knowledge."[54] Existential environmentalism, like existential nationalism, is an idealization of a past that never existed and thus a form of romanticism, as Tillich defines it.[55]

The rise of the environmental movement coincides historically with the rise of consumerism. Like consumerism, the success of environmentalism derives from its compatibility with the global network economy. Like consumerism, existential environmentalism finds meaning in the exercise of agency in economic consumption and the recognition and validation of these acts by others. Where environmentalism and consumerism differ is in

---

53. Taylor, *Confidence Games*, 148–49; Friedman, *Lexus and the Olive Tree*, 62; Boyle, *Who Are We Now?*, 71–72.

54. Dunlap, *Faith in Nature*, 118, 149.

55. Tillich, "Realism and Faith," 75.

the meanings that are signified by acts of economic consumption. According to Dunlap, environmentalists are motivated by an experience of "horror at the destruction of a world they felt was essential to our physical survival and our spirit."[56] Since existential environmentalists seek to ground their personal meaning in relationship to nature, the destruction of nature confronts them with the existential threat of meaninglessness.

Environmentalism borrowed the idea that reality and meaning are to be found in nature from nineteenth-century Romanticism. This belief is exemplified by Ralph Waldo Emerson. According to Dunlap,

> Emerson regarded Nature as at once the radically Other and the gateway to ourselves. Outside society, unaffected by humanity's tricks and shams, nature did not deceive. Uniquely real, it transforms us.... Our ties to nature were more than personal or physical—they were metaphysical. Two elements divided the world between them, Nature and Soul, and there is "a radical correspondence between visible and human thoughts.... Every natural fact is a symbol of some spiritual fact.... The whole of nature is a metaphor of the human mind. The laws of moral nature answer to those of matter as face to face in a glass."[57]

Two forebears of the environmental movement, John Muir and John Burroughs, echoed Emerson's view of nature as ultimate or primal reality. In environmentalism, meaning exists in relation to the whole of the life process, which includes the birth and death of individuals and the natural emergence and extinction of species. As an existential strategy, therefore, environmentalism answers the threat of meaninglessness but it fails to answer the anxiety of death. Like Marxism and nationalism, environmentalism offers a collective immortality but not an individual immortality.[58]

Like nationalism, environmentalism is practical rather than theoretical. Environmentalists seek practical ways of living with nature that can guide individual lives and inspire social change. Dunlap identifies two practical strategies that environmentalists have adopted: green consumerism and bioregionalism. "Green consumerism tried to change society from within, while bioregionalism looked for a new kind of daily life outside the established economy and in tune with the land." [59] Green consumers reinter-

---

56. Dunlap, *Faith in Nature*, 117.
57. Ibid., 47; quoting Emerson, "Nature," 6, 15, 17.
58. Dunlap, *Faith in Nature*, 51–55, 121.
59. Ibid., 42, 97.

pret consumer decisions as moral choices that can preserve or destroy the natural world. Bioregionalists do not seek to escape society, but to create enough distance from the consumer culture that they can achieve a purity of life that can have an evangelical effect upon the mainstream culture, in the same manner as monastic communities. In practice, bioregionalists have found even a limited withdrawal from the global economy more difficult than they anticipated.[60]

As an existential strategy, environmentalism faces two risks: co-option by consumerism and historical refutation. The term "green consumerism" suggests the possibility of a synthesis between environmentalism and consumerism in which environmentalism becomes a consumable lifestyle rather than a ground of personal meaning. Advertisers have recognized consumers' increasing expression of environmental values and learned to present the natural world and environmental responsibility as consumable amenities. Environmentalism is vulnerable to co-option by consumerism precisely because both existential strategies are mediated by acts of economic consumption and social validation. Seemingly contradictory evidence in opinion polls suggests that most professed support for the environment reflects a "green" form of consumerism rather than existential environmentalism. Dunlap acknowledges that "while people told public-opinion pollsters they thought pollution was a major problem, they bought bigger houses and bigger SUVs and continued to believe that endless economic growth was possible and necessary."[61] Because the narrative of environmentalism points towards a this-worldly utopia, it is also vulnerable to historical refutation in the same manner as Marxism. The world's ongoing environmental deterioration threatens environmentalists' hope in the eventual historical realization of a harmonious environmental utopia, and the erosion of hope undermines a commitment to environmental practices.[62] The difference between the Marxist and environmentalist utopias lies in the fact that the latter remains a historical possibility, despite increasingly grim forecasts to the contrary.

60. Ibid., 39, 106–10.
61. Ibid., 151, 158.
62. Ibid., 143.

The Religious Significance of Recent Developments in Western Culture

Developments in Institutional Religion

In Tillich's analysis, the decisive event underlying the search for meaning (and the despair of it) in the twentieth century was the loss of God in the nineteenth century. Ludwig Feuerbach explained God away in terms of the infinite desire of the human heart. Karl Marx dismissed God as an ideological attempt to rise above the given reality. Friedrich Nietzsche interpreted belief in God as a weakening of the will to live. The result was the pronouncement "God is dead," and with God, the whole axiomatic system of Judeo-Christian values and meanings that Westerners once took for granted. Secularization, however, did not mean that Western cultures had lost their religious substance, but that this substance was increasingly expressed outside the explicitly religious sphere. Accompanying this shift, Tillich saw a hollowing out of the explicitly religious elements in culture, a process by which they were emptied of religious substance and could no longer answer the question of meaningful personal existence.[63]

Tillich attributed the rise of existential nationalism and Marxism in the 1930s to the inherently unstable void of meaning created by secularization in the churches. Nationalist movements easily co-opted the secularized Protestant churches that had sought to rationalize Christianity in the service of economic progress. In Europe, only the Roman Catholic and Barthian Protestant churches—with their heteronomous claims to an authority that superseded the absolute claims of the state—were able to survive the Nazi era intact. However, in Tillich's view, these heteronomous churches had no power to resist the autonomous spirit of capitalism.[64] The modern spirit's desire for autonomy makes consumerism more attractive than heteronomous religion as a strategy to secure meaningful personal existence.

The tendency in the present world situation for individuals to locate agency and identity in their economic consumption activity has amplified the spirit of autonomy that Tillich observed in capitalist cultures. Persons who construct their identity primarily in terms of economic consumption tend to view their decisions in the explicitly religious sphere as free sovereign acts, in the same manner as they view their consumer decisions. Network capitalism's increased availability of information, its disruption of community through increased labor mobility and family breakdown, and

---

63. Tillich, *Courage to Be*, 142; Tillich, "Religious Situation in Germany," 365.

64. Tillich, "On the Boundary," 51; Tillich, "Religious Situation in Germany," 364; Tillich, "Continental European Development," 302–3; Tillich, "End of the Protestant Era?" 228–29; Tillich, *Religious Situation*, 171–72.

its diminishment of trust in institutions also undermine the authority and existential significance of traditional religious organizations.

In Europe, these forces have emptied the churches, accelerating the processes of secularization that Tillich described. The churches lack the power to recreate the axiomatic belief in God and church that was sustained by the medieval European cultural consensus. In the absence of axiomatic belief, the consumer culture's autonomous consumer has largely rejected Europe's heteronomous churches. Secularization is now the norm in traditionally Roman Catholic as well as traditionally Protestant European nations. Heteronomous Islam has grown in Europe in recent decades, but this phenomenon is associated with immigrant subcultures from Islamic nations that are largely unassimilated into the dominant European consumer cultures.

In the United States, the heteronomous Roman Catholic Church has also suffered secularization because it does not respond to the demands of autonomous consumers. This is seen in declining membership, contributions, and intensity of church participation among native-born Americans. At the same time, overall Catholic numbers in the United States have been replenished by immigration from traditionally Roman Catholic nations.[65] Like Islamic immigrants in Europe, many first-generation Roman Catholic immigrants in the United States belong to subcultures that are relatively isolated from the dominant consumer culture.

Protestant religious institutions in the United States have proved more responsive to the religious demands of the consumer culture than in Europe. In the Protestant churches, the shift from production-centered to consumption-centered identity has been accompanied by a shift from production to consumption in attitudes towards the church. Wuthnow observes that Americans "used to . . . spend their time working for religious committees and guilds; they now let professional experts—writers, artists, therapists, spiritual guides—be the producers while they consume what they need in order to enrich themselves spiritually."[66] Those institutions that do not provide a spiritual product that is compatible with a consumption-centered lifestyle are subject to abandonment and withdrawal of financial support by a population increasingly willing to shop around in the religious marketplace. Frequently, Wuthnow observes, the churches have submitted

---

65. Putnam, *Bowling Alone*, 75–76, 126.
66. Wuthnow, *After Heaven*, 7–8.

to these pressures, following the path of least resistance to avoid giving offense to congregants upon whom clergy salaries depend.[67]

What U.S. consumers seek in the religious marketplace depends significantly upon how successful they have been at sustaining a sense of personal significance through their economic consumption. As I noted above, the economic rewards of the global economy are increasingly unequally distributed, and the U.S. government has done less and less to mitigate these differences. This growing differentiation of society into economic winners and economic losers separates U.S. demand for religious institutions into two market segments. Wuthnow identifies one segment with the pursuit of economic success, and the other with seeking comfort in the face of economic failure. Each of these segments, however, demands a certain compatibility with the culture's association of identity with economic consumption. The result has been the creation of two distinct syntheses between Christianity and consumer culture. Religious consumers in both market segments seek institutions that affirm rather than challenge their economic decisions. They seek religious institutions that affirm consumerism's vision of the good life as material prosperity, ease, and social esteem. They seek institutions that affirm their sovereign consumer will as the only measure of truth and value.[68]

The market segment for economic winners demands a form of institutional religion that is compatible with success in the global network economy. Since their consumer lifestyle is validated socially, persons in this market segment do not approach organized religion with the attitude that there is any flaw in themselves or any need for teaching. Rather, they seek a religion that helps them to fulfill the roles they are already playing, and to feel better about themselves in the process. Because their demands upon organized religion are slight, they are likely to abandon it if they cannot find something useful to their consumeristic form of life. This explains why sociologists have found that those who drop out from organized religion tend to have higher economic and social status than those who remain.[69] Where identity and meaning are associated with economic consumption, success in one's work means the ability to earn as much money with as little effort as possible. The labor market in the global economy demands optimism, flexibility (including moral flexibility), and social conformity. Those who

---

67. Wuthnow, *God and Mammon*, 9.
68. Ibid., 5–7, 33–34, 48, 127–30, 149; Wuthnow, *After Heaven*, 80–81, 92, 132–33.
69. Wuthnow, *God and Mammon*, 46–47; Putnam, *Bowling Alone*, 76–77, 124–26.

have successfully adapted to these demands seek religious teachings that help them, in Wuthnow's words, "fit in and ... roll with the punches, rather than taking ... [themselves] too seriously."[70] Organized religion that meets the demands of this market segment serves a private, therapeutic role, the purpose of which is to offer unconditional moral affirmation and reassurance. The economically successful look to religion to legitimate their wealth and happiness, given the poverty and misery of others. Therapeutic religion's affirmation of every individual's conduct de-links spirituality from morality. Therefore this form of organized religion has little effect upon conduct, particularly in the economic sphere. A psychologized spirituality also undermines the communal aspect of organized religion.[71]

What is valued in therapeutic religion is the usefulness of teaching and practice to one's psychological well-being, which each consumer determines for himself or herself. This leads to an increasingly syncretistic approach to spirituality, in which individuals adopt beliefs and practices a la carte from many religious traditions.[72] The synthesis of consumerism and cafeteria spirituality is a form of "psychological polytheism." Following psychologist James Hillman, Wuthnow defines psychological polytheism as the fragmentation of a personal identity that "has many different claims made on it and that is able to find small truths in many places, rather than deriving answers from a single source."[73] A fragmented identity can readily accommodate a functionally polytheistic synthesis between consumerism and many religious traditions, so long as the monotheistic tenets in the Jewish, Christian, and Islamic traditions are ignored at the practical level.

The market segment for economic losers demands a form of institutional religion that compensates for failure in the global network economy. Like those in the segment of economic winners, individuals in this market segment define the good life in terms of a prosperous consumption lifestyle in this world, along with its associated social recognition and validation. Therefore, they seek a form of organized religion that offers—or at least promises—a second chance at economic prosperity and social esteem in this world, another path to consumeristic success for those who see little chance at gaining a prosperous lifestyle and social esteem through

---

70. Wuthnow, *God and Mammon*, 6.

71. Wuthnow, *After Heaven*, 77–79, 96–101; Wuthnow, *God and Mammon*, 14, 77; Roof and McKinney, *American Mainline Religion*, 32–33; Putnam, *Bowling Alone*, 74.

72. Wuthnow, *After Heaven*, 15, 149; Taylor, *Confidence Games*, 313.

73. Wuthnow, *After Heaven*, 160.

economic processes alone. This form of synthesis between consumerism and institutional Christianity is found most commonly among evangelical and Pentecostal churches, whereas the mainline Protestant churches are more likely to offer therapeutic religion. Since those who fail to succeed economically have fewer secular options for spiritual self-affirmation than the economically successful, and since the global network economy has shrunk the ratio of economic winners to economic losers, U.S. membership in the evangelical and Pentecostal churches has grown faster than national population growth, even as mainline churches declined. Moral self-control is the means that the "second chance" religious institutions offer those who have experienced economic failure to achieve consumeristic success. They promise a divinely guaranteed moral order in which purity of life is eventually rewarded in this life with material prosperity and social recognition. This moral discipline is primarily identified with sexual restraint. These "second chance" religious institutions minimize those elements of biblical teaching that call into question the compatibility of Christian faith with the goals of consumerism. Like the synthesis between Christianity and consumerism in the market segment for economic winners, the synthesis in the market segment for economic losers is fully compatible with an existential commitment to seek meaning through economic consumption.[74]

Existentialism and Postmodernism

Existentialist philosophy, in Tillich's view, was the theoretical movement that best expressed the postwar situation of the end of culture, that is, a culture that no longer expressed any religious substance. Tillich described existentialism as a protest against the spirit of capitalist society that was motivated by capitalist society's threat to individual personal existence. However, the existentialist critique of the spirit of capitalism failed to change the course of Western culture as significantly as Tillich had hoped. This failure was due to the inadequacy of philosophical existentialism as a means to ground the meaning of personal existence. Philosophical existentialism could say "No" to the capitalist spirit, but it provided nothing apart from technical knowledge to which an individual could say "Yes."[75] To choose a life with no ground of meaning was, and is, impossible. To

---

74. Putnam, *Bowling Alone*, 76–77, 161; Wuthnow, *After Heaven*, 92–93, 110.

75. Tillich, "Religion and Secular Culture," 60; Tillich, *Courage to Be*, 137–38; Tillich, *Systematic Theology*, vol. 1, 100.

choose the meaning of one's life arbitrarily by fiat of the autonomous will is likewise inadequate as a ground of meaning because an arbitrarily chosen meaning cannot be validated by others.

Tillich described existentialism as a protest against the depersonalizing threat of industrial capitalism to the individual self. The rise of a new kind of capitalism in the 1970s signaled the end of this protest. The sovereign consumer of the global network economy is not threatened with the loss of personality altogether, as Tillich believed the worker in industrial society was. He or she is threatened with meaninglessness, with the loss of a personal center, and with the loss of community. Tillich's Christian existentialism can address this situation but philosophical existentialism cannot.

The emergence of global network capitalism has been accompanied by the emergence of theoretical movements that are compatible with this economic order. Much of what falls under the label "postmodernism" belongs to this category. Since the term "postmodernism" covers a broad array of intellectual currents, it is possible to find exceptions to almost any generalization attempting to cover all of its various movements. My aim here is simply to identify the most significant elements within postmodern thinking that disclose its compatibility with consumerism. These elements are most clearly seen in the work of post-structuralist thinkers like Jacques Derrida and Mark C. Taylor.

Boyle argues that postmodernism and consumerism are inseparable. One way in which their compatibility is seen is in many postmodern thinkers' wholesale rejection of meta-narratives, and the consequent fragmentation of meaning into discrete acts of subjective interpretation. In a similar fashion, consumerism has been accompanied by a refusal to recognize the contemporary economy's historical contingency and the causal factors that led to its development. A second point of compatibility between consumerism and postmodernism is their disintegration of the modern understanding of a unitary personal identity. In consumerism, personal identity is spatially and temporally discontinuous. The institutions that formerly provided continuity to identity have faded in significance. Meaning exists in discrete acts of consumption and discrete events of recognition by other persons. This parallels the postmodern belief that there is no unity of the self, and indeed no such thing as the self.[76]

A third point of compatibility between consumerism and postmodernism is that both ignore and obscure the bodily foundation of human

---

76. Boyle, *Who Are We Now?*, 82–83.

existence. They thereby fail to recognize the existential threat of death and the necessity (for most persons) of work in order to live. In the consumer society, Boyle argues, advertisers and marketers promote the idea that the self is purely a consumer. So consumerism encourages self-concealment. The awareness that we must eventually pay for our consumer freedom through further restraints on our working conditions would destroy the illusion of pure sovereign agency in the act of consumption. Postmodern thought shares this concealment of human finitude. It promises that the human past or our own individual lives may be given an infinite number of possible meanings.[77]

A final point of compatibility between consumerism and postmodernism is that both deny the significance of the existential question of meaning, obscuring their adherents' actual ground of meaning. In consumerism, advertisers portray life as an unending series of commercial pleasures, in which the buyer can be recognized as uniquely distinguished by identifying with meaning-laden consumer products. But consumers are only invited to view the false picture of an easy purchase of meaningful life, not their own desperate longing for spiritual affirmation which makes this implausible invitation tempting. In postmodernism, Boyle observes, the idea of the "crisis of the sign" signifies the "loss of confidence in the notion of truth and a virtual divinization instead of the media of communication."[78] These movements are also found in consumerism. The loss of confidence in objective truth exacerbates the existential problem of securing an objective personal significance. Taylor provides an example of the postmodern dismissal of meaning when he writes, "If reality turns out to be virtual, who can really be sure what is real and what is not? . . . Life in all its complexity remains a confidence game in which the abiding challenge is not to find redemption but to learn to live without it."[79] The affirmation of meaningless as an existential strategy is a contradiction in terms that ignores the depth of the problem of human existence. If sincere, Taylor's statement reflects a profound lack of self-understanding. While he rightly argues that meanings grounded in nations, heteronomous churches, and high art are radically undermined by the global network economy,[80] this by no means eliminates all of the potential grounds of meaning that are available to him, a professor

77. Ibid., 120, 153–54.
78. Ibid., 84.
79. Taylor, *Confidence Games*, 13.
80. Ibid., 3, 25–30, 40, 94–98, 310.

who holds a relatively affluent, unusually secure, and prestigious job in the world's richest nation. To proclaim the ease of affirming meaningless life when one has never done so is not a serious proposal.

Because of its affinities with consumerism, postmodernism is incapable of serving as the basis for a critique of the consumer culture. Nor are there any other significant theoretical critiques of consumerism in Western culture today. The theoretical Marxist critique has been discredited, and the philosophical existentialist critique addresses a different world situation. Within the explicitly religious sphere, there are no significant theoretical critiques of consumerism because the existing critiques are based on obsolete economic worldviews and flawed models of consumerism. I will describe the five main types of flawed consumerism models in chapter 3.

3

Types of Consumerism Theories

THE MANY DIVERSE THEORIES that theologians, ethicists, social scientists, and social theorists have offered to describe Western consumerism can be classified into five main types. These types propose, respectively, that consumerism is motivated by:

1. *greed*, i.e., consumers' intemperate materialistic hedonism;

2. *status signaling*, i.e., consumers' desire to communicate superior social status by emulating the consumption patterns of a dominant social class;

3. *manipulation* of consumers by the producers of economic goods through marketing and mass media advertising;

4. *imaginative hedonism*, i.e., consumers seeking emotional pleasure through the imaginative identities that they associate with consumer goods; or

5. *parental concern*, specifically, parents' desire to maximize their children's well-being by acquiring the best possible education, relative to other children, through their housing and college expenditures.

Each of these types of consumerism theories accepts the premise that primary moral agency belongs to the individual person, even if that agency may be subject to others' domination through coercion or lies. This premise ensures these theories' compatibility with most Christian understandings of the human being, which hold that persons are at least partially free, at least partially self-determined, and, to the degree that they are self-determined, responsible for their character and their actions.

The most significant recent attempts by Christian theologians and ethicists to describe consumerism have all conformed to one or more of these types. For example, in *Being Consumed: Economics and Christian Desire,* William Cavanaugh offers contradictory descriptions of the motive of consumerism. Consumerism is, on the one hand, the individualistic association of the self with novel imaginary identities, and on the other hand, the consequence of the powerful formative influence of advertisers' efforts to create dissatisfaction. Cavanaugh does not validate either position or attempt to reconcile the two. Likewise, in *Consuming Religion: Christian Faith and Practice in a Consumer Culture,* Vincent Miller makes uncritical use of contradictory accounts of consumerism's motivation, including status signaling, manipulation, and imaginative hedonism. Like Cavanaugh, Miller makes no attempt to validate the various positions that he incorporates or to reconcile their contradictions. In *The Market Economy and Christian Ethics,* Peter Sedgwick uncritically adopts the position of sociologist Colin Campbell that consumerism is a matter of imaginative hedonism without offering any validation of his position.[1] The failure of these writers to validate a theory of consumerism's motivations undermines their proposals for how the churches or society as a whole should lessen the influence of consumerism. Without understanding consumerism's motivations, their proposals are either ineffective or impossible to implement.

In this chapter I explain the five types of consumerism theories by exploring the thought of paradigmatic thinkers for each model. John Paul II represents the greed theories, Thorstein Veblen the status signaling theories, John Kenneth Galbraith the manipulation theories, Colin Campbell the imaginative hedonism theories, and Elizabeth Warren and Amelia Warren Tyagi the parental concern theories. This sequence represents the order in which the five types of theories emerged historically. In this chapter I explain these thinkers' views of consumerism, show how their theories contrast, and evaluate the conditions under which their theories could be adapted to describe contemporary Western consumerism. I also identify other social theorists who have presented significant or recent examples of the five theoretical types. I leave a more formal empirical testing of these theories to chapter 4.

---

1. Cavanaugh, *Being Consumed*; Miller, *Consuming Religion*; Sedgwick, *Market Economy and Christian Ethics*. These authors' critiques of rival theories do not and cannot validate their own positions, since they do not and cannot demonstrate that the theories they consider are the only possible explanations of consumerism.

Consumerism as Greed

The theorists who interpret consumerism as greed understand greed to mean an immoderate hedonistic desire for the direct material utilities the consumer receives from his or her economic goods. As in standard economic theory, the greed theory sees desires for consumer goods arising wholly within the individual. That is, the individual is independent of other consumers and producers except insofar as they contribute to the individual's adoption of a consumeristic form of life in the first place.[2] The greed theorists understand consumer desires to be conscious but not rational. They associate consumer desires with the lower faculties of appetite and instinct rather than the higher intellectual or spiritual faculties. The thinkers who interpret consumerism as greed include most theologians and ethicists in the Christian tradition, including John Paul II, whose thought I will explore in detail. It also includes thinkers in secular disciplines like sociologists Werner Sombart and Daniel Bell, cultural critic Terry Eagleton, and evolutionary psychologist Peter Whybrow.

The greed theorists generally consider contemporary Western consumerism to be a continuation—if an extreme example—of a form of life that has always existed so long as there have been economic surpluses and luxury goods. The fact that they associate consumerism with luxury goods indicates that they consider consumerism to be a behavior of persons who subsist above the level of economic necessity: first elites, and now in the West the middle and working classes as well.

John Paul II's theory of consumerism is a logical extension of the oldest and most broadly held perspective in Christian ethics on the relationship of persons to material possessions. While this perspective is not limited to Roman Catholics, John Paul II is heir to the most influential thinkers in this intellectual tradition and fully incorporates this tradition into his thought. According to this tradition, the right relationship between persons and economic goods is to use goods in a manner that is fitting to humanity's proper end, not to desire them or become attached to them. Thus John Paul II writes, "We must . . . distinguish that which is merely a condition for a truly human life from that which is decisive for such a

---

2. In the terminology of philosopher Harry Frankfurt, the greed theorists hold that first-order desires—ordinary choices among possible courses of action—are autonomous while second order desires—choices about one's desired character—are subject to social influences. Frankfurt, *Importance of What We Care About*, 12–16.

life."[3] The criterion that John Paul II proposes for the correct use of goods is that they contribute "to the realization of the human vocation as such."[4] Economic consumption within a market economy may or may not meet this criterion, depending on the form that such consumption takes.

In his 1991 encyclical *Centesimus Annus*, John Paul II does not condemn consumption as such or rising living standards, but the wrong personal relation to consumption. "It is not wrong to want to live better; what is wrong is a style of life which is presumed to be better when it is directed towards 'having' rather than 'being,' and which wants to have more, not in order to be more but in order to spend life in enjoyment as an end in itself."[5] Thus consumerism transgresses the proper use of economic goods because the consumeristic person seeks to enjoy goods as an end in itself. This position is consistent with Thomas Aquinas, who condemns treating temporal goods as an end. It likewise agrees with Augustine's position that temporal goods are designed to serve the end of temporal peace, not the pursuit of pleasure.[6]

John Paul II understands consumerism to be a desire for material goods that is not only directed towards the wrong end, but is wrongly directed in immoderate or intemperate degree. Thus, in his 1987 encyclical *Sollicitudo Rei Socialis*, he describes consumerism as "a crass materialism, and at the same time a radical dissatisfaction, because one quickly learns—unless one is shielded from the flood of publicity and the ceaseless and tempting offers of products—that the more one possesses the more one wants, while deeper aspirations remain unsatisfied and perhaps even stifled."[7] In this respect, John Paul II's analysis of consumerism reflects Aquinas's definition of the vice of covetousness as exceeding the measure of external riches necessary for life by wishing to acquire or keep them immoderately.[8] However, John Paul II specifically attributes the insatiability of consumerism's desires to its failure to satisfy deeper human aspirations.

I have assumed, provisionally, that consumerism has become sufficiently prevalent in Western cultures to generate observable effects on national economic statistics. However, consumerism can only be a widespread

3. John Paul II, "Constitution of Culture," 268.
4. John Paul II, *Sollicitudo Rei Socialis*, 28.
5. John Paul II, *Centesimus Annus*, 36.
6. Aquinas, *Summa Theologica* I-II.99.6; Augustine, *City of God* 19.13–14.
7. John Paul II, *Sollicitudo Rei Socialis*, 28.
8. Aquinas *Summa Theologica* II-II.118.1.

social phenomenon in a society that has achieved mass affluence. In such societies, the *necessary* utilities of consumer goods are relatively unimportant to most persons because they can be taken for granted. Thus defined, consumerism does not becomes significant in Western society until the twentieth century. John Paul II takes a contrary position. In describing the phenomenon of consumerism in concepts similar to those used by Augustine and Aquinas, he assumes substantial historical continuities in the relationships between persons and economic goods. In his view, contemporary consumerism is qualitatively similar to hedonism, avarice, and covetousness as they were expressed in Roman and medieval European societies.

In *Sollicitudo Rei Socialis*, John Paul II associates consumerism with materialism. Materialism, as used by John Paul II, means two things. First, there is a practical preoccupation with material goods and pleasures. In materialism, "the only goal which counts is the pursuit of one's own material well-being.... 'Quality of life' is interpreted primarily or exclusively as economic efficiency, inordinate consumerism, physical beauty and pleasure."[9] Second, there is an ideological element that defines the human being and the human good solely in terms of economics and the satisfaction of material needs. In *Centesimus Annus*, John Paul II denounces the consumer society and the Marxist society as equally materialist in this sense. John Paul II describes the practical preoccupation with material goods as an idolatry of material goods, and the ideological element as an idolatry of the market. Only the former, strictly speaking, belongs to John Paul II's definition of consumerism, but the latter is found in conjunction with it in societies in which consumeristic culture is widespread.[10]

John Paul II identifies the aim of the consumeristic individual's materialist pursuits as enjoyment, and the perceived good of consumerism as pleasure. In other words, the motivation for consumerism is hedonistic. In consumerism, he argues, people become slaves to immediate gratification through the multiplication or continual replacement of possessions. In his view, the consumer society equates freedom with absolute license. However, freedom is only free, he argues, when it is obedient to the truth about God and humanity. Thus for John Paul II hedonism and freedom are opposites. Nevertheless, he claims, the individual enslaved to the culture of

---

9. John Paul II, *Evangelium Vitae*, 23.

10. John Paul II, *Centesimus Annus*, 19; John Paul II, "Address to the Tribunal of the Roman Rota," 5; John Paul II, "Address to Margus Laidre."

consumerism retains a residual freedom due to the transcendent nature of the human being.[11]

John Paul II condemns the hedonistic motive of consumerism for two further reasons. In the first place, he asserts, it appeals to a false, secular picture of what the human being is, and thereby prevents the individual enmeshed in a consumerist lifestyle from recognizing, seeking, or attaining his or her true end. In his account, the human being possesses interior and spiritual dimensions to which the material and instinctive dimensions should be subordinated. But the consumeristic culture makes direct appeal to persons' instincts while ignoring the reality of their intelligence and freedom. John Paul II singles out advertisers for particular criticism when they encourage a view of the human being that is purely appetitive and instinctual. However, in exhorting people not to succumb to advertisers' temptations, he places the primary responsibility for adopting a consumeristic form of life with the individuals who consent to the advertisers' seductions.[12]

Instead of finding happiness, John Paul II contends, the individual who embraces a purely instinctual picture of human nature suffers a fragmentation of spirit, a breakdown of interpersonal relationships, and an existential loneliness and meaninglessness. Moreover, he argues, this view of the human being is an obstacle to faith because it dulls and distracts the intellect, and it closes the self to the possibility of the transcendent.[13] Even where religion and its ethical demands are not explicitly rejected, when freedom is lived as "a blind acquiescence to instinctive forces and to an individual's will to power" the result is "a life which, even in its more significant moments and more decisive choices, is lived as if God did not exist."[14] The consequences of living without reference to God, John Paul II contends, are dehumanization, fear, selfishness, moral confusion, and relativism. Absent an acknowledgment of offense against God, he argues, individuals lose a sense of sin against their fellow human being. What remains, is growing moral subjectivism and a practical lack of any ethical principles. The person who rejects God rejects the high dignity of the human being expressed in the

---

11. John Paul II, *Centesimus Annus*, 41; John Paul II, *Memory and Identity*, 34; John Paul II, *Sollicitudo Rei Socialis*, 28; John Paul II, *Veritatis Splendor*, 53.

12. John Paul II, *Centesimus Annus*, 36; John Paul II, *Dilecti Amici*, 13.

13. John Paul II, "Address to the Bishops of Angola," 7; John Paul II "Address to the Bishops of Japan," 4; John Paul II, "Address to the Pontifical Academies," 3.

14. John Paul II, *Pastores Dabo Vobis*, 8.

Christian doctrines that humanity is created in God's image and that God became human in the person of Jesus Christ. In rejecting these, both the high respect that is due other persons and self respect are rejected as well.[15]

In the second place, John Paul II condemns consumerism's hedonistic motives because they foster a selfish, exaggerated individualism that undermines the moral imperatives of family responsibilities, solidarity with persons in need, and ecological stewardship. In defining consumerism as individualistic and its motivation as hedonistic, John Paul II denies that there is a relational element to consumeristic desires.[16] To the contrary, he argues, consumerism acts to undermine relationships and isolate the individual. In the family, he asserts, consumerism leads to the desire for individual gratification rather than a happy and fruitful shared life. The hedonistic person tends to objectify others and to treat them as possessions, a phenomenon which John Paul II labels "concupiscence." John Paul II's condemnation of concupiscence has a philosophical parallel in the second form of Immanuel Kant's categorical imperative, to treat persons as ends in themselves rather than means.[17] The desire to use other persons to further one's own hedonistic ends is precisely the opposite of the virtue of solidarity, which John Paul II defines as "a firm and persevering determination to commit oneself to the common good; that is to say to the good of all and of each individual, because we are all really responsible for all."[18] He declares that "the building of . . . a global culture of solidarity is perhaps the greatest moral task confronting humanity today."[19] Thus the consumeristic attitude that opposes the spirit of solidarity is an obstacle to humanity's present moral task. With respect to the environment, consumeristic individualism yields a "culture of waste" that ignores the limited availability of natural resources, the poverty of fellow human beings, and the duty of sharing. In John Paul II's view, the anthropological error responsible for ecological de-

---

15. John Paul II, "Address to the Bishops of Italy," 2; John Paul II, *Centesimus Annus* 11; John Paul II, *Memory and Identity*, 111; John Paul II, "Message for World Mission Sunday 1998," 2; John Paul II, *Reconciliation and Penance*, 18.

16. The individualism of consumeristic motivations is distinct from the question of the social reproduction of the consumeristic form of life, for which John Paul II recognizes the influences of family, associates, and cultural institutions. See John Paul II, *Centesimus Annus*, 38, 41.

17. John Paul II, "Letter to Families," 20; John Paul II, "Message for the 1993 World Day of Peace," 3; Kant, *Groundwork of the Metaphysics of Morals*, 96.

18. John Paul II, *Sollicitudo Rei Socialis*, 38.

19. John Paul II, "Address to the United Kingdom Ambassador."

struction not only holds too high a view of human self-sufficiency, it holds too low a view of human worth. Disregard for the environment reflects a prior disregard for the value of human life.[20]

In defining consumerism as excessively individualistic, John Paul II once again displays his belief in the continuity between contemporary consumerism and historical relationships between human beings and material goods. For example, in a 1961 essay he associates the sin of excessive individualism with modern liberalism and capitalism generally, not just with consumerism. Likewise, in a 2001 exhortation, John Paul II identifies nineteenth-century capitalist culture as "industrial, consumer society," indicating that he sees a basic continuity between industrial capitalism and consumer capitalism.[21]

In contrast to the interpretation of consumerism that I presented in chapter 2, John Paul II argues that consumerism is characterized by the absence of religion and of existential meaning. In his 1990 encyclical *Redemptoris Missio*, for example, he explicitly places consumerism in opposition to the search for meaning: "While on the one hand people seem to be pursuing material prosperity and to be sinking ever deeper into consumerism and materialism, on the other hand we are witnessing a desperate search for meaning, the need for an inner life, and a desire to learn new forms and methods of meditation and prayer."[22] In this analysis, consumerism serves as a means of avoiding the search for meaning rather than an alternate means of seeking meaning. John Paul II thereby implies that it is possible to choose to live a life without meaning, a position that fails to acknowledge the seriousness of the human existential predicament and the strength of the psychological and spiritual drives to escape it. In similar fashion, in *Centesimus Annus*, John Paul II asserts that consumerism intentionally and successfully excludes any religious dimension.[23] As with the search for meaning, John Paul II understands the religious aspect of life to belong to the category of an activity that can be freely chosen or avoided, rather than an essential and inescapable dimension of human existence.

A parallel to John Paul II's discussion of consumerism can be found in Werner Sombart's discussion of luxury consumption. Sombart identifies

---

20. John Paul II, "Jubilee of the Agricultural World," 8; John Paul II, "Message for the 1989 World Day of Peace," 13.
21. John Paul II, *Ecclesia in Oceania*, 26; John Paul II, "Thomistic Personalism," 174.
22. John Paul II, *Redemptoris Missio*, 38.
23. John Paul II, *Centesimus Annus*, 19.

luxury as unnecessary consumption driven by materialistic and selfish motives. Like John Paul II, Sombart sees the desire for luxuries existing alongside the desire for necessary consumption throughout Western history, but assuming greater prominence in the modern era. Like John Paul II's view of consumerism, Sombart views luxury consumption to be materialistic and hedonistic in its motivation. Like John Paul II, Sombart describes the hedonism that drives luxury consumption as an improper subordination of higher ideals to baser natural instincts. Unlike John Paul II, however, Sombart recognizes that social ambition may also drive luxury consumption. Still, he sees this motive as subordinate to hedonism.[24]

Like Sombart, Daniel Bell does not explicitly discuss consumerism. Nevertheless, his description of middle-class American life in the 1970s shares many features with my definition of consumerism. First, he observes, consumption has become unmoored from any objective standard of need. Second, because desires for luxury goods are psychological rather than biological, they are insatiable. Third, these desires are not restrained by any transcendent ethic. Like John Paul II, Bell describes the modern middle-class consumer culture as hedonistic and materialistic in both the practical and ideological senses. On the one hand, the individual in the consumeristic society is controlled by baser appetites. On the other hand, unrestrained instinctual behavior is reinforced by postmodern theorists who see it as liberation from neurotic repression and by politicians who define the society's end as an ever-increasing material prodigality. Advertisers, in Bell's view, do not manipulate consumers so much as teach them the consumption lifestyles appropriate to their status. Like John Paul II, Bell sees a preoccupation with license, one that substitutes individual impulse for any transcendent purpose. Bell is also consistent with John Paul II's description of consumerism when he characterizes the modern middle-class lifestyle as one of self-absorption and self-idolatry. This entails a belief in self-created identity and a shift toward self-grounded moral norms.[25]

Like John Paul II, Terry Eagleton describes individual motives in the consumer culture in terms of a hedonistic self-gratification of instinctive desires. In Eagleton's portrayal, the consumeristic individual surrenders his or her will to his or her desires and passions. The natural self, encompassing the desires and passions, assumes the role of "surrogate deity." The individual sees his or her natural self and its unconstrained impulses as an

---

24. Sombart, *Luxury and Capitalism*, 59–61, 81–85, 95, 117.
25. Bell, *Cultural Contradictions of Capitalism*, 18–22, 37, 49–51, 69, 75, 89, 132.

independent source of meaning and value. In consequence, the culture's commodities become aesthetic goods, marketing becomes semiotic—i.e., marketers transform consumer goods into signs—and consumer goods are eroticized. In contrast to John Paul II, who sees continuity between contemporary consumerism and premodern hedonistic materialism, Eagleton holds that the consumer society that exists today emerged in the West during the postmodern period. Like John Paul II, Eagleton does not restrict this form of life to a particular social class. Eagleton also shares John Paul II's view with respect to the consumer culture's loss of transcendent meaning. The consumer culture, he argues, restricts meaning to consumer desire and individual choice, thereby eliminating any transcendent symbolic foundations for a collective identity associated with nation, religion or cultural tradition. As a result, Eagleton argues, individuals lose their capacity to act in accordance with some greater good, and the social order loses any objective rationale for its continued existence.[26]

Peter Whybrow, like Sombart and Bell, does not specifically use the term consumerism. However, his description of contemporary American life closely follows my definition of consumerism. First, he argues, material ambitions have become unmoored from any standard of objective need. Second, this striving overrides consciously held values so that other goods are sacrificed for greater material affluence. The goods sacrificed for consumption include freedom from debt, time for intimate relationships, family and community cohesion, leisure time, adequate sleep, physical fitness, and freedom from anxiety and stress. Like John Paul II, Whybrow claims that human beings' instinctive desires are selfish. Unlike John Paul II, however, Whybrow contends that reason is naturally subordinate to instinctive desires. Whybrow attributes the human capacity to control and regulate instinctive desires to socially-learned behaviors and their associated emotions. Self-restraint, empathy, and conforming to social hierarchies through the influence of pride and shame are learned by imitation in stable families and communities. Human beings thus traditionally lived in a dynamic tension between self-assertion and social restraint. Greed arises in contemporary American society, Whybrow argues, because the culture has failed to reproduce social restraints on self-assertion. This failure is partly due to advertisers' legitimation of consumers' insatiable desires, but Whybrow does not credit advertisers with creating these desires. Like John

---

26. Eagleton, *Idea of Culture*, 72–75, 84, 125–26; Eagleton, *Crisis of Contemporary Culture*, 2–3, 6–10.

Paul II, Whybrow defines greed as an excess over and above a natural and appropriate desire for material goods. John Paul II considers reason, rather than socialized emotions, to be the restraint on material appetites that consumeristic culture overrides, but otherwise Whybrow's description is comparable to John Paul II's.[27]

Consumerism as Status Signaling

The second group of theorists attributes consumerism's motivation to the desire to maintain or advance social status, which, they claim, is signified by an individual's pattern of consumption. The theories of Thorstein Veblen, Georg Simmel, Pierre Bourdieu, Juliet Schor, and Shira Boss all conform to the status signaling type. These theorists generally agree that consumerism is mainly found in the upper and upper-middle classes—a claim that I will evaluate empirically in chapter 4. However, they differ with respect to the timing of its historical emergence. According to Veblen consumerism arises with the modern industrial age, but Schor situates its historical emergence in the late twentieth century. In contrast to the greed theories, the status signaling theories consider the primary utility of consumer goods to be semiotic rather than material. That is, consumer goods are valued for what they signify, not for the direct services they provide. In contrast to the imaginative hedonism theorists, the status signaling theories stress the importance of communicating the meanings signified by consumer goods to other persons. They do not consider these meanings significant only in relationship to oneself. The status signaling theories consider social status to be the sole, universally-recognized positional good. This also contradicts the imaginative hedonism theories. By positional good, I mean a good that is valued primarily for how it compares with goods in the same category that are possessed by others. Unlike the greed and imaginative hedonism theories, the status signaling theories deny that the consumer's motives are fully conscious. In this respect, the status signaling theories agree with the manipulation theories and with the position that I present in chapter 5.

I will examine the position of Thorstein Veblen in detail because his theory is the original and most influential example of the status signaling type. While Veblen does not use the term consumerism, he identifies a closely related concept that he calls "conspicuous consumption." Like

---

27. Whybrow, *American Mania*, 2, 6–8, 25, 37, 106, 128, 158–59, 176–77.

consumerism, conspicuous consumption refers to an inherently unlimited pattern of consumption that subverts consciously-held ethical beliefs in determining an individual's action. Conspicuous consumption, like consumerism, reflects consumption far in excess of that which can be explained by the need for the direct material utilities of consumer goods and services. These similarities are sufficient to ask whether Veblen's late-nineteenth-century theory of conspicuous consumption can account for the motivation of contemporary consumerism.

Veblen proposes that conspicuous consumption is motivated by an instinct of emulation. By "emulation," Veblen does not mean simple imitation, but comparing oneself with others for the sake of besting them in a competition for social rank. Veblen calls the comparison that serves this function an "invidious" comparison. He uses the term invidious "in a technical sense as describing a comparison of persons with a view to rating and grading them in respect of relative worth or value."[28] The individual, in Veblen's view, does not merely seek to be like the person of higher social status but to take his or her place. The invidious comparison is the means by which this competition takes place.

By referring to emulation as an instinct, Veblen means an immutable, hereditary, physiologically-grounded, psychological drive. According to Veblen's definition, an instinct drives the will toward an end, but the intellect determines the means for achieving that end. In Veblen's view, emulation is one of the strongest motives of economic behavior, second only to the instinct of self-preservation. However, Veblen believes that the instinctive motives governing human behavior should not be understood singly. In addition to emulation and self-preservation, Veblen proposes that human conduct aims to achieve the ends of a predatory instinct, an aggressive or sporting instinct, an instinct of workmanship, a parental instinct, and an instinct of idle curiosity. The interaction of multiple ends and the indeterminacy of means to achieve these ends mean that Veblen's concept of instinctive motivation does not simply and directly determine conduct.[29]

What determines conduct in Veblen's theory is the interaction of habit and social institutions with an individual's cultural situation. Over time, Veblen argues, societies develop institutions that represent historically-tested and conventionalized means of achieving instinctive ends. These

28. Veblen, *Theory of the Leisure Class*, 40.
29. Veblen, *Instinct of Workmanship* 3–5, 13, 29; Veblen, *Theory of the Leisure Class*, 85; Tilman, *Intellectual Legacy of Thorstein Veblen*, 78, 99.

institutions are both practical and theoretical. Habitual practices aimed at achieving instinctive ends are institutionalized, but so are the habits of thought that consider these habitual practices to be good, useful, socially appropriate, and morally right. In practice, individuals tend to govern themselves according to these conventional institutions and to lose sight of the ends that they are intended to achieve. Thus their ultimate motivations may become almost entirely subconscious. While human beings remain free to determine individually the means to achieve their instinctive ends, Veblen believes that the forces of social institutions to conform behavior make deviation from convention very difficult. Not only is there a threat of disapprobation or ostracism for those who break with convention, but, because conventions tend to be absorbed into individuals' common sense notions of what is right and good, deviation from convention is rarely even contemplated. At the level of populations, Veblen's theory allows little freedom for a society to deviate from the dynamics of institutional reproduction and Darwinian adaptation.[30]

Unlike instincts, in Veblen's account, social institutions may change. What causes institutions to change is a process of natural selection in which institutions that adapt sufficiently to a changing cultural environment are able to survive. However, the cultural environment is capable of rapid change, while the adaptation of institutions to a new environment tends to lag behind. Therefore the institutions present in a given society at a given point in history are just as likely to represent adaptation to earlier cultural environments as to the current environment.[31]

Veblen considers conspicuous consumption to be an example of a social institution that evolved as a means for achieving the instinctive end of emulation. Conspicuous consumption originates when "relative success, tested by an invidious pecuniary comparison with other men, becomes the conventional end of action.... Purposeful effort comes to mean, primarily, effort directed to or resulting in a more creditable showing of accumulated wealth."[32] By attributing conspicuous consumption to emulation, Veblen proposes a psychological or spiritual motive, rather than a concern with material utility as in John Paul II's theory. Accordingly, persons who have been socialized in the conventional norms of conspicuous consumption

---

30. Veblen, *Instinct of Workmanship*, 6–8; Veblen, *Theory of the Leisure Class*, 86.

31. Veblen, *Instinct of Workmanship*, 16–18; Veblen, *Theory of the Leisure Class*, 132–33.

32. Veblen, *Theory of the Leisure Class*, 40.

will consider consumption aimed at securing social esteem to be just as necessary as consumption that satisfies physical needs. Because the end sought in emulation is psychological and relative, it is inherently unlimited. Conspicuous consumption has two particular aims that serve the end of emulation in Veblen's theory. First, the conventional norms of conspicuous consumption dictate that one must at least possess the material signs of one's own social class in order to preserve one's social standing. To possess visibly the signs of material decency is to possess the respect of one's community. To fail to meet this standard results in a loss of others' esteem and a loss of self-esteem. The second aim of conspicuous consumption is to advance one's social status and to gain the greater esteem associated with a higher social class by possessing and displaying the material signs of that higher class.[33]

Veblen creates a narrative of human history to explain how conspicuous consumption serves as an evolutionary adaptation of institutional means to the end of emulation. At a certain point in human history, Veblen argues, advances in agricultural technology required fixed settlement and created an economic surplus, enabling a division of labor in which not all members of a community had to engage in food production. Competition with other communities for sustenance made exploits of individual prowess highly valuable to these communities. Successful aggression, therefore, became the basis for social status. Veblen locates the origin of private property in the seizure of slaves in early warfare. Because it originated in exploit, private property served to signify the prowess and high status of its owner. It retained this signification even after it was no longer acquired through aggression. A high-status "leisure class" emerged that shunned routine labor and limited its activities to competitive acts of aggression. The spirit of the leisure class was dominated by the instinct of emulation and the pursuit of individual interest.[34]

In the early modern era, in Veblen's theory, the emulative instinct of the leisure class was redirected to pecuniary ends. Status no longer depended upon prowess in acts of aggression, but upon accumulation of the signs of prowess, i.e., property. The property-owning leisure class remained distinct from the laboring classes. The working classes possessed only the necessary means of life, while all luxury and superior goods were reserved

33. Ibid., 38–39, 70–72, 80–81.
34. Veblen, *Instinct of Workmanship*, 160–61; Veblen, "Irksomeness of Labor," 87–94; Veblen, *Theory of the Leisure Class*, 25, 34, 159.

for the leisure class, which subsisted on the labor of others. Leisure and not exploit was the characteristic feature of leisure-class life in this stage. The dominant social institution of this period was status: property owners were esteemed while the working classes were disesteemed.[35]

The industrial age, in Veblen's theory, is characterized by the transition to large-scale, standardized industrial enterprises, a concentration of private commercial wealth, and a further division of labor that separates the ownership and management of enterprises. The owners and managers are governed by pecuniary concerns that lead to an intensified focus on emulation and an intensified pecuniary competition. In this stage, the captain of industry replaces the hereditary landlord as the highest status member of the leisure class and assumes the functions of conspicuous leisure and conspicuous consumption of what is produced by others.[36]

According to Veblen's historical narrative, the leisure class engaged in emulative competition for status for thousands of years. The reason that this competition now involves economic consumption as the means of invidious comparison is due to the value that property originally held as the visible sign of successful aggression. Property's signification of "success" remains in the modern period, even though this comes to mean pecuniary success rather than successful violent exploits.

Because its purpose is to put into evidence the pecuniary strength of its owner, Veblen contends, conspicuous consumption is deliberately wasteful, deliberately unusual, and deliberately visible to others in one's social environment. Waste is not valued for itself, but for what it communicates, namely, prima facie evidence of pecuniary strength. Therefore the motives of emulation and of serviceability work at cross purposes in consumer decisions. If consumer goods and services have material utility they are less effective at signaling pecuniary strength and making an invidious comparison with others.[37] On this point, Veblen contradicts the greed theories, which claim that consumption is motivated by desire for goods and services' direct material utilities.

Veblen associates conspicuous consumption with conspicuous leisure. The two are different aspects of the same emulative behavior. Conspicuous

---

35. Veblen, *Theory of the Leisure Class*, 37, 44, 61, 136.

36. Veblen, *Absentee Ownership*, 105–14; Veblen, *Instinct of Workmanship*, 220, 277–81.

37. Veblen, "Economic Theory of Woman's Dress," 69–72; Veblen, *Theory of the Leisure Class*, 42, 86, 120.

leisure is not idleness but activity that does not serve productive ends and thus provides "evidence of pecuniary ability to afford a life of idleness."[38] There is emulative advantage in consumption patterns that signal a large amount of time has been spent on consumption—as, for example, in the cultivation of tastes for fine clothes, fine wines, or opera. Other types of consumption—including travel, hobbies, and dabbling in scholarship or the arts—are useful in displaying nonproductive use of time directly. Consumption and leisure do not have to be direct in order to serve an emulative purpose. According to Veblen, wives, children, and paid servants engage in vicarious consumption and vicarious leisure that put the pecuniary strength of the male head of household into evidence. Certain forms of philanthropy such as endowed clergy and endowed scholarship also serve the function of vicarious leisure in Veblen's theory.[39]

While the members of the leisure class are the complete exemplars of conspicuous consumption and leisure, Veblen maintains that the middle and working classes only partly exhibit these behaviors. The reason that they engage in conspicuous consumption at all is because the leisure class sets the social norms of reputability and status for the entire society. These norms exert a coercive influence on the lower classes. "The norm of reputability imposed by the upper class extends its coercive influence with but slight hindrance down through the social structure to the lowest strata. . . . The members of each stratum accept as their ideal of decency the scheme of life in vogue in the next higher stratum, and bend their energies to live up to that ideal."[40] However, Veblen contends, the direct influence of industrial labor provides a countervailing influence on those who must work for a living. For the working classes, industry promotes a peaceful and workmanlike character, although the motive of emulation is also present. In the lower classes the impact of the industrial process is more immediate, while in the upper-middle classes the influence of the leisure class is more immediate and the relationship with industrial processes less direct. Veblen's theory therefore predicts that emulation diminishes in its importance to consumer motivation as one descends the social scale.[41]

38. Veblen, *Theory of the Leisure Class*, 46.

39. Veblen, "Economic Theory of Woman's Dress," 68–71; Veblen, *Theory of the Leisure Class*, 49–59, 201, 246.

40. Veblen, *Theory of the Leisure Class*, 70.

41. Veblen, *Theory of Business Enterprise*, 309; Veblen, *Theory of the Leisure Class*, 162–63.

Veblen claims that his portrayal of conspicuous consumption is a morally neutral historical and economic analysis. However, Veblen's claim to moral objectivity cannot be accepted at face value because he considers morality nothing more than a cultural artifact of other-regarding traits that survives from pre-agricultural human societies.[42] In fact, Veblen's viewpoint contains two closely related normative criteria. He understands the good in terms of utility to the society as a whole, where utility is not equated with subjective desires and aversions but with objective human welfare. Accordingly, "the test to which all expenditure must be brought . . . is the question whether it serves directly to enhance human life on the whole—whether it furthers the life process taken impersonally."[43] Veblen finds value only in the life process of the human species, not in individuals. So far as he is concerned, the existential question of the meaning of individual existence does not arise. Veblen's second criterion rests on his theory of social evolution: what is right is to adapt to the present cultural environment. In the modern industrial period this means adaptation to the conditions of industrial life. For Veblen, this implies a peaceable, cooperative, and workmanlike character rather than an emulative one.[44]

Veblen's theory of social institutions is deliberately historical and contextual. In describing conspicuous consumption, he specifically intends the phenomenon as it occurs in the late nineteenth century among the elite class of absentee owners of large-scale business enterprises in the Western industrialized nations. Thus, any application of Veblen's theory to contemporary consumerism would have to explain why one believes the present situation is substantially similar to that which Veblen observed, or why one believes conspicuous consumption is universal rather than the evolving historical phenomenon that Veblen describes. The former route is complicated by the fact that Veblen anticipated ongoing cultural change.[45] It is further complicated by cultural developments since Veblen proposed his theory. First, mass media technologies have opened a much broader scope for invidious comparisons, including comparisons with fictional reference characters. It has also facilitated market segmentation in which the meanings associated with consumer goods are more complex than their significance to an elite class. Second, the greatly expanded participation

---

42. Veblen, "Mr. Cummings's Strictures," 23; Veblen, *Theory of the Leisure Class*, 150.
43. Veblen, *Theory of the Leisure Class*, 79.
44. Veblen, *Theory of the Leisure Class*, 176; Diggins, *Bard of Savagery*, 79–80.
45. Veblen, *Theory of the Leisure Class*, 233.

of women in economic production resists a description that reduces their social role to specialists in vicarious consumption. Third, consumption and leisure are increasingly exclusive of one another in contemporary Western societies. This raises the question whether a theory associated with a leisure class has any validity in a society in which consumption is primarily a function of those who work. Finally, the affluence of the middle classes in Western nations now makes it implausible to view consumerism as primarily an upper-class phenomenon. I examine this final point empirically in chapter 4. While Veblen allows for middle-class conspicuous consumption, he attributes both leisure-class and middle-class conspicuous consumption to status competition. In a society in which consumerism is mainly found among the middle class, it may be difficult to demonstrate this unity of motivation.

Georg Simmel presents a theory of fashion that can be understood as a particular case of Veblen's conspicuous consumption. Fashion, according to Simmel, is driven by two motives: imitation and self-differentiation. Imitation corresponds to the aspirational element of Veblen's instinct of emulation. The middle classes mimic the consumption of the upper classes in order to gain their prestige, power, and sense of importance. Self-differentiation corresponds to the defensive element of emulation. The upper classes seek to maintain the privileges of their social distinction and thus strive continually to differentiate themselves from those who aspire to their status from below. This effort is conducted through the continual purchase of fashionable new possessions. Like Veblen's conspicuous consumption, Simmel views fashion as a modern phenomenon. He observes several features of modern society that bring fashion into importance: the sameness of the modern world, the tendency of mass society to efface individuality, the rapid pace of social change, and the modern belief in social progress. Like Veblen's conspicuous consumption, Simmel views fashion as a phenomenon of the upper and upper-middle classes. This is because imitation that spreads too broadly fails to serve the function of reinforcing social distinctions. In contrast to the imaginative hedonism theorists, Simmel views the motives driving fashion consumption as peripheral to individual identity. While fashion expresses distinction, Simmel argues, it is always a group distinction. The man or woman who follows fashion has sacrificed the possibility of individual attention and distinction in order to receive a share of a group attention and group distinction.[46]

46. Simmel, "Fashion," 135, 138–41, 145–46, 151–52.

Pierre Bourdieu's observations of 1960s France share much in common with Veblen's observations of the late-nineteenth-century United States. Like Veblen, Bourdieu sees the middle and upper classes engaging in insatiable consumption driven by competition for the status signified by luxury goods. Unlike Veblen, however, he does not consider the working classes to be influenced by the consumption norms of the higher classes. In Bourdieu's theory, income and employment determine one's taste. He defines taste as a semiotic system in which material differences provide the code for differences in meaning. Bourdieu defines a status signaling lifestyle in terms of both conspicuous consumption and conspicuous taste. As a sign system, Bourdieu observes, an individual's lifestyle must be validated by others. This encourages consumers to sort themselves into lifestyle affinity groups. Like Veblen, Bourdieu sees a single semiotic system of positional goods and a single criterion of value that drives economic consumption. Bourdieu names that criterion "distinction," a term which signifies both relative social status and invidious comparison. The semiotic hierarchy of consumption lifestyles corresponds to a social hierarchy of status distinctions.[47]

Bourdieu agrees with Veblen that consumption is driven by a good's utility as a sign of status rather than its material utility. He argues that consumer goods do not have objective value or meaning. Rather the consumer helps to produce the product by completing its meaning.[48] Because products function as signs in a positional competition, the imperative of consumption is unbounded. For Bourdieu, there is no difference between the motives of status defense and status seeking because "the groups involved in the race . . . cannot conserve their position . . . except by running to keep their distance from those immediately behind them, thus jeopardizing the difference which distinguishes the group immediately in front."[49] In both cases, the desire for distinction is grounded in a desire for social identity.[50] Bourdieu thus agrees with the imaginative hedonism theorists insofar as he sees a desire to assert an identity behind the motivation of consumerism, but he differs from them in limiting the relevant content of identity and the object of personal striving to social rank.

---

47. Bourdieu, *Distinction*, 1, 13, 31, 163, 174–75, 241, 246, 250–51.
48. Ibid., 86, 100.
49. Ibid., 161.
50. Ibid., 172.

Juliet Schor provides a status signaling theory for contemporary U.S. consumerism. She identifies consumerism by its insatiable economic consumption, lack of any objective standard of need, and sacrifice of consciously-held values and non-economic goods for the sake of status good consumption. Among the values and goods that consumeristic individuals sacrifice are time for family, social relationships, and community; savings; public spending on education, recreation, the arts, social programs, and public safety; environmental quality and sustainability; and moral injunctions against material excess, debt, deceit, and theft. Several elements of Schor's theory follow Veblen's. Schor considers consumption to be semiotic and the meaning conveyed by conspicuous consumption to be social status. She agrees that consumption must be visible to others to serve this semiotic function, and that both the objects consumed and the manner of consumption convey meaning. Like Veblen, she recognizes a role for vicarious conspicuous consumption, although she identifies this primarily with spending on one's children rather than one's wife and servants. Schor agrees with Veblen that both status defense and status seeking drive conspicuous consumption. She agrees with Veblen that consumers are not generally conscious of their motives. In fact, she claims that consumers are not generally conscious of their consumption behavior either.[51]

Schor identifies a "new consumerism" that has taken hold in the United States since 1980, defined by "an upscaling of lifestyle norms; the pervasiveness of conspicuous, status goods and of competition for acquiring them; and the growing disconnection between consumer desires and incomes."[52] She attributes the new consumerism to a shift in consumers' reference groups due to rising economic inequality, declining social connections, and the greater visibility of higher classes in the workplace and on television. Schor's new consumerism differs from Veblen's conspicuous consumption in its late-modern historical emergence and its social location in all classes of American society. There are other differences between Schor's description of consumerism and Veblen's theory. Schor argues that the upper-middle class now sets the standard for material success that every lower class seeks to emulate. Schor also observes a growing pluralism in consumption ideals. The meanings signified by consumer goods now

---

51. Schor, "New Politics of Consumption," 7–14, 28–30; Schor, *Overspent American*, 5–7, 19–21, 30–34, 40–45, 82–85, 108.

52. Schor, "New Politics of Consumption," 7.

vary by the social and historical location of the observer.[53] This semiotic pluralism conflicts with Schor and Veblen's claims that consumerism is driven by status concerns, since the meaning of status is hierarchical and one-dimensional.

Although she does not employ Veblen's terminology, Boss offers another comparable account of contemporary U.S. consumerism. Like Veblen, she considers the appearance of relative wealth, not absolute wealth, to be the source of individuals' subjective sense of well-being. Unlike Veblen, Boss locates consumeristic behavior exclusively in the upper and middle classes. Nevertheless, Boss recognizes the same motives and behaviors as Veblen. Persons seek to maintain their social status or to achieve higher status by putting wealth into evidence through conspicuous consumption and conspicuous leisure. The status for which persons feel they must maintain appearances may be set by those persons with whom one associates. It may be set by fictional references on television or in movies. Or it may be set by an individual's subjective sense of desert or entitlement. Boss describes advertisers' influence as a reinforcement of individuals' existing tendencies to make invidious comparisons and seek relative advantage. She thereby situates a historical development not addressed by Veblen within the framework of a status signaling theory.[54]

Consumerism as Manipulation

The third group of theorists attributes the motivation of consumerism to some combination of deception and coercion employed by economic producers to manipulate consumers. While these theorists consider consumers to be free formally, in practice they see the vast majority of consumers conforming their economic behavior to the needs of economic producers either because they fail to see through marketing deceptions or because they do not choose to suffer the social consequences of nonconformity. I will explore the thought of John Kenneth Galbraith in detail as exemplifying a manipulation theory. Max Horkheimer, Theodor Adorno, Herbert Marcuse, and Jean Baudrillard are other influential thinkers whose theories conform to this type. These theorists consider consumerism a purely middle-class phenomenon since, they claim, the upper classes are the

53. Schor, "New Politics of Consumption," 13; Schor, *Overspent American*, 3–4, 9–13, 39–41.
54. Boss, *Green With Envy*, 8, 16, 31, 85, 111, 119, 167–70.

agents of manipulation and the lower classes lack the means to participate. While they all associate consumerism with corporate capitalism and mass communication, Horkheimer and Adorno see consumerism emerging as early as the Enlightenment and Baudrillard as late as the 1970s. Like the status signaling theories, the manipulation theories accept the possibility that consumer motivations are not fully conscious. However, the manipulation theories differ from the other types in the degree to which they minimize personal freedom and thereby absolve individuals of responsibility for living a consumeristic form of life. Like the status signaling theories and unlike the greed theories, the manipulation theories attribute the perceived utility of a consumer good to its signifying function rather than the good in itself. Unlike the status signaling theories, however, the manipulation theories do not confine the meaning of consumer goods to status. Instead, they claim that marketers and advertisers associate meanings with consumption at two levels. At one level, they claim, marketers and advertisers create associations between consumer goods and a variety of goods that are not directly exchangeable—for example, freedom, comfort, power, esteem, sex, and friendship. At a second level, they indoctrinate consumers in an ideology in which accumulation of the output of economic producers is associated with success or fulfillment, and thus accepted as the aim of life. At both levels, the meanings generated by advertisers are socially enforced.

Galbraith presents his account of consumer motives in the context of a critique of the neoclassical economic theory of consumer demand. Galbraith considers the widespread affluence in Western societies in the twentieth century to be a new historical situation. Prior to the twentieth century and outside the West, Galbraith argues, the normal human experience has been economic scarcity and deprivation. He characterizes earlier cultures' economies as purely needs-based, implying a hierarchy of economic desires in which physical needs like food and shelter take precedence over psychological desires. This contradicts Veblen's view that luxury consumption already existed in pre-industrial societies to serve the end of emulation. In modern society, Galbraith argues, affluence becomes the norm for the majority of citizens. This contented majority is motivated by self-regard to defend tenaciously its self-satisfied form of life.[55]

Galbraith attributes the new situation of affluence to industrialization and its accompanying cultural changes. Industrialization fosters a greater division of labor, which has important consequences. Galbraith lists these

55. Galbraith, *Affluent Society*, 1, 126; Galbraith, *Culture of Contentment*, 15–17.

consequences as first, increased time required for product development; second, increased capital intensity of production; third decreased flexibility in the tasks of individual workers; fourth, increased specialization of labor skills; fifth, an increased need for organization; and sixth, an increased need for planning. These conditions make the industrial economy particularly favorable to the emergence of large industrial corporations. The emergence of these corporations plays a central role in Galbraith's account of modern society because of the power that they exercise through a combination of size and planning.[56] The mature corporation "alone can deploy the requisite capital; it alone can mobilize the requisite skills;" it alone can plan its market outcomes and takes steps to ensure that its plans become reality; it alone has the power to determine its markets and bend its customers to its needs.[57] Organization, rather than technology, is the key innovation of the Industrial Revolution, in Galbraith's view.[58]

For large industrial corporations, Galbraith challenges the view that control lies with the shareholders. In his account, control passes to the organization of managerial and technical professionals. This is because shareholders are more easily replaced than managerial and technical organizations and because these organizations can coordinate their actions more easily than shareholders. Within the corporate hierarchy, Galbraith does not locate control with the executive, but with the professional managers, engineers, technicians, scientists, designers, financiers, accountants, and marketers with whom the firm's specialized technical and organizational knowledge resides. Galbraith labels this group the "technostructure." The technostructure holds power as an organization—a corporate personality—and not in its individual members. He attributes the technostructure's power to its ability to pool and test the information that is needed to make decisions. The power of the technostructure is directed to two primary goals. First, it seeks the preservation of its power and autonomy by maintaining a secure minimum of corporate earnings. Since high earnings accrue to others, its decisions are biased towards risk-aversion. Second, the technostructure seeks corporate sales and earnings growth to enhance opportunities for career advancement and prestige.[59]

---

56. Galbraith, *New Industrial State*, xii, 32–34.
57. Ibid., 24.
58. Ibid., 76.
59. Ibid., 64, 74–92, 170–74.

Shopping for Meaningful Lives

As a class, Galbraith argues, the technocrats' control of the dominant cultural institutions gives them preeminent influence in society. Thus the technocratic class supersedes Veblen's leisure class in prestige. Leisure becomes disreputable and the leisure class difficult to identify. Galbraith characterizes the technocratic class by its high level of education and its sense of identification with its work. This is a different relationship to work than either the leisure class or the laboring classes in Veblen's theory. In Galbraith's affluent society, consumption also differs from Veblen's account. Galbraith considers the use of consumption to signal class status less effective than Veblen claims. With growing general affluence, Galbraith argues, non-elite classes are increasingly able to purchase the same luxury goods consumed by elite classes and they feel entitled to the same quality of economic consumption. In Galbraith's affluent society, consumer demand rises in step with production, with no evidence of slackening as basic wants are fulfilled and no evidence that consumers will forego higher consumption levels for any larger purpose. Galbraith observes that consumption in the affluent society is biased towards private goods and services at the expense of public goods like education, infrastructure, and environmental protection.[60] Thus he accounts for both the insatiability of consumerism and its sacrifice of noneconomic goods for the sake of consumption.

The insatiability of consumer demand amidst rising affluence represents a failure of neoclassical economic theory, Galbraith argues. The theory of diminishing marginal utility states that "the urgency of desire is a function of the quantity of goods which the individual has available to satisfy that desire. The larger the stock, the less the satisfaction from an increment."[61] So long as consumers make decisions to purchase some goods prior to others, this demonstrates that the goods purchased sooner have higher priority (i.e., utility) and those purchased later have lesser utility. However, consumption no longer follows the theory of diminishing marginal utility. In pre-industrial societies human beings tended to increase their leisure as wants were satisfied, but this tendency is not found in modern society. This contradicts the neoclassical proposition that wants originate independently in the consumer. To explain the insatiability of modern consumer demand, Galbraith draws a distinction between physical needs and psychological wants. He argues that physical needs for food, shelter and clothing are innate, necessary, and urgent to persons who live under

60. Galbraith, *Affluent Society*, xxvi, 189–90, 247–51.
61. Ibid., 115.

conditions of scarcity, but are easily satiated and diminish in importance for the affluent. Psychological satisfactions are neither necessary nor urgent, according to Galbraith, but they are insatiable. Because psychological wants are not urgent, Galbraith argues, they are readily manipulated by others. In the affluent society, he claims, most persons are so far removed from physical needs that they are subject to persuasion and manipulation.[62]

Galbraith's explanation for unnecessary consumption is that corporate technocrats manipulate affluent consumers through advertising and marketing operations to produce the demand for their corporations' products. With some qualifications, then, Galbraith attributes consumerism to producers' effective control of consumers. He claims that demand control arises in mature corporations from their long product planning horizons, high capital investment, great specialization, large-scale inflexible organizations, and desire to avoid market uncertainty. Unless a corporation can eliminate its market risk, Galbraith argues, it cannot plan. Therefore it must and does control its markets.[63] Galbraith's argument suffers from a peculiarly binary interpretation of certainty. Unless a corporation knows everything about future market outcomes, then, he claims, it knows nothing and cannot plan. But the typical situation for corporate planning decisions is partial knowledge and partial uncertainty. There is an even more basic problem with Galbraith's logic. He argues that because a corporation's personnel *should* dominate consumers in order to plan, then they are *able* to do so. This is a category confusion. A factual conclusion cannot be drawn from a normative proposition.

Galbraith does not claim that corporate demand management controls the individual decisions of every consumer, only that those who resist successfully are rare enough that consumers as a population are effectively conformed to corporate need and intent. Thus, individual moral agency is formally preserved in Galbraith's theory, even though it is effectively subverted through commercial propaganda. As evidence of corporate control, Galbraith cites the research of Tibor Sciotovsky and Jerome Rothenburg that demonstrates that advertisers influence consumer decisions. He also points to the scale of effort and expenditure by corporations to influence

---

62. Galbraith, *Affluent Society*, 117–19, 126; Galbraith, "Economics as a System of Belief," 472n; Galbraith, *New Industrial State*, 201–2, 264.

63. Galbraith, "Economics as a System of Belief," 472; Galbraith, *New Industrial State*, 40–43, 201.

consumer decisions as evidence of their effectiveness.[64] Again, Galbraith's argument suffers from logical confusion. The fact that corporations act to influence consumers does not demonstrate their effectiveness in achieving that end. Galbraith also ignores the distinction between influence and control. What Sciotovsky's and Rothenburg's research demonstrates is influence, not the complete domination of consumers by advertisers.[65] Whether corporate influence is sufficient that it is indistinguishable from control, is an empirical question that I will examine in Chapter 4.

Advertising plays an important but not exclusive role in corporations' management of consumers, according to Galbraith. Demand management consists in market research, sales and merchandising personnel, corporate sales strategies, product design oriented towards sales strategies, and comprehensive, compelling, and repetitive communication to consumers. This communication function was greatly facilitated by the development of radio and television. In addition to its role in influencing individual purchase decisions, Galbraith argues, advertising collectively establishes a belief in the importance of consumer goods and their relationship to happiness. This leads individuals to behave as though privately-produced consumer goods were the measure of human achievement, even though they do not consciously profess this belief.[66] Thus Galbraith explains the subversion of consciously-held moral beliefs, a key characteristic of consumerism.

While emulation is not as significant in Galbraith's theory as in Veblen's, it does serve to increase the effectiveness of corporate demand management. For evidence of this, Galbraith points to the leveling of consumption differences between economic classes in the affluent society. Galbraith subordinates emulation to manufactured demand because, he argues, emulation cannot explain the origin of wants for goods that do not yet exist. Instead, it serves to multiply wants for goods that already exist and have already generated some consumer response. Emulation contributes to consumer insatiability because consumption that satisfies one person's wants simultaneously creates wants in her or his neighbors. Galbraith refers to the work of James Duesenberry to argue that the comparisons made in modern emulation are both intertemporal and interpersonal. However,

---

64. Galbraith, "Economics as a System of Belief," 473–74; Galbraith, *New Industrial State*, 203–8; Galbraith, "Time and the New Industrial State," 374.

65. Sciotovsky, *Papers on Welfare and Growth*, 241–49; Rothenburg, "Consumers' Sovereignty Revisited," 279–80.

66. Galbraith, *Affluent Society*, 189–90; Galbraith, *New Industrial State*, 200–209.

Duesenberry's findings are that persons expect their consumption to rise as the society's production rises. This is a purely intertemporal comparison with the individual's own prior condition. It does not involve invidious comparisons with others. Galbraith extrapolates from Duesenberry's argument the conclusion that people expect to maintain a constant level of social prestige as a society's production and incomes rise.[67] This implies that the consumer expects the relationship of his or her consumption to an average or reference level to remain the same, which is the same claim as Veblen's imperative of status preservation.

Galbraith's works reflect an understanding of the social good that is part collective, part utilitarian. The first priority of any society, he contends, must be its survival. To ensure its survival, he argues, a society must invest in education and scientific and technological development. It must also seek peace, international cooperation, and environmental preservation. Beyond the goal of survival, Galbraith writes, the good society should give every individual the opportunity for a "rewarding life." He leaves each individual to determine the content of a rewarding life for himself or herself. The state's role is to provide the means for individuals to pursue their own utility, whatever it is. Galbraith's interpretation of individual utility is hedonistic. Thus, he argues, an affluent society should choose to increase leisure or make work more pleasant rather than produce more consumer goods.[68]

Like Veblen, Galbraith views economic theory as historically and culturally contextual.[69] Because his theory is historically and culturally contextual, it is subject to empirical evaluation to test whether it has contemporary validity. With respect to his central claim that corporations control consumer behavior through advertising and sales techniques, I have already argued that Galbraith failed to demonstrate this fact empirically at the time that he wrote. A number of economists have agreed with Galbraith's proposition that advertising influences consumer behavior, while contradicting his claims regarding the degree to which that influence extends.[70] Nor have the intervening years been kind to Galbraith's other empirical claims. Among the evidence that Galbraith cites for corporate

67. Galbraith, *Affluent Society*, xxvii–xxviii, 122–23; Duesenberry, *Income, Saving and Consumer Behavior*, 28.

68. Galbraith, *Affluent Society*, 243, 255–59; Galbraith, *Good Society*, 23, 31, 82.

69. Galbraith, *New Industrial State*, 214.

70. See, for example, Duffy, "Advertising and the Distribution of Demand, 1062–68; Hodgson, "Hidden Persuaders," 169–72; Munier and Wang, "Consumer Sovereign and Consumption Routine," 72–75.

manipulation is the stability of consumer demand, as reflected in stable prices, stable earnings, and the stable positions of mature corporations in the industrial system.[71] However, the past four decades have seen substantial price inflation in most industries (and deflation in others), frequent corporate losses, significant turnover in the Fortune 500 list of the largest U.S. corporations, and significant inroads by foreign corporations into U.S. (and foreign) markets formerly dominated by U.S. corporations. All of these developments point to the weakness of U.S. corporations' market power rather than their strength. Any contemporary application of Galbraith's manipulation theory to explain consumerism would have to demonstrate the power of the global corporate sector as a whole, rather than the power of individual firms, sectors, or national industries.

Horkheimer and Adorno describe "late capitalist" industrial society in terms that are similar to Galbraith's affluent society. Horkheimer and Adorno describe three means by which late capitalist elites dominate the lower classes: an ideology of Enlightenment rationalism, an ideology of affluence, and manipulation by the entertainment industry and mass media technologies. The ideology of Enlightenment rationalism teaches individuals to see universal reason in the order of society, so that subordination to the ruling class is understood as subordination to reason. The myth of economic success leads workers willingly accept the goals of material affluence that the elite class imposes on them to ensure diligent labor and the consumption of industrial production. Beneath this ideology, Horkheimer and Adorno see a real economic coercion that links individuals' material standard of life to the degree to which they accede to the system. Horkheimer and Adorno see mass communications technologies as the means through which elites impose their ideologies. They point to the one-way nature of television and radio communication, their cultural ubiquity, the imperative nature of their communication, and their oligopolistic control by corporate conglomerates. They see no distinction between the offerings of the entertainment industry and advertisement. Advertisement and entertainment use style to conceal their social norming function and they employ symbolic associations to circumvent any reasoned response. Like Galbraith, Horkheimer and Adorno formally preserve individuals' moral agency by viewing their subordination to the imperatives of corporate producers as a willing consent to advertisers' manipulation.[72]

71. Galbraith, *New Industrial State*, 94, 194.

72. Horkheimer and Adorno, *Dialectic of Enlightenment*, 22, 120–25, 131–37, 150, 159–63.

Types of Consumerism Theories

Marcuse does not use the term consumerism, but he describes a society in which consumers strive after an ever-rising luxury consumption to the exclusion of other ends. Marcuse's "advanced industrial society" is similar to Galbraith's affluent society. It is characterized by a constantly rising economic productivity and a constantly rising standard of economic consumption. In order to achieve this rising standard of living, it must rationalize human beings in their roles as economic producers. To ensure the consumption of their increasingly productive output, corporations must also scientifically control their demand. According to Marcuse, corporate owners and managers dominate individual freedom through an ideology of technological and economic progress, and through marketing techniques for particular consumer goods. The technological-economic rationalization of society is established as the natural, objective order of things, so that individuals do not resist domination but identify with society and adopt its goals of rising productivity and rising affluence. Like Galbraith, Marcuse cites the existence of mass media advertising and marketing techniques as evidence that consumer behavior is directed by corporate manipulation. In response to advertisers' manipulations, the consumer not only purchases the product, he or she subjectively appropriates the values that the advertiser associates with it so that his or her subjective identity is linked to the products that he or she consumes.[73] This connection between consumption and identity bears some resemblance to the imaginative hedonism theories, but the fact that it is an imposed identity makes Marcuse's description a manipulation theory. Like the theories of Galbraith and Horkheimer and Adorno, Marcuse's theory is subject to empirical critique on the question of the degree of advertisers' control over consumer decisions.

Baudrillard describes "consumption" in contemporary Western societies in terms that are consistent with consumerism.[74] The purchase of economic goods, in Baudrillard's view, is only consumption, "where the commodity is immediately produced as a sign . . . and where signs (culture) are produced as commodities."[75] Under this definition, Baudrillard sees consumption as insatiable, dissociated from goods' material utility,

---

73. Marcuse, *One-Dimensional Man*, 5, 10–12, 17, 22–23, 49, 158.

74. My reading of Baudrillard's theory of consumption focuses on the works that he produced between 1968 and 1973, including "The System of Objects," *The Consumer Society, For a Critique of the Political Economy of the Sign*, and *The Mirror of Production*. These works collectively describe a fairly consistent theoretical position, in contrast to his later writings.

75. Baudrillard, *Political Economy of the Sign*, 147.

and unconstrained by any morality but its own. Baudrillard views the consumption stage of capitalism as a historical development that emerges in the 1970s. He locates consumption primarily in the middle classes. He exempts the elite classes due to their mastery over the meaning system of consumption, and he exempts the lower classes because they lack the means to engage in symbolic exchange.[76] These assertions are subject to empirical critique, which I take up in chapter 4.

What is consumed in Baudrillard's description of consumption is not material goods, but signs. He portrays a ubiquitous code of commodified signs that controls both culture and interior life. This code signifies relative social status through differences in the array of objects consumed and the manner of their consumption. Because status claims create both positive and negative social distinctions and because the status signs are unreal, consumption is inherently unlimited. Unlike Veblen, Baudrillard does not attribute the semiotic status system to instinctual and evolutionary factors. To the contrary, he sees the code as a means of social control by elites who hold monopolies on the code's meanings and on the mass media by which they are communicated. This enables elites to dominate middle-class consumers, subordinating their demand to the needs of economic production. Control is not only maintained by persuasion but also by threatening consumers with social exclusion if they do not "play the game." In general, however, no coercion is necessary. The code imposes a group morality that overrides individuals' conscious moral and rational restraints. Subjectively, the individual consumer experiences his or her domination as hedonistic freedom. In using the code, the consumer seeks to claim a social status identity, and to legitimate this identity through social recognition. But the consumer is controlled, even though she or he participates willingly.[77] This justifies the classification of Baudrillard's theory as a manipulation type.

Consumerism as Imaginative Hedonism

The fourth group of theorists attributes the motivation of consumerism to the pleasures afforded by private fantasies of identities, relationships, and

---

76. Baudrillard, *Consumer Society*, 59, 83; Baudrillard, *Mirror of Production*, 127–28; Baudrillard, *Political Economy of the Sign*, 38, 67; Baudrillard, "System of Objects," 28.

77. Baudrillard, *Consumer Society*, 61–62; Baudrillard, *Mirror of Production*, 121–32; Baudrillard, *Political Economy of the Sign*, 40–42, 68, 85, 162; Baudrillard, "System of Objects," 19–26.

experiences that are signified by the goods and services one consumes. This group includes Colin Campbell, Paul Oppenheimer, and Virginia Postrel. They associate consumerism with the middle classes, but they differ on the timing of its historical emergence. For Campbell consumerism arises in the early modern period, but for Postrel it is postmodern. According to these theorists, consumption is semiotic but not communicative. That is, consumer goods are consumed for the sake of the meanings that they signify, but these meanings reside in the consumer's interior life. They are neither imposed on the consumer by advertisers nor addressed to other persons. Like the greed theories, the imaginative hedonism theories consider the consumer's motivation to be a conscious pursuit of the pleasures that he or she can obtain from consumer goods, without reference to other persons. Unlike the greed theories, however, these pleasures do not arise from the goods as such but from the goods as signs. This understanding of consumer goods as signs agrees with the status signaling and manipulation theories. In contrast to those types, however, the imaginative hedonism theories permit an infinite number of meanings to be associated with a particular good. Like Bourdieu and Baudrillard, the imaginative hedonism theorists associate consumerism with a desire for identity, but in contrast to Bourdieu and Baudrillard they maintain that identity can be established by subjective assertion alone.

Campbell does not use the term consumerism but he defines a closely related concept that he calls "modern consumption." The desire for novelty and the insatiability of desire distinguish modern consumption from traditional consumption. In contrast to Veblen, Campbell identifies modern consumption solely with the middle class. Campbell also critiques Veblen's insistence that consumer goods only signify social status and nothing else. Instead of imitating elites, Campbell argues, groups competing for status seek to set up alternative meaning systems in relation to consumption that are favorable to themselves. In contrast to John Paul II, Campbell considers the meanings associated with economic goods to be the principal driver of consumer demand. In Campbell's theory, these meanings are consciously chosen by the consumer on the basis of both rational and affective considerations. However, they are chosen in the context of advertisers' efforts to provide meanings in association with their products. Campbell recognizes no distinction between motives and justifications—i.e., the reasons or accounts that one offers for one's action after one has acted.[78] He therefore fails

78. Campbell, "Character and Consumption," 42; Campbell, "Reception of a Thesis," 37; Campbell, *Romantic Ethic*, 8, 37–39, 48–54.

to acknowledge the possibility that persons may act in response to drives that they are later unable or unwilling to identify.

Like Veblen, Campbell employs a genetic method. He seeks to characterize modern consumption through a study of the factors that shaped its origins. The social and historical location to which he looks for these origins is late-eighteenth-century England. Because the origins of the Romantic consumption ethic and the nature of contemporary Western consumerism are both unknown, Campbell claims, "the problem of explaining the conduct of modern consumers—and that of accounting for events in the eighteenth century—is, at root, one and the same."[79] This argument displays flawed reasoning. Campbell assumes, but does not present any evidence to show, that contemporary consumerism is the same phenomenon as that which emerged in eighteenth-century England. There is no logical necessity that two unknowns have the same explanation. Campbell's choice of socio-historical origin is not dictated by the characteristics of contemporary consumerism but by his intention to address a missing element in Max Weber's *The Protestant Ethic and the Spirit of Capitalism*. Weber explains the origin of an ethic of production in the Protestant nations in which the Industrial Revolution took place, but he does not explain the origin of a complementary ethic of consumption. Campbell argues that it impossible to have an Industrial Revolution without a consumption revolution that matched the rapid growth in the supply of consumer goods with an equally rapid growth in consumer demand. Campbell observes that the great expansion of consumption during the early Industrial Revolution can be traced to the consumption of luxuries by the middle classes. Mass-produced luxury consumer goods were by far the most common items produced by the new industrial capacity of England. Campbell associates much of this new consumption with a concurrent emergence of middle-class leisure activities.[80]

Campbell argues that a new Romantic consumer ethic emerged in the English middle classes alongside the Puritan ethic. Campbell's evidence for associating the spirit of modern consumerism with Romanticism lies in the historical and social proximity of Romanticism to an emerging modern consumer ethic. Puritanism was a source for the Romantic spirit, according to Campbell, despite their apparent contradiction. It gave the individual a capacity for emotional self-regulation, and an attention to his or her

79. Campbell, *Romantic Ethic*, 36.
80. Ibid., 17, 25–26.

subjective emotional state. A second source was the early modern character of the dandy, who sought reputation in the expression of refinement and elegance in dress and deportment. The dandy ethic linked identity to an individual's manner of consumption alone, and not to class or birth. A third source was the optimistic moral anthropology of the Cambridge Platonists and deists, who emphasized the individual realization of divine moral qualities rather than the question of salvation. During the Enlightenment, the subjective turn in philosophy included a subjective turn in aesthetics that prefigures the autonomous character Campbell ascribes to Romanticism. The turn to subjective aesthetics and the deists' moral optimism were retained by Romanticism, even though in many ways Romanticism was a reaction against the Enlightenment.[81]

In eighteenth-century England, Campbell contends, the middle classes, influenced by the Cambridge Platonists and the Enlightenment, rejected Calvinism in favor of Sentimentalism. Sentimentalism combined a cultivation of the moral sentiments of benevolence and pity with a belief in human beings' natural goodness. Since the Sentimentalists considered it natural for human beings to take pleasure in beauty and for benevolent dispositions to be beautiful, they viewed pleasure as a sign of morality. The aim of the Sentimentalist life was *sensibility*—a susceptibility to feeling that represents both a moral and an aesthetic ideal. Campbell describes the Sentimental life as one occupied with the pleasures obtained from one's imagination and moral disposition. The Sentimentalist self-consciously and artificially stimulated her or his emotional response to a situation to enhance the pleasure she or he could obtain from it. However, Sentimentalists retained a concern with social validation through external signs. Campbell locates Sentimentalism's contribution to the Romanic spirit in its imaginative interiority and emotional hedonism.[82]

Campbell interprets Romanticism as a further development of Sentimentalism. His description of Romanticism encompasses both a popular movement focused on emotionality and an elite intellectual idealism. Romanticism borrowed from deism a belief in a non-personal divinity that could be discovered in nature and in the self. The Romantic elites claimed a quasi-divine aesthetic faculty of imagination that enabled a select few men of genius to perceive the real aesthetically and to express the real in their

---

81 Campbell, "Reception of a Thesis," 44; Campbell, *Romantic Ethic*, 117–29, 156, 168–70, 182–83.

82. Campbell, *Romantic Ethic*, 134–35, 139–41, 144, 151–52.

artistic creations. The Romantic moral ideal was a character of altruism, benevolence, and sympathy, motivated by an imaginative identification with others. The Romantic cultivated this ideal by imaginatively entering into the cultural creations of the Romantic geniuses and being moved emotionally by these experiences. The Romantic elites believed that transforming persons through imaginative aesthetic experiences would ultimately lead to a social utopia.[83]

In Campbell's account, Romanticism sought truth in the emotional pleasure experienced in response to the beauty of social harmony and sympathy for others' emotions. Thus the criterion of ethical truth was subjective and aesthetic. Because pleasure served as the criterion by which ethical truth could be discerned, this was a form of hedonism. There were no shared transcendental or existential experiences in Romanticism that would enable others to judge or validate one's interior experience. In fact, Romanticism categorically rejected the idea of objective norms. As a result, the willingness to defy conventional morality served as a secondary criterion by which the Romantics believed they could discern ethical truth. This counter-cultural element found social expression in the Bohemian movement, a subculture in which Romantics sought mutual support in their revolt against an increasingly rationalized and utilitarian society. The desire for mutual support is evidence that the Romantic spirit contained an element that seeks social validation, despite Campbell's identification of the Romantic spirit with interiority. This same tension can be found in Campbell's description of fashion as providing a common aesthetic standard for ordered and meaningful interaction.[84] Campbell accounts for a demand for novelty but he does not account for why a Romantic, whose aesthetic and ethical values are purely subjective, should consider a common aesthetic standard or ordered and meaningful social interaction to be necessary.

Campbell's thesis is that modern consumption is a process of autonomous self-illusory hedonism that is a legacy of the Romantic movement. Modern consumption is autonomous, Campbell contends, in that the individual has mastery over her or his daydreams, over the meanings that she or he attaches to them, and over her or his emotional responses to them. Both the meanings of objects and the emotional content of experiences must be entirely conscious and subjective in order to be subject to imaginative manipulation. Campbell implies that meanings and identity do not

83. Ibid., 179–87.
84. Ibid., 158, 177–78, 190, 195.

require validation by others to assure the individual of their certainty. In fact, he denies a relational dimension to meaning and identity altogether. Campbell also contends that the consumer acts independently of advertisers. While advertisers suggest meaning associations for their products, he claims that these suggestions are only aids for the consumer's daydreaming. Modern consumption is hedonistic, he argues, in that it is motivated by pleasure that one receives from the desire to fulfill the daydreams that one associates with consumer goods. Since desire and not the satisfaction of desire is the source of pleasure, modern consumption seeks to create new desires, not merely to satisfy existing ones. According to Campbell, three conditions must be met for illusory hedonism to function effectively as a source of pleasure. First, it can only be pursued in the absence of any actual unmet needs. Second, since pleasure is a subjective response to external stimuli, it requires continually varying stimuli to continue to prompt responses. Third, it requires control over one's emotional response to stimuli. This control can only be maintained in an environment in which there are no external stimuli that prompt strong emotional responses. Individuals must withdraw from engagement with real life in order to pursue pleasures found only in daydreams.[85]

Campbell proposes that modern hedonism is distinct from traditional hedonism in that pleasure is received from emotions rather than sensations, and the source of these emotions lies in the imagination. This requires a creative process of emotional self-manipulation through daydreaming. Daydreaming anticipates the imagined meanings that the individual associates with a desired object becoming real. Campbell argues that the imaginative aspect of modern consumerism accounts for its search for novelty. It is easier to attach imagined pleasures to objects of which one has no direct experience that could interfere with the illusion. To the extent that the actual attainment of desired objects destroys their illusory pleasures, new objects of desire are needed to which to attach imaginary pleasures. Objects of desire that are never attained likewise lose their ability to give imagined gratification, Campbell maintains. Therefore, new objects of desire are continually needed to renew the pleasures produced by daydreaming.[86]

Campbell fails to demonstrate the relationship he hypothesizes between Romanticism and contemporary consumerism. While he shows a relationship between Romanticism and the ideal type he calls "the spirit of

85. Ibid., 11, 61–64, 70–72, 81, 86, 90–93, 221–22.
86. Ibid., 69, 84–86, 90, 95.

modern consumption," he has no comparable demonstration that his ideal type corresponds to anything that exists in the contemporary world. His argument rests on his claim that his ideal type explains the novelty-seeking character of consumerism better than the three alternative theories he addresses—the neoclassical account of consumer demand, Veblen's status signaling theory, and a manipulation theory.[87] However, novelty-seeking is not the only characteristic of contemporary consumerism, and the three theories he addresses do not exhaust the possible alternate explanations for consumerism. Without linking his ideal type to contemporary consumer behavior, Campbell's thesis remains speculative.

Like Veblen and Galbraith, Campbell interprets consumerism as a phenomenon specific to a particular culture and historical period. Therefore, even if Campbell demonstrated that the Romantic ethic directed the consumption patterns of the eighteenth- and nineteenth-century English middle classes—which he does not[88]—this does not demonstrate that nineteenth-century English middle-class consumption is motivated by the same factors as contemporary Western consumerism. To attribute contemporary consumerism to a Romantic-inspired imaginative hedonism, his theory would have to explain the many differences that exist between nineteenth-century English middle-class consumption and contemporary Western consumerism. For example, if consumerism is tied to the legacy of Calvinist theology, then how does it arise in traditionally Roman Catholic, Lutheran, or Orthodox nations? How does a lifestyle that Campbell claims was practiced by a nineteenth-century English middle-class cultural elite come to transcend boundaries of age, class, sex, and nationality? How could an ethic defined by its rejection of social convention become the social convention?[89] Can a form of life defined in the absence of mass communications technologies and advertising techniques be unchanged by their introduction? Campbell believes that it can, but he defends this by asserting that the function of advertising is only to draw attention to possible experiences offered by new products.[90] This is a claim subject to empirical

---

87. Campbell, "Reception of a Thesis," 43.

88. Gordon Marshall notes that Campbell's description of the Romantic ethic derives wholly from cultural artifacts such as novels and poetry. Campbell does not show that these cultural works represent either the norms or life practices of actual historical social groups. Marshall, "Culture of Capitalism," 258.

89. See Campbell, *Romantic Ethic*, 177–79.

90. Campbell, "Reception of a Thesis," 38.

validation that I will address in chapter 4. I will also examine the question of consumerism's social location empirically in chapter 4.

For Campbell's theory to be applicable today, it would be necessary to claim that the present cultural situation remains modern rather than postmodern. Campbell is quite clear that he is describing a *modern* theory of consumption, in which "modern" is understood analytically as implying particular intellectual commitments.[91] For example, the desire for novelty, which Campbell considers the characteristic trait of modern consumption, is intimately bound up with the modern idea of human progress, which values the new because it signifies humanity's gradual historical realization of perfection.[92] I argued in chapter 2 that this idea of progress is now largely discredited. The modern worldview sees the individual self as autonomous. It privileges the material realm over the spiritual as the domain of knowledge. Likewise, it privileges culture over nature as the domain of human autonomy and progress.[93] Thus Campbell's modern consumer chooses a material cultural artifact to which to attach his or her autonomous daydreams. In a postmodern culture, the autonomy of meanings from economic goods and thus the autonomy of individuals to establish the meaning of their consumption can no longer be assumed.

Although Campbell consistently claims that the modern consumer attaches her or his autonomous hedonistic daydreams to economic goods, he never explains *why* this should be so. Why does autonomous hedonistic daydreaming lead to economic consumption? Campbell's argument that the daydreamer needs an object that he or she perceives to be new is not specific enough to motivate economic consumption.[94] According to this criterion, the daydreamer could simply watch clouds and be spared the distraction of having to earn the means to consume. One possible explanation is that Campbell has overstated his claim concerning the modern consumer's autonomy. The desire to justify the Romantic ethic's morality to others, the desire for a common aesthetic standard in fashion, and the formation of Bohemian communities to provide mutual support all point to a desire for social validation in Romanticism. Thus a truly Romantic form of life cannot be understood as purely autonomous. The degree of

---

91. Ibid., 41.
92. Gronow, "What is 'Good Taste'?," 294.
93. Askegaard and Firat, "Material Culture," 115–16.
94. See Campbell, "Consuming Goods," 146–47.

inner-directed versus outer-directed motivation present in consumerism is an empirical question that I will address in chapter 4.

Campbell adopts an apologetic role in his description of the spirit of modern consumption. For example, he argues that it was necessary for the Romantic ethic to displace the Protestant ethic of frugality in order to absorb the output of industrial capitalism and ensure its continued growth. The premise of this argument is that ensuring the output of industrial capitalism is a social good sufficiently important that it should determine individuals' consumption choices. Campbell's unquestioned acceptance of the imperative of economic growth belongs to the ideology of economic progress, which identifies the social good with ever-increasing material affluence. Elsewhere, he defends modern consumerism as an expression of social idealism because, he claims, the daydreaming associated with modern consumption is part of the aspiration toward a better world. Campbell praises modern consumption as the means to achieve an individual good of identity-formation, self-expression, creativity, and aesthetic idealism.[95] In linking identity solely to personal consumption, Campbell tacitly assumes the consumer's autonomy from productive activity. For the vast majority of consumers who must generate the means of consumption through paid labor, Campbell's imaginary consumer-identity would require a suppression of self-knowledge.

Campbell claims that the imagined identities of the illusory hedonist are sufficient for the formation of individual personality because "the hedonist's sense of identity can easily become so molded by this process as to come to depend upon a belief in a real similarity."[96] In making this argument, Campbell adopts the subjectivist ethic that he describes, equating identity with the individual's subjective self-image. Campbell grants this subjective self-image divine status. "This 'self' is an inner god or goddess who demands that the individual act in ways that ensure its 'manifestation' or 'release' . . . [by] giving expression to powerful wants and desires."[97] Campbell's flattering language notwithstanding, the ethic he is describing is simply egoism, or in religious terms, self-idolatry. Campbell argues that the hedonistic dimension of consumerism is ethically legitimated by the consumer's moral self-image. "Imagining oneself 'doing good' and 'being good,'

---

95. Campbell, "Considering Others," 214–15, 224; Campbell, "Reception of a Thesis," 47; Campbell, *Romantic Ethic*, 78.

96. Campbell, *Romantic Ethic*, 214.

97. Campbell, "Considering Others," 223.

often constitutes an important part of the pleasures of day-dreaming. . . . The pleasures associated with imagining 'perfected' scenarios relate directly to imagining oneself as a 'perfected' person, exemplifying certain ideals."[98] This argument again illustrates Campbell's adoption of the subjectivist ethic he is describing. Only a subjectivist ethic would consider "imagining oneself doing good" morally equivalent to "doing good." Only a subjectivist ethic would consider having ideals—*any* ideals—as sufficient to defend a form of life as ethically good. While Campbell acknowledges that autonomous imaginative hedonism fosters withdrawal from a shared social world, he fails to acknowledge any consequences that it may have beyond the life of the subject—presumably because they have no relevance to a subjectivist ethic.

Like Campbell, Oppenheimer views contemporary Western consumerism to be a modern phenomenon characterized by insatiability and a desire for novelty. Oppenheimer attributes the emergence of consumerism to the exaggerated importance that Western culture gives to material desires. He claims that the diminished modern view of human beings' role in the universe leads persons to adopt a form of life characterized by a desire for novelty that is insatiable and unconstrained by morality.[99] While Oppenheimer attributes the motivation of consumerism to desire, it is not the desire for pleasure, as with Campbell, but the desire to avoid a negative emotion called *noia*. Following Giacomo Leopardi, Oppenheimer defines *noia* as "'an emptiness of the soul' . . . [that is] 'inseparable from yearning and desire and the failure of huge imaginative passions.'"[100] According to Oppenheimer, *noia* arises in response to the implications of the Copernican universe for human self-understanding. The scale of the modern universe "stimulates boundless desires, yet it recompenses them only with a lax and smothering blank. The result is that the desires themselves seem far more absorbing than the infinite universe that induces them."[101] *Noia* thus differs from the anxiety of meaninglessness to which I attribute consumerism. First, it is an emotion rather than an existential condition. Second, it is a response to a contingent cultural and historical situation rather than a universal experience.

98. Campbell, "Reception of a Thesis," 46–47.
99. Oppenheimer, *Infinite Desire*, 91–94, 107.
100. Ibid., 106.
101. Ibid., 94.

Oppenheimer, like Campbell, describes the imperative to consume as a duty to an inner god. This inner god of infinite desire produces infinite guilt because it can never be satisfied or appeased.[102] Oppenheimer calls this "the divine incarnation of solipsism. . . . The individual human mind . . . has replaced the universe."[103] But the individual who lives the life he describes sees this as "a form of health," or even the "ideal destiny of all human beings."[104] This idealization of a life driven by powerful desires echoes Campbell idealization of the spirit of modern consumption.

Postrel's theory of consumerism belongs to the same category as Campbell's because she describes contemporary Western consumption as primarily inner-directed, hedonistic, and tied to subjective identity. Like Campbell, Postrel rejects the status signaling and manipulation theories. She asserts that "we buy aesthetic models because we like what we see and feel. Exposure, not manipulation, creates demand."[105] For Postrel, as for Campbell, advertising serves only to expose consumers to new products. While Campbell describes consumerism as a modern phenomenon, Postrel considers it postmodern in its rejection of universals, emphasis upon plural subjective perspectives, and fragmentary meanings. Postrel also dissociates consumers' desire for novelty from the modern era. Citing historian Anne Hollander, she locates the origin of fashion in the Middle Ages.[106]

While Campbell considers the pleasures of consumerism to be purely semiotic, Postrel holds that they are aesthetic as well. Aesthetically pleasing forms have positive meaning associations, she claims, that are another source of aesthetic pleasure for the person who identifies with them. Unlike Campbell, Postrel considers goods to have social signification as well as interior meaning. What consumer goods signify is personal and social identity. While Campbell sees the pleasures of modern consumption as rationally-directed, Postrel describes consumption's aesthetic pleasures as immediate and pre-rational, and its meanings as subliminal. Consumer goods may either reflect the individual's subjective sense of self or the individual's aspirations. Unlike Campbell, Postrel holds that aspirational identities may be unconscious as well as calculated. Like Campbell, she treats identity as purely subjective.[107] Postrel's theory, like Campbell's, is vulner-

102. Ibid., 110–12.
103. Ibid., 108–9.
104. Ibid., 92.
105. Postrel, *Substance of Style*, 57.
106. Ibid., 9, 82.
107. Ibid., 6, 95–102, 108, 113, 117.

able to a critique that questions why consumer goods should be implicated in a process of taking pleasure in imaginary identities. Postrel's answer that "commerce just makes things easier"[108] is inadequate. It fails to explain why the meanings associated with consumer goods should be preferred to those of other imaginative experiences.

Consumerism as the Product of Parental Concern

The theory advanced by Elizabeth Warren and Amelia Warren Tyagi represents a final type that attributes the motivation of consumerism to parental concern. Warren and Tyagi specifically examine the condition of the U.S. middle class. Their definition of the middle class excludes the top few percent of U.S. households that are rich enough to afford a second home and the lower income households that are too poor to own a primary home. Warren and Tyagi aim to demonstrate that all spending by the U.S. middle class is necessary spending. Toward that end, they analyze the U.S. Bureau of Labor Statistics Consumer Expenditure Survey data from 1972 to 2001. These data show that real (inflation-adjusted) household spending on food, clothing, major appliances, and household furnishings have declined substantially over a generation. On the other hand, real household spending has increased significantly for housing, higher education, health care, automobiles, air travel, and home electronics.[109]

Warren and Tyagi seek to show that expenditures in those categories in which spending has grown significantly are necessities. Their main argument for the necessity of middle-class consumption concerns housing and education. They claim that housing has become more and more expensive for middle-class households because households with children engage in a bidding war for houses in good school districts out of concern for the future well-being of their children, which would be furthered by a good education. The concern for good schools results in a bidding war, they argue, because the supply of good public schools is inadequate to meet the demand and there are no adequate alternatives. Warren and Tyagi argue that automobile expenses must be viewed as a necessary consequence of changing lifestyles, regulations, and social norms. Households need more

---

108. Ibid., 118.
109. Warren and Tyagi, *Two-Income Trap*, 17–20, 42–43, 47, 109, 196–98.

cars, they argue, because of the entry of women into the workforce and families' relocation to the suburbs. They need larger and more expensive cars because of increased safety regulations and stricter social norms for child safety. Spending on home electronics and air travel can be ignored, according to Warren and Tyagi, because of their small contributions to the family budget.[110]

Two observations should be noted with regard to Warren and Tyagi's claims. First, they are claiming that the market for elementary and secondary education has insurmountable barriers to entry. In a free market, an excess of price-inelastic demand for high quality schools would result in market entry by new participants—for example, by private schools offering high quality education. Second, what Warren and Tyagi consider a good or decent school is subject to a shifting definition. At first they argue that a good school is merely one that avoids the problems of violence and underperformance that characterize urban schools serving the economic underclass.[111] This standard is potentially measurable by absolute metrics such as test scores, college admission rates, and frequency of violent incidents. Later, however, Warren and Tyagi shift to a positional or relative standard for what constitutes a good school: "As parents increasingly believe that the differences among schools will translate into differences in lifetime chances, they are doing everything they can to buy their way into the *best* public schools."[112] They also describe a positional measure of quality in the market for higher education: "The number of students aiming for a spot in a *decent* four-year institution is rising every year, while the number of openings at the *major* public and private universities stays essentially the same."[113] For positional goods, demand is directed towards those suppliers perceived as relatively better, no matter what the quantity or absolute utility of supply in general. Warren and Tyagi write that middle-class life is characterized by home ownership, decent schools, college, a safe car, and health insurance.[114] Since the education and housing components of this definition are positional, middle-class status in their argument is defined by a positional standard of consumption.

---

110. Ibid., 19–28, 47–48.
111. Ibid., 26.
112. Ibid., 33 (emphasis mine).
113. Ibid., 42 (emphasis mine).
114. Ibid., 41, 109, 113.

The highest good for persons in the U.S. middle class, according to Warren and Tyagi, is the well-being of their children. Thus, they only include households with children in their understanding of the middle class. It is the pursuit of children's well-being, they claim, that justifies middle-class households engaging in positional competition with one another to buy the most expensive home—which, they assume, is bundled with the best public schools—and the most expensive college education they can afford. However, Warren and Tyagi's own arguments demonstrate that middle-class parents are inconsistent in pursuing their children's well-being. According to their theory, middle-class parents are willing to send two workers into the workforce so they can spend everything they can on housing and the associated public schools, which have instrumental value for their children's future well-being. But those same parents are unwilling, they concede, to save adequate amounts to mitigate the risks to their children's future well-being inherent in spending most of both parents' paychecks on fixed expenses like mortgage payments, car payments, health insurance, and tuition. In the event of a parent's death, disability, unemployment, or divorce, a two-income household that has committed most of both parents' paychecks to fixed expenses is more likely to fail financially than a household that has only one parent in the workforce or a household that has committed its second paycheck to savings and variable expenses. Such financial failures have significant and lasting negative effects on the children. Yet Warren and Tyagi acknowledge that this risk does not lead two-income households to save more. The imperative of middle-class parents' concern for their children's future is not honored in their risk management practices, despite the role that Warren and Tyagi claim for this imperative in housing and education consumption.[115]

In describing positional housing and educational expenses as *necessary*, it is clear that Warren and Tyagi do not mean logical necessity. By definition, a positional good cannot be possessed by everyone who demands it, and therefore it cannot logically be necessary for those who demand it. Nor do Warren and Tyagi mean necessity in the sense that John Paul II, Galbraith, and Campbell use this term—i.e., as consumption that comprises an objective condition to sustain human life. While the first dollar that a household spends on shelter is a human necessity, the last or marginal dollar that a U.S. middle-class household spends on housing is not. Warren and Tyagi do not claim that the lives of those in the United States who rent their

115. Ibid., 62–68, 172–79.

homes, drive second-hand cars, and fail to attend college are unsustainable or subhuman; they claim that such a life is not desirable. By acknowledging that U.S. consumers may choose not to engage in positional competition in housing and education, Warren and Tyagi admit that such forms of consumption are neither logically nor humanly necessary.[116] When they describe all housing and educational expenses as necessary, then, Warren and Tyagi are using the term "necessary" to mean *normative*. Since they acknowledge that not all middle-class consumer spending is logically or humanly necessary, their theory does not challenge the current existence of consumerism, which is defined in part by its rejection of any standard of sufficiency. What they do instead is propose a new theory of the motivation of consumerism.

In order to demonstrate their theory, Warren and Tyagi would have to demonstrate that consumeristic spending in the U.S. middle class is confined to spending on children. They offer no analysis that demonstrates that positional competition in housing consumption is limited to parents with school-aged children. To the contrary, they acknowledge that real housing costs have also risen for households without children, though not as steeply. They assert that the difference is due to concern for children, but they do not demonstrate this, nor do they explain the increase for other households.[117] Likewise, Warren and Tyagi do not demonstrate that middle-class parents' spending on their children is motivated solely by concern for their children's well-being. Without further validation, Veblen offers an equally plausible theory: that spending on one's children is vicarious conspicuous consumption intended to demonstrate the wealth and status of the head of household. Veblen's theory is also consistent with the pattern of spending that Warren and Tyagi observe, in which real consumption grows for some goods but not others. To Warren and Tyagi these patterns show concern for children, but in Veblen's theory the goods subject to increased spending—housing, education, cars, travel, and electronics—are those best suited to putting pecuniary prowess and social rank into evidence.

Warren and Tyagi's thesis is subject to a high standard of proof because they insist that concern for children explains *all* significant increases in consumer spending. Thus, for example, they claim that only safety concerns drive increased per vehicle spending on automobiles, and not any desire that consumers may have to associate themselves with the power, status, freedom, and sexual desirability that advertisers associate with

116. Ibid., 63, 164–72.
117. Ibid., 22.

automobiles. To demonstrate their thesis that consumer motivation is concerned solely with children's well-being, Warren and Tyagi would have to demonstrate that these other associations have no significant impact on consumer behavior. They do not.

Although Warren and Tyagi have failed to prove the superiority of their theory, that does not disqualify it either. In order to test their theory's relative adequacy, several empirical tests are possible. First, if their theory is correct, positional competition for housing in the best school districts should be limited to households with preschool- and school-aged children, since public education has no expected value for households that do not have or expect school-aged children. Second, to the extent that education is valued for its perceived utility, as Warren and Tyagi argue, and not as an indicator of status, there should be an upper limit on the amount that households will spend on housing to secure a "good" education under the law of diminishing marginal utility. Third, the existence of high quality private schools can be readily shown, which suggests that Warren and Tyagi have overstated the lack of substitute goods for public education and the barriers to market entry in education. If Warren and Tyagi are correct that housing spending is driven by the perceived utility of public schools, the existence of high quality private education should impose an upper limit on the premium that households will spend on housing to secure "good" public schools that is equal to the price of a "good" private education. I will explore these empirical questions in chapter 4.

4

An Empirical Evaluation of Current Consumerism Theories

THEOLOGICAL ETHICS SHOULD BE practical. Whether it is descriptive or normative, ethics reflects on human beings' moral judgments and actions—both actual and potential—in the experience of real persons and communities. Ethical arguments make claims about how individuals and communities exercise moral judgment and act or how they should do so. Any reflection on human judgment and action that fails to relate itself to the practical experience of real persons and communities is merely speculative. A demonstration of the practical applicability and significance of an ethical argument is a necessary—though not sufficient—component of any complete ethical analysis. A complete theological ethical analysis of an existing socioeconomic phenomenon like consumerism must be multidisciplinary. It must combine an empirical socioeconomic analysis of what is going on with a theological ethical analysis of its moral significance. Since social scientific interpretations and theological ethical interpretations each contain normative and descriptive elements, this is not a straightforward task.

Consumerism cannot be described in purely empirical terms because it is a creation of the human spirit. Paul Tillich observes that the actions of the human spirit are characterized by reflexive self-observation and free self-determination. They are therefore normative as well as descriptive. They contain both logical forms and a judgment of their significance. This applies to any act of interpreting the activity of the human spirit as well, since the act of interpretation is also an act of the human spirit.[1] Many economists

---

1. Tillich, *System of the Sciences*, 38–39, 137, 146.

An Empirical Evaluation of Current Consumerism Theories

and sociologists have sought to establish an understanding of consumerism within their own disciplines without acknowledging that their evaluations incorporate moral judgments as well as empirical observations. As a result, they misunderstand consumerism and misunderstand the status of their own interpretations. Because consumerism is an act of the human spirit, any evaluation of consumerism includes moral judgments regarding its significance, even if these judgments are not made consciously. Since my aim in this book is to describe consumerism theologically and to ask how it might be changed, I consciously evaluate consumerism from a particular Christian ethical standpoint. This adds a reflexive layer of normative evaluation to the moral judgments already incorporated into social scientific descriptions of consumerism.

If it is impossible to understand consumerism in purely empirical terms, it is equally impossible to describe it in purely normative terms without any empirical understanding. In James Gustafson's reflections on the methodological issues that arise in multidisciplinary work, he observes that avoiding empirical evaluation confines the theological ethicist to fruitless discussions of ideology and epistemology. To untangle the empirical observations of the social scientist from the observer's presuppositions, Gustafson argues, the empirical research must be engaged on its own terms.[2]

Tillich considers theological ethics and science to be completely separable, since the questions that each seeks to answer occupy different dimensions. The object of the theological ethicist is the religious depth dimension of culture, while science is concerned with the observable characteristics and processes of finite objects. Therefore, he argues, the theological ethicist's findings do not condition those of the scientist, nor do the scientist's findings condition those of the theological ethicist.[3] Gustafson takes a contrary view, that there is significant overlap between the work of the theological ethicist and the scientist because there is overlap in their objects of study. In his view, the findings of each should qualify what can be claimed by the other.[4] I propose that this disagreement should be settled by the principle that the relationship between different modes of inquiry should reflect the relationship between their objects of understanding. Therefore, I agree with Gustafson that the work of the theological ethicist and the social scientist

---

2. Gustafson, *Intersections*, 131.

3. Tillich, "Idea of a Theology of Culture," 20–23; Tillich, "Relationship between Science and Religion," 154–55.

4. Gustafson, *Intersections*, xii–xvii.

invariably overlap, but I also agree with Tillich that the questions each seeks to ask are properly distinct. I attribute the overlap between the disciplines not to an overlap in their objects but to the mutual dependence of their objects as means to achieve understanding. Since the objects of inquiry are mutually dependent, their corresponding modes of inquiry are mutually dependent.

What does this mean in practice? The social scientist who engages in empirical research does not randomly decide what phenomena to observe and what attributes of those phenomena to classify, compare, and report. She or he is guided by an intention to disclose what a social phenomenon *means*. But she or he cannot do so without making normative judgments about what is significant and why, and basing these judgments upon some system and ground of meaning. Thus every social scientist makes meaning claims and every social scientific meaning claim rests on a metaphysics and an ethics that lie outside the realm of empirical social scientific observation. Similarly, the theological ethicist cannot make ethical interpretations of the observable world and practical proposals for that world without basing his or her interpretations upon descriptions of the observable world that overlap the scientific community's objects of empirical observation and interpretation.

Since the overlap of theological ethical and social scientific disciplines does not arise from an overlap in the questions they are suited to answer but from the inability of either discipline to establish complete meaning in isolation from the other, each discipline should condition the findings of the other's practitioners within its own proper domain of inquiry. The theological ethicist should constrain the judgments and proposals of the social scientist to the degree that these judgments rest upon metaphysical and ethical presuppositions, but the theological ethical critique must limit itself to metaphysical and ethical matters. Likewise, the social scientist should constrain the judgments and proposals of the theological ethicist to the degree that these judgments and proposals rest upon empirical claims and social scientific criteria of validity, but the social scientific critique must limit itself to these empirical matters. My project would be incoherent if I attempted to incorporate the moral evaluations of the social scientists whose work I reference along with my own normative Christian ethical standpoint. To maintain a consistent Christian ethical standpoint, I must either perform my own social scientific analyses, guided by the normative aims of my study, or I must identify and bracket the moral claims and presuppositions of the social scientists whose work I appropriate.

An Empirical Evaluation of Current Consumerism Theories

The analytic tasks of Christian ethics are conditioned by social scientific descriptions of actual human behavior. These descriptions can provide empirical validation for the *possibility* of Christian anthropological claims. I disagree with Gustafson when he claims that experience can demonstrate that Christian anthropological claims are true.[5] My claim is more limited. Empirical evidence can offer only a negative validation. Empirical evidence can *invalidate* Christian anthropological theories if the empirical evidence shows that people behave otherwise than the theological theories predict. Or it can demonstrate that actual human behavior is *consistent* with a particular theological description. But it cannot demonstrate that a particular theological description of human behavior is true.

For my purposes, it is possible to examine empirically how different groups of people actually consume, as well as what goods they forego and what norms they violate in order to consume. It is possible to evaluate empirically the consequences of different patterns of consumer behavior to the common good, given a particular theological account of the common good. And it is possible to judge empirically what practical limits and tradeoffs must be recognized with respect to alternate proposals for consumer behavior and the means needed to achieve them. These findings should condition Christian normative proposals in order for these proposals to meet the standards of general intelligibility and practicability.

The five theories of the motivation of consumerism that I presented in chapter 3 provide anecdotal support, at best, to demonstrate their practical relevance. John Paul II offers no empirical evidence whatsoever. His theory is wholly deductive. Veblen's theory rests on anecdotal descriptions of a small group of upper-class U.S. households in the late nineteenth century and a speculative theory of social evolution. Galbraith's theory rests on an untested assumption regarding the effectiveness of corporate attempts to control their markets. Campbell relies on Romantic literature as evidence of a broadly-practiced contemporary practical form of life, even though this is not empirical. Warren and Tyagi rely on anecdote, assertion, and limited data that lack the scope and precision to confirm or contradict their arguments. All of these thinkers fall short of demonstrating their theories' empirical possibility, let alone their empirical superiority over the rival theories.

In this chapter, I provide the missing empirical evidence to evaluate the practical possibility and relative empirical superiority of the five

---

5. Ibid., 23.

theories of consumerism's motivation that I presented in chapter 3. To the extent that previous studies of consumerism developed empirical data at all, their authors' moral judgments are embedded in the premises, scope, and methods of their analyses. To accept these moral judgments *a priori* would beg the question of consumerism's motivation. Therefore I develop my own empirical analyses that establish premises, scope, and methods according to my own normative perspective and ethical questions. My analyses must still meet the criterion of descriptive veracity. The evidence that I develop here is intended to demonstrate the empirical inadequacies of the five theories from chapter 3 in describing contemporary Western consumerism, the need for an alternate theory, and the empirical constraints by which this alternate theory will be bound if it is to meet the conditions of empirical possibility and practical contemporary relevance.

Consumerism's Historical and Social Location

Consumerism as I have defined it is an ideal type of a form of life chosen and practiced by individuals interacting with cultural processes. As such, it cannot be measured directly. However, to the extent that this ideal type approximates an existing form of life, the widespread presence of this form of life in a particular society should produce economic behaviors consistent with its motivations. In order to find the clearest evidence of consumer motivations, I will limit my examination of U.S. historical data to the period up to and including the peak of the business cycle in 2007. The Great Recession of 2007–9 was responsible for a dramatic rise in the rates of unemployment, underemployment, discouraged workers, negative home equity, home foreclosures, and personal bankruptcies, and these rates remain elevated in 2013. To the extent that the Great Recession changed U.S. consumer behavior between 2007 and 2013, these behavioral changes coincide with significant changes in the material constraints upon consumers. This makes it very difficult to isolate the effects of any changes in consumers' motivations from the effects of changes in consumers' material constraints since 2007.

I use two behaviors as markers that suggest the prevalence of a consumeristic form of life in a particular historical and class location: namely, the preferences for leisure and savings as incomes rise. Both leisure and savings represent goods that, in modern Western societies at least, are widely held to be valuable apart from economic consumption, and are readily measurable through official government statistics.[6] The broad cultural consensus that most, if not all, people value leisure and savings is reflected in the assumptions of economic theory. Mainstream economic theory holds that as incomes rise, the marginal utility of consumption diminishes and leisure time becomes relatively more valuable.[7] If this theory is correct, one would expect average work hours to decline as affluence increases. If and when work hours increase as affluence increases this suggests the suppression of competing values and insatiability which characterize consumerism. Similarly, mainstream economic theory holds that the diminishing marginal utility of consumption raises individuals' propensity to save as incomes rise.[8] If and when the saving rate declines as income rises this would also suggest the suppression of competing values and insatiability which characterize consumerism. Both the leisure and savings measures are limited in their ability to demonstrate consumeristic behavior to households above the official poverty line. Since the official poverty line constitutes an objective measure—however contested—of economic sufficiency and since part of the definition of consumerism is that it transgresses objective standards of economic sufficiency, consumeristic motives cannot be demonstrated through revealed preferences below this level. In 2007, 9.8 percent of U.S. households had incomes below this threshold.[9]

For the purpose of my analysis, leisure time includes all hours not spent in paid employment. According to this definition, leisure time includes all activities chosen for the sake of non-pecuniary motives, including unpaid labor for dependent care and housekeeping, time spent with family and friends, time spent in recreation, and time spent in volunteer and community activities. It also includes activities that are unpaid but linked to paid employment, like commuting. Paid employment hours are the product of the percentage of working-aged persons who are employed

---

6. To be more precise, savings are valued for reasons in addition to future consumption—for example, providing an emergency reserve and making bequests. See Friedman, *Theory of the Consumption Function*, 16.

7. Samuelson and Nordhaus, *Economics*, 86–90. In economic theory, the influence of this *income effect* on work hours may be offset by a *substitution effect* in which rising real wages create a greater incentive to work. Ibid., 247–49. The substitution effect is inseparable from the phenomenon I wish to explore, since the aim of an individual or household choosing longer work hours is generally to increase consumption.

8. Ibid., 458–63.

9. DeNavas-Walt, Proctor, and Smith, *Income, Poverty, and Health Insurance: 2007*, 13.

and the average number of hours that they work. The civilian labor force participation rate for U.S. civilians aged sixteen and older is plotted in Figure 1. These employment trends are broken out in Figure 2 according to whether U.S. employment was full- or part-time, and whether part-time work was voluntary or involuntary. Figure 1 shows that U.S. labor force participation rates increased significantly between 1948 and 2006, and more particularly between 1970 and 2000. Figure 2 shows very little change in the share of full-time employment during this period in which U.S. labor force participation was rising sharply. Therefore, the change in leisure time can be analyzed solely with reference to the labor force participation data shown in Figure 1.

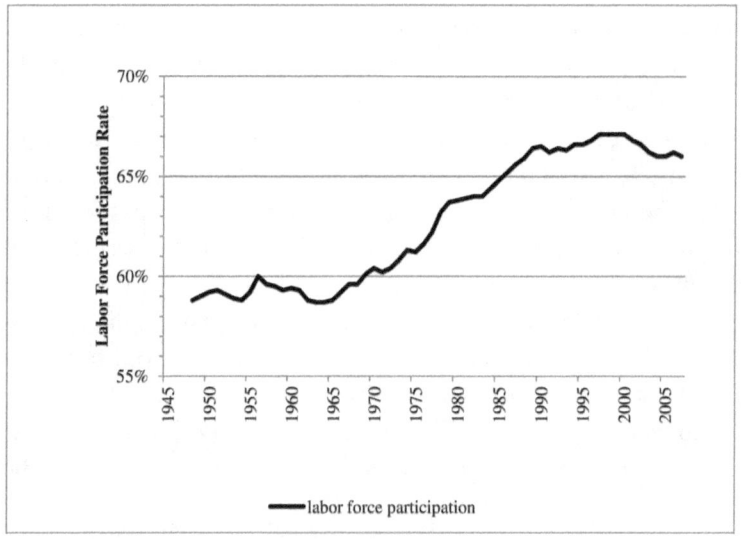

FIGURE 1: U.S. labor force participation rate, 1948–2007.
Source: U.S. Department of Labor, Current Population Survey.

An Empirical Evaluation of Current Consumerism Theories

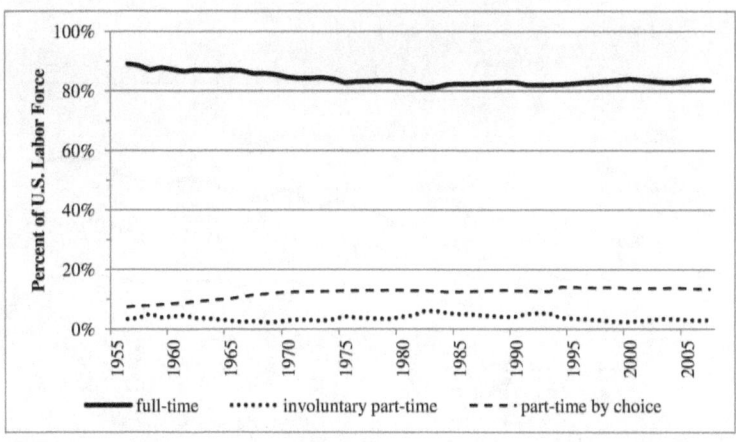

FIGURE 2: U.S. employment by full- or part-time classifications, 1956–2007. *Source*: U.S. Department of Labor, Current Population Survey.

To compare leisure time to income growth, Figure 3 shows real (inflation-adjusted) income growth over the same period for the 20th, 40th, 60th, and 80th percentiles of U.S. families by income. During the 1970–2000 period, Figure 3 shows that real U.S. family incomes grew at all levels of the income distribution, although they grew much faster for upper-income families. The increase in labor force participation during a period of rising incomes contradicts the prediction of standard economic theory that persons prefer more leisure as incomes rise. Even though some of the increase in labor force participation may be in response to stagnating real wages among lower-income families, this cannot explain why lower-income families would choose to increase labor force participation above and beyond the level needed to maintain their households' standard of living, sacrificing more leisure time than needed to maintain real income.

Shopping for Meaningful Lives

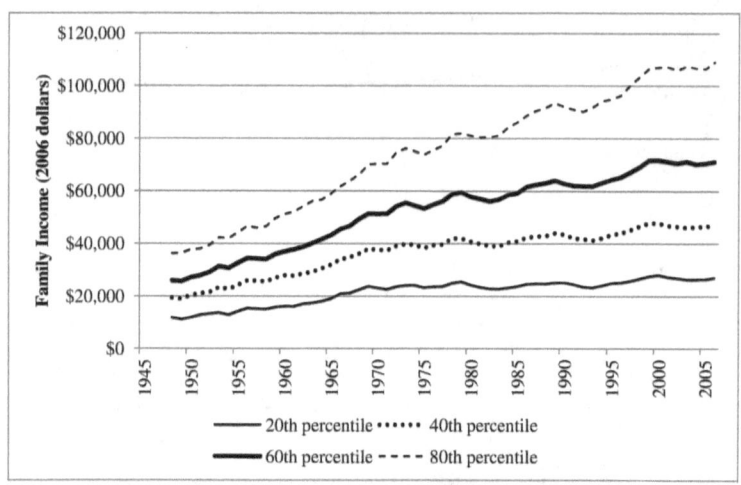

FIGURE 3: U.S. real family income by income percentile, 1948–2006.
Source: U.S. Census Bureau, Current Population Survey.

In order to assess the motives behind this behavior, it should be recognized that the increase in U.S. labor force participation was entirely the result of increased participation by women. While men's labor force participation declined from 80 percent to 75 percent between 1970 and 1998, women's labor force participation rose from 43 percent to 60 percent over the same period.[10] This increase in women's employment cannot be attributed to non-pecuniary motives. Robert Putnam analyzes DDB Needham survey data and concludes that during the period 1978–99, "virtually all the increase in full-time employment of American women ... is attributable to financial pressures, not personal fulfillment."[11] U.S. labor force participation increased between the 1970s and 1990s out of a desire for economic means to fund household consumption, despite rising real incomes during this period. This is consistent with an increase in the prevalence of a consumeristic form of life during this period.

The U.S. savings rate and disposable personal income are defined by the Department of Commerce. Personal income is "the income that persons receive in return for their provision of labor, land, and capital used in current production and the net current transfer payments that they receive from business and from government," disposable personal income is equal

10. Fullerton, "Labor Force Participation: 1950–98," 4.
11. Putnam, Bowling Alone, 197.

An Empirical Evaluation of Current Consumerism Theories

to personal income minus personal taxes, personal savings "is equal to personal income less personal outlays and personal taxes," and the personal savings rate is the ratio of personal savings to disposable personal income.[12] Figure 4 shows the historical relation between the personal savings rate and real (inflation-adjusted) disposable personal income. The standard economic model accurately predicts the savings behavior of U.S. consumers between 1952 and 1982. As real per capita incomes rose steadily from $8,500 to $17,400 in 2000 dollars, the savings rate rose from 8.4 percent to 11.2 percent of disposable personal income. However, 1982 represents an inflection point. Between 1982 and 2007, U.S. consumers' real per capita incomes continued to rise steadily, from $17,400 to $28,700 in 2000 dollars, but the savings rate fell from 11.2 percent in 1982 to 0.5 percent in 2007. The declining savings rate during a period of rising income is consistent with a large increase in the prevalence of a consumeristic form of life after 1982.

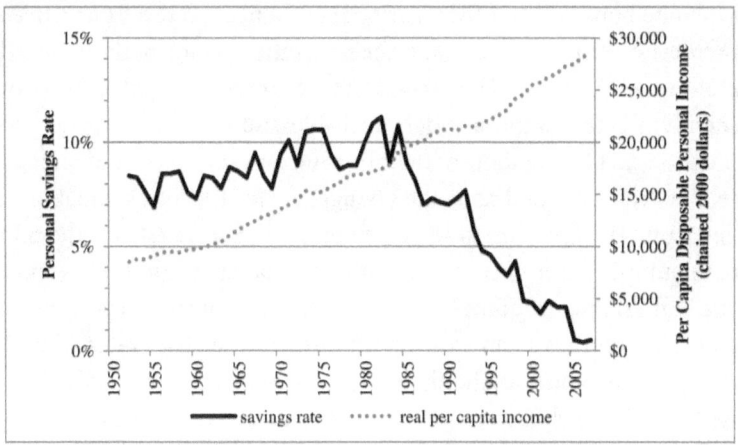

FIGURE 4: U.S. personal savings rate vs. real per capita disposable personal income, 1952–2007. *Source*: U.S. Department of Commerce, National Income and Product Accounts.

The Commerce Department's aggregate income data mask changes in the distribution of income and spending. According to the U.S. Census Bureau, the Gini coefficient—a measure of household income inequality—rose from 0.412 in 1982 to 0.463 in 2007, meaning that the share of U.S. national

---

12. U.S. Department of Commerce, *Concepts and Methods of the National Income and Product Accounts*, 2-6, 2-12.

income controlled by wealthier households increased over this period.[13] The standard economic model predicts that aggregate savings should increase from this trend since the law of diminishing marginal returns leads higher income groups to save at a higher rate. Despite increasing income inequality, however, the data show the opposite trend in the nation's aggregate savings rate. Thus the changing distribution of income adds weight to the conclusion that U.S. consumer behavior changed fundamentally in the early 1980s. To attribute this changed behavior to consumerism is to claim that a change in cultural values led a significant proportion of U.S. households to increase the value that they assigned to current consumption and reduce the value that they assigned to future consumption, insurance against risk, and providing bequests.

There are two other hypotheses that could explain the declining savings rate. The first is that savings rates have fallen since the early 1980s due to greater availability of credit. If this were correct, it should only affect low-income households whose marginal propensity to save is negative and whose desire to spend more than their income was formerly impeded by lack of access to credit. Higher-income households might borrow more frequently if credit is more widely available, but their motives for paying their debts and placing some of their income into savings would remain the same. Between 1980 and 2005 the savings rate for the lowest income quintile fell from -32.8 percent to -61.0 percent, the savings rate for the middle income quintile fell from 10.7 percent to -2.1 percent, and the savings rate for the highest income quintile fell from 26.0 percent to 23.0 percent.[14] The easy credit hypothesis can explain why negative savings rates would decline for low-income households, but it cannot explain why middle-income households would shift from positive to negative savings rates.

The second competing hypothesis to explain the declining savings rate is that savings preferences have fallen because of rising wealth. However, the magnitude of this wealth effect was not large enough to produce declining savings rates in the United States between 1952 and 1982, when household wealth was growing. Other factors, such as the income effect, were evidently more significant. If the wealth effect was the main determinant of the savings rate, the change in savings rate would be inversely

13. U.S. Census Bureau, Current Population Survey. The Gini coefficient ranges from 0 to 1, where a 0 value indicates perfect income equality and a 1 value indicates all the income in a society is earned by one household. For a more precise definition, see Hicks, *Inequality and Christian Ethics*, 247–51.

14. Bunting, "Saving Decline," 287.

related to the business cycle. Asset appreciation accompanied the economic expansions of 1983–90, 1991–2000, and 2002–7, while asset devaluation accompanied the recessions of 1990–1 and 2001. Figure 4 shows that the savings rate leveled off during the recessions of 1990–1 and 2001 when asset values were falling, but resumed its downward trend when each of these recessions was over. This suggests that the substitution effect can be considered a contributing factor but not the most significant cause of the declining U.S. savings rate since 1982.

The National Opinion Research Center conducts a triennial Survey of Consumer Finances for the U.S. Federal Reserve Board which tracks U.S. household balance sheet information. An increasing willingness to incur debts—particularly debts that are not matched by comparable gains in assets—would indicate that competing values were being sacrificed for the sake of rising consumption. The Survey of Consumer Finances is ideal for measuring changes by income class because it uses a dual-frame sample design that over-samples wealthy households and weights accordingly. This makes it possible to calculate precise estimates of household financial indicators for the wealthy classes as well as for the much more populous middle and lower classes. The survey's sample design and questionnaire have remained relatively constant only since 1989.[15] Thus, there are too few historical data points to conduct time-series regressions on the survey data. However, an inspection of the data still provides an indication of recent changes in debt tolerance among U.S. households by class location.

Real (inflation-adjusted) total household debts from the Survey of Consumer Finances are plotted in Figure 5 by income quintile and Figure 6 for upper-income groups. Figures 5 and 6 show that U.S. real household debts grew between 1989 and 2004 across all income classes. The growth rate of debt was highest for the bottom income quintile (8 percent per year) and richest one percent (7 percent per year), and lowest for the fourth and fifth income quintiles (4 percent per year), which primarily represent the upper-middle class.

---

15. Kennickell, *Over-Sampling the Wealthy*.

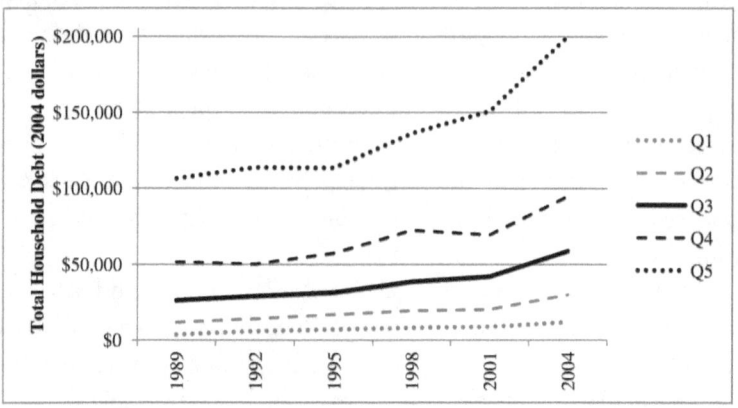

FIGURE 5: U.S. real total household debt by income quintile, 1989–2004. *Sources:* U.S. Federal Reserve Board, Survey of Consumer Finances; U.S. Department of Labor, Consumer Price Index.

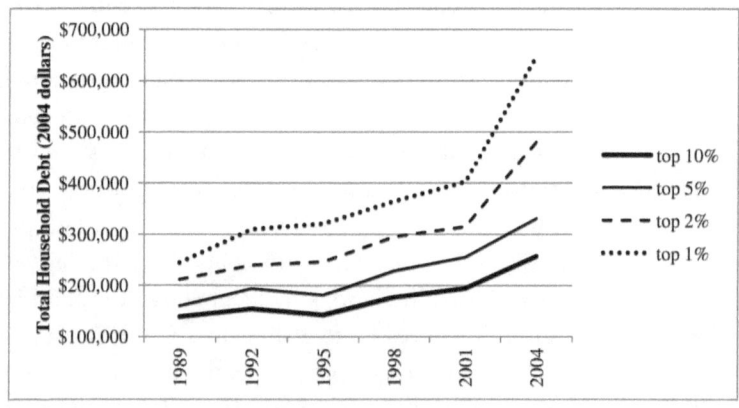

FIGURE 6: U.S. real total household debt for upper-income households, 1989–2004. *Sources:* U.S. Federal Reserve Board, Survey of Consumer Finances; U.S. Department of Labor, Consumer Price Index.

While rising household debt implies a gap between household income and spending on consumption and investment, it does not in itself indicate deepening financial distress since households' ability to repay their debts may be growing as well. One fairly strict measure of the relationship between debt and the capacity to repay it is the ratio of debt to income. Since income is more liquid than household assets and since income volatility is lower than the price volatility of real estate, financial assets, and businesses—which comprise the great majority of household assets[16]—the use of income to repay debts is more typical than the use of assets.

Figures 7 and 8 plot the debt-to-income ratios of U.S. households for income quintiles and upper-income groups respectively. Figures 7 and 8 show that the debt-to-income ratio for U.S. households grew between 1989 and 2004 across all income classes. While household debts rose steadily over time, the growth in the debt-to-income ratio is more variable, indicating that other causal factors influence income besides the historical trend. The shapes of the upper-income plots suggest that the debt-to-income ratio is strongly dependent on the business cycle for these groups. This is because a larger share of the income of high-income households is investment and business income rather than wages and salaries. Investment and business income vary more strongly with the business cycle than wage and salary income. Despite this business cycle effect, even the highest income percentiles show a pattern of higher lows and higher highs, suggesting an upward trend in the debt-to-income ratio. This means that U.S. households in all income classes accepted increasing levels of financial risk during the 1989–2004 time period in order to maintain spending growth.

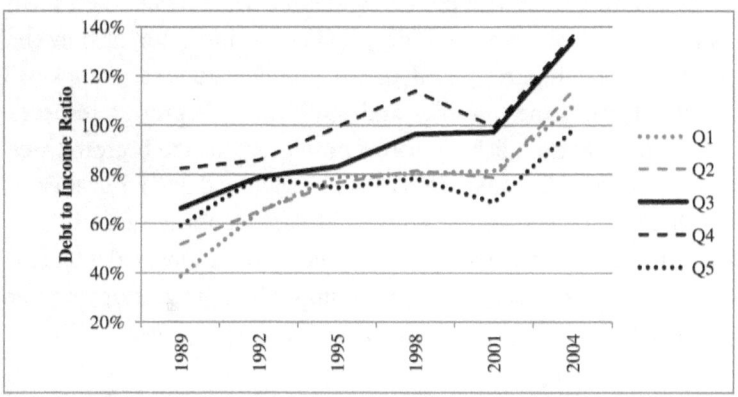

FIGURE 7: U.S. household debt-to-income ratio by income quintile, 1989–2004. *Source*: U.S. Federal Reserve Board, Survey of Consumer Finances.

---

16. Real estate, financial assets, and business assets collectively comprise at least 75 percent of total household assets for every income quintile of the U.S. population between 1989 and 2004. U.S. Federal Reserve Board, Survey of Consumer Finances.

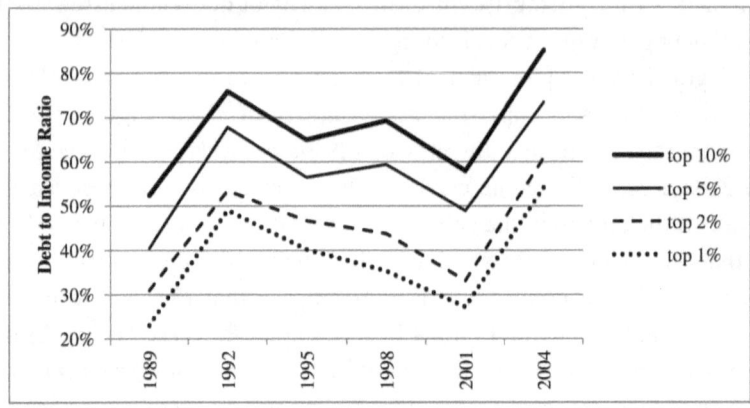

FIGURE 8: U.S. household debt-to-income ratio for upper-income households, 1989–2004. *Source*: U.S. Federal Reserve Board, Survey of Consumer Finances.

The debt-to-assets ratio is a broader measure than the debt-to-income ratio of the relationship between households' debt and their capacity to repay it. More importantly, the debt-to-assets ratio provides a measure of households' net indebtedness. Where the debt-to-income ratio provides an indicator of households' risk of having to sell assets to meet their financial obligations, the debt-to-assets ratio provides an indicator of households' risk of insolvency. Figures 9 and 10 plot the debt-to-assets ratios of U.S. households for income quintiles and upper-income groups respectively. Figure 9 shows that the debt-to-assets ratio grew for the bottom three income quintiles of U.S. households between 1989 and 2004, but there is no evident historical trend in the household debt-to-assets ratio for the top two income quintiles during this period. Nor is there any evident historical trend in the debt-to-assets ratio for the upper income groups represented in Figure 10.

An Empirical Evaluation of Current Consumerism Theories

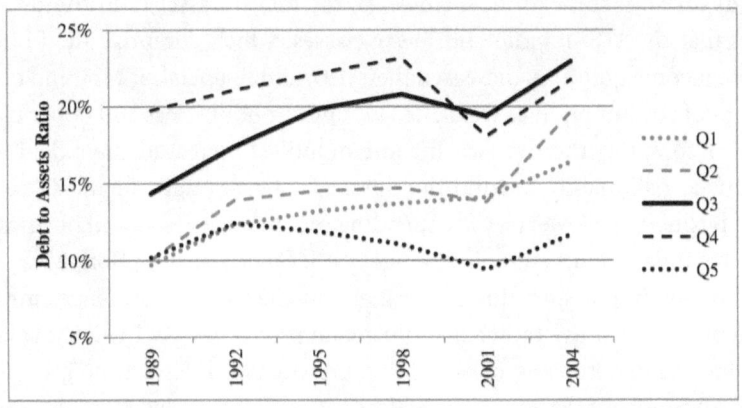

FIGURE 9: U.S. household debt-to-assets ratio by income quintile, 1989–2004. *Source*: U.S. Federal Reserve Board, Survey of Consumer Finances.

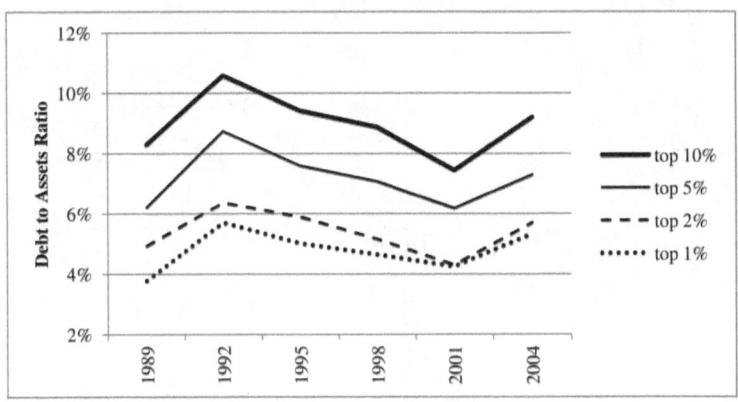

FIGURE 10: U.S. household debt-to-assets ratio for upper-income households, 1989–2004. *Source*: U.S. Federal Reserve Board, Survey of Consumer Finances.

In order better to interpret these ratios, it is also helpful to examine the trends in real (inflation-adjusted) household asset ownership. The changes in U.S. real total household assets are plotted in Figures 11 and 12 for income quintiles and high income groups respectively. Figures 11 and 12 show that household assets grew across all income classes. As I noted earlier, these household assets are primarily real estate, financial assets, and businesses. Therefore at least part of U.S. households' increased debt and financial risk between 1989 and 2004 can be attributed to the purchase of real estate, financial assets, and businesses. This observation holds for all income groups. However, the debt-to-asset ratio trends suggest that the U.S. middle and lower classes, which comprise the bottom three income quintiles, increased their debt and financial risk to fund other forms of consumption as well. The U.S. upper-middle class and upper class, which comprise the top two income quintiles, increased their debt and financial risk mainly to fund the purchase of real estate, financial assets, and businesses. However, only spending on financial assets and businesses can be understood as pure investment rather than consumption. Most real estate spending is spending for primary and secondary residences for the household's own use rather than for rental properties. As I will show later in this chapter, housing consumption grew for all U.S. income groups in the 1989–2004 time frame. Therefore, even those upper-income groups whose spending primarily increased to fund the purchase of assets showed significant consumption growth from 1989 to 2004.

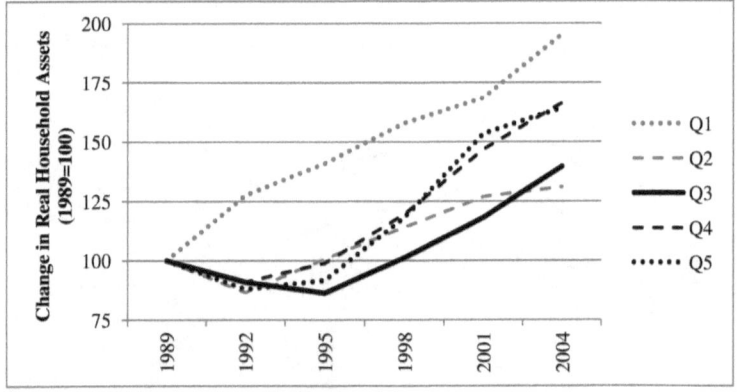

FIGURE 11: U.S. real total household assets by income quintile, 1989–2004. *Sources*: U.S. Federal Reserve Board, Survey of Consumer Finances; Department of Labor, Consumer Price Index.

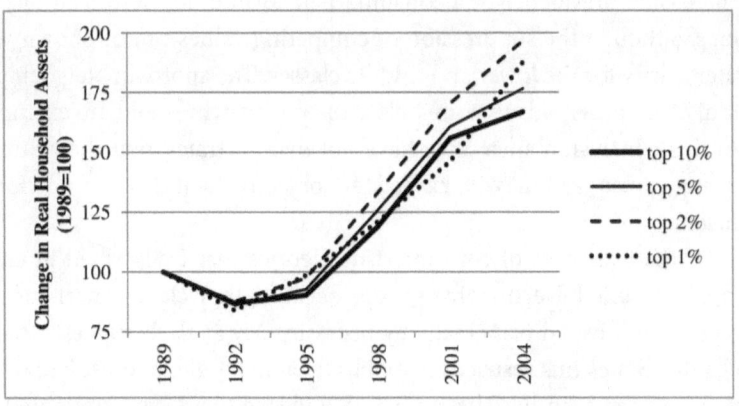

FIGURE 12: U.S. real total household assets for upper-income households, 1989–2004. *Sources*: U.S. Federal Reserve Board, Survey of Consumer Finances; Department of Labor, Consumer Price Index.

My analyses of leisure preference and savings preference show a historical discontinuity in individual economic behavior that occurred in the U.S. in the 1970s and early 1980s. During this transition, the values represented by leisure time and savings were increasingly sacrificed for the sake of greater financial means and greater consumption. This is consistent with the emergence of consumerism as a dominant form of life in the United States during this time period. Among the exemplars for the five consumerism theories, only Warren and Tyagi locate the emergence of consumerism in this time period. Neither John Paul II nor Campbell consider consumerism in the postmodern era to be distinct from modern consumption, while Veblen and Galbraith predate the 1970s. However, only the greed theories as a class exclude the possibility of a historical emergence of consumerism in the postmodern period. Schor claims a postmodern date for the emergence of consumerism in a status signaling theory, Baudrillard provides an example in a manipulation theory, and Postrel provides an example in an imaginative hedonism theory.

My class analysis of trends in U.S. households' tolerance of debt and financial risk shows that during the late twentieth and early twenty-first centuries, U.S. households accepted greater debt burdens and greater financial risk in every income category in order to fund increased spending. For the lower and middle classes, this risk-taking is even more pronounced than for the upper-middle and upper classes. This pattern is consistent with an increasing prevalence of a consumeristic form of life across all income groups, although the suppression of competing values can be shown with greater clarity for the lower and middle classes. The approximately ten percent of U.S. households that are below the poverty threshold are exempted from this conclusion since they have not demonstrated that their pursuit of rising consumption will exceed an objective standard of economic sufficiency.

Of the five types of consumerism theories that I described in chapter 3, all exclude lower-income groups because, they claim, lower-income groups are motivated principally by necessity. My analysis suggests that in the United States this restriction applies to, at most, the poorest half of the bottom income quintile. The empirical evidence that I have presented for the presence of consumeristic forms of life among the lower-middle and working classes demonstrates a key weakness of all five types of motivation theory in explaining contemporary consumerism. This problem is particularly acute for the status signaling theories because these theories claim that consumerism is driven by a single competition, with a single standard of semiotic value—pecuniary prowess and its associated status—that is established by the upper class, and a single motive—emulation, or desire for status. The further an individual's income lies from the upper class, the less plausible it is that he or she would choose to enter into consumeristic behavior in order to make status comparisons according to standards established by the upper class. These comparisons would be unlikely to reflect favorably on the individual. If the standard of social comparison is identical for everyone, it is impossible to make a flattering comparison looking down the social hierarchy without at the same time making an unflattering comparison looking up the social hierarchy. The net effect for the poorer classes would not be a comparison that anyone could be expected to seek out intentionally.

The empirical evidence that I have presented for the presence of consumerism in the upper classes calls into question the contemporary applicability of the manipulation and imaginative hedonism theories, since they associate consumerism exclusively with the middle classes. This is a particular problem for the manipulation theories, since these theories must identify some persons or groups as the manipulators who are themselves exempt from manipulation because they are aware of the deceptions they employ. This role is invariably assigned to the upper classes, along with their agents in the advertising, marketing, and mass media professions.

An Empirical Evaluation of Current Consumerism Theories

When the upper classes widely engage in consumeristic forms of life, as I have shown, it is difficult for the manipulation theorists to explain how the wealthy classes are themselves manipulated by their own manipulations.

The Interpersonal Dimension of Consumer Motives

Both the greed theories and the imaginative hedonism theories claim that persons seek subjective happiness through the pleasures they obtain through economic consumption. These theories further maintain that these pleasures are solely due to individuals' relationships to the economic goods, and not to their relationships with other persons. If these theories are correct, one would expect to find a positive correlation between rising consumption expenditures and rising subjective happiness. Figure 13 plots U.S. Department of Commerce statistics for real (inflation-adjusted) per capita personal consumption expenditures. Subjective happiness has been measured in the U.S. since 1972 by the General Social Survey conducted by the National Opinion Research Center. This survey asks the question, "Taken all together, how would you say things are these days—would you say that you are very happy, pretty happy, or not too happy?" The responses to this question are plotted in Figure 14.

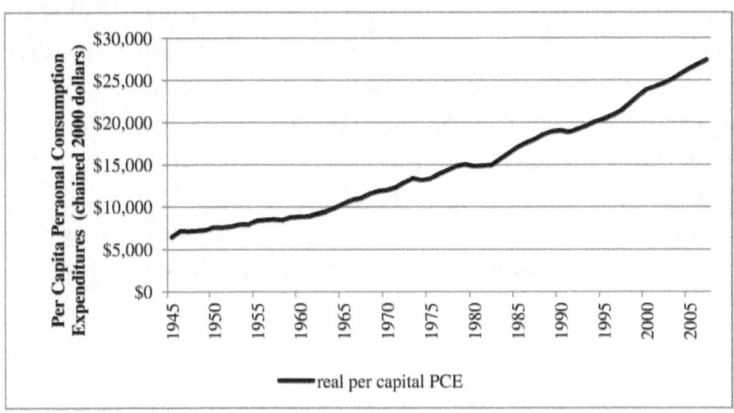

FIGURE 13: U.S. real per capita personal consumption expenditures, 1945–2007. *Source*: U.S. Department of Commerce, National Income and Product Accounts.

Shopping for Meaningful Lives

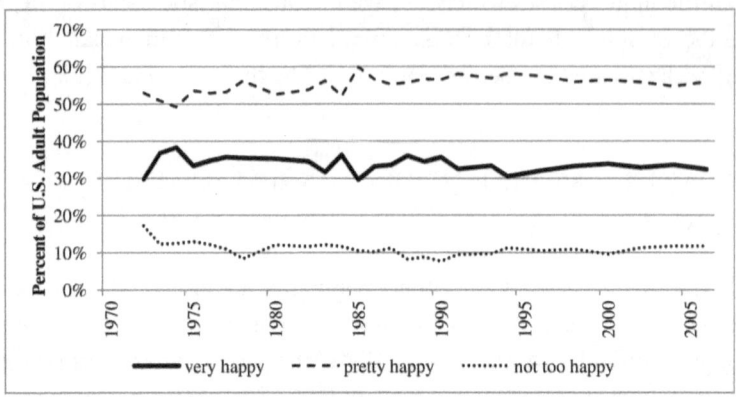

FIGURE 14: U.S. subjective happiness in the non-institutionalized English-speaking population age 18 and older, 1972–2006. *Source*: National Opinion Research Center, General Social Surveys.

The data in Figures 13 and 14 show that subjective happiness in the United States was essentially unchanged over the period 1972–2006, despite steadily rising levels of real personal consumption. Real per capita personal consumption expenditures more than doubled over this period, but U.S. consumers were not significantly happier in 2006 than in 1972. This suggests that, at least in relatively affluent societies, there is no demonstrable relation between consumption and happiness. This observation is confirmed by a simple time-series regression of the percentage of U.S. consumers who report themselves very happy against real (inflation-adjusted) per capita personal consumption expenditures. The regression shows no significant relationship between the variables.[17] Economist Richard Easterlin identifies similar results for consumers in Western Europe and Japan between the late 1950s and late 1980s.[18]

Easterlin's results have been the target of a detailed critique by Betsey Stevenson and Justin Wolfers, who claim to show that happiness is

---

17. In this regression, the t-statistic for real per capita consumption is -1.47. The same result is found in examining the relation between happiness and proportional differences in real per capita consumption. When the percentage of U.S. consumers who report themselves very happy is regressed against the natural logarithm of per capita personal consumption expenditures, the t-statistic for ln (real per capita consumption expenditures) is -1.51.

18. Easterlin, "Will Raising the Incomes of All Increase the Happiness of All?," 38–40.

positively correlated to income.[19] However, there are several reasons to question whether Stevenson and Wolfers's claim can be applied to the richest Western countries. First, Stevenson and Wolfers's strongest evidence of time-series correlations between subjective happiness and income are derived from regressions on survey data that include developing countries, newly-industrialized countries, and former Comecon nations. Developing countries would not be expected to have a large enough share of their population engaged in a consumeristic form of life for this to be reflected in aggregate national statistics. Furthermore, the rapid political and economic liberalization that many of these nations experienced during the study period could be expected to influence subjective happiness independently from rising affluence. Second, Stevenson and Wolfers cannot demonstrate that rising subjective happiness in Western Europe was caused by rising affluence because they do not control for other factors that could influence subjective happiness, such as the unemployment rate, income variance, income inequality, class mobility, security, political rights, health, education, and gender parity. Without controlling for other factors that could influence subjective happiness, the study's conclusions are significantly determined by the analysts' hypotheses. Third, Stevenson and Wolfers do not evaluate other possible relationships between income and subjective happiness. The Eurobarometer survey data that they rely on for Western European nations show that the business cycle has far greater influence on subjective happiness than the secular trend. This suggests that change in income is more relevant to subjective happiness than absolute income. Fourth, Stevenson and Wolfers concede that some nations, including the United States, show no positive correlation between subjective happiness and income. In fact, another study by Stevenson and Wolfers demonstrates that subjective happiness among U.S. women has fallen significantly during the period 1972–2006, when U.S. women's income was rising rapidly due to increased labor force participation.[20]

The data that show no significant time-series correlation between consumption and subjective happiness pose a serious problem for the hedonistic theories of consumerism. The greed and imaginative hedonism theories could only be valid if persons consume for the sake of happiness despite their repeated experience over a lifetime that, on average, consumption does not make them any happier. It remains possible that consumers

19. Stevenson and Wolfers, "Reassessing the Easterlin Paradox."
20. Stevenson and Wolfers, "Paradox of Declining Female Happiness."

are driven by a zero-sum competition to gain happiness at others' expense,[21] but this would violate the hedonistic theories' claim of consumer autonomy. A simpler and more plausible explanation is suggested by Easterlin: namely, that "the material norms on which judgments of well-being are based increase in the same proportion as the actual income of the society."[22] This does not settle the question of the origin and function of these consumption norms, but it does imply that they do not arise autonomously. If consumption norms *could* be generated autonomously, each individual could simply choose to be happy by choosing a norm at or below his or her present standard of living. Therefore, the lack of any proven time-series correlation between consumption and subjective happiness in developed Western nations suggests that consumerism cannot be understood as a function of an individual's relation to economic goods without reference to other persons.

Standard economic theory assumes that each individual's utility function arises independently from producers and other consumers.[23] The strongest challenge to this assumption has come from economists like Fred Hirsch and Robert Frank who argue that at least some economic goods—*positional goods*—have social utilities as well as direct material utilities. According to Hirsch, the consumer's individual utility is derived from a *material economy* of goods and services that yield increased satisfaction to the consumer, while the consumer's social utility is tied to a *positional economy* that "relates to all aspects of goods, services, work positions, and other social relationships that are either (1) scarce in some absolute or socially imposed sense or (2) subject to congestion or crowding through more extensive use."[24] Frank defines positional goods in relation to the first of Hirsch's conditions, scarcity. "'Positional goods' . . . [are] goods that are sought after less because of any absolute property they possess than because they compare favorably with others in their own class. . . . Positional goods are, by their very nature, things in fixed supply."[25] However positional goods may be scarce in a social rather than a physical sense. "Social scar-

---

21. Income and happiness are only unrelated over time. At a given point in time, higher income persons are happier than lower income persons. See Easterlin, "Income and Happiness: Toward a Unified Theory," 467–69.

22. Easterlin, "Will Raising the Incomes of All Increase the Happiness of All?," 44.

23. G. Becker, *Accounting for Tastes*, 3–4.

24. Hirsch, *Social Limits to Growth*, 27.

25. Frank, *Choosing the Right Pond*, 7.

city," according to Hirsch, "expresses the idea that the good things of life are restricted not only by physical limitations of producing more of them but also by absorptive limits on their use. Where the social environment has a restricted capacity for extending use without quality deterioration, it imposes social limits to consumption."[26] Frank describes this deterioration in quality of one's consumption attributable to others' consumption as a negative externality of consumption.[27]

Some examples of goods that are significantly positional in character are suburban houses, whose value diminishes as a suburb become less exclusive and more congested, and higher education, which becomes a less valuable certification of relative intelligence, motivation, and discipline as the number of certified persons increases. Status itself is a pure positional good. The consumerism theories of Warren and Tyagi and of Veblen both assume competition for positional goods. However, the status signaling and parental concern theories do not exhaust the possibilities for a theory of consumerism's motivation that explains positional competition. Among the possible motives of positional competition, Adriaan Soetevent identifies jealousy, the desire for approval, the desire for prestige, peer pressure, social norms, group loyalty, herd behavior, and signaling. Amartya Sen adds that positional goods may be necessary for social inclusion.[28]

Positional competition, according to Hirsch, is "competition that is fundamentally for a higher place within some explicit or implicit hierarchy and that thereby yields gains for some only by dint of losses for others. Positional competition, in the language of game theory, is a zero-sum game: what winners win, losers lose."[29] The scope of the market for this zero-sum game of positional competition is determined by consumers' *reference groups*. A reference group, Frank observes, is any group "with whom one might reasonably be viewed as competing for resources."[30] Reference groups influence an individual's aspirations and perceptions of relative standing. Reference groups are disproportionately likely to be composed of persons with whom one has direct contact, such as neighbors or coworkers,

---

26. Hirsch, *Social Limits to Growth*, 3.

27. Frank, "Frames of Reference," 82.

28. Hirsch, *Social Limits to Growth*, 38, 47–48; Soetevent, "Identification of Social Interactions," 196–97; Sen, "Poor, Relatively Speaking," 161–62.

29. Hirsch, *Social Limits to Growth*, 52.

30. Frank, *Choosing the Right Pond*, 96.

but they may also be composed of distant persons with whom one shares some salient characteristics, such as age, education level, or profession.[31]

The composition of an individual's reference groups significantly affects the quantity of resources that she or he devotes to positional competition. For example, in Veblen's status signaling theory, an individual's reference groups consist of members of his or her socioeconomic class as well as the next highest class. If this were valid, the increase in income inequality in the United States from 1982 to 2007 would explain increased positional competition. As I will elaborate in Chapter 5 in my proposed theory of the motivation of consumerism, individuals generally seek reference groups of their peers in order to maximize the likelihood of receiving recognition and validation. However, these self-selected reference groups are never independent of broader cultural influences that associate meanings with positional goods and stimulate positional competition.

Positional goods are characterized by a high income elasticity of demand. Consumer demand for them rises faster than for nonpositional goods as income rises. At the same time, their price elasticity of supply—the increase in the amount of equivalent quality that is produced as prices rise—is zero. In other words, the market only produces inferior substitutes for those who fail to obtain positional goods. The result is intensified competition for positional goods as consumers become more affluent and the demand for positional goods exceeds the supply. The market for positional goods can only match supply to demand by destroying excess demand. Demand for positional goods can be destroyed through rising prices or market barriers that block would-be consumers' access to them. Therefore, the first effect of positional competition is rising prices for positional goods relative to the prices of nonpositional goods. Second, because consumers face a tradeoff between increasingly costly positional goods and relatively less costly nonpositional goods they tend to over-consume positional goods and under-consume nonpositional goods from the perspective of their collective preferences. This offers a potential explanation for why persons in an affluent culture may sacrifice nonpositional goods like leisure, savings, safety, and insurance for the sake of ever-greater consumption of goods that are significantly positional, like cars, housing, and higher education. Third, because positional competition is zero sum by definition, consumption of positional goods yields no net gain in utility for consumers as a group. Therefore, the higher the share of rising income devoted to positional

---

31. Ibid., 8, 30.

competition, the less the general effect of rising affluence on consumers' utility or happiness.[32]

One piece of empirical evidence that positional concerns affect consumers' relative consumption of positional and nonpositional goods, Frank argues, is that union workers purchase a significantly larger share of nonpositional goods like insurance and pension benefits than nonunion workers, who lack a collective mechanism to improve their overall utility by enforcing limits on positional competition amongst themselves.[33] A second important piece of empirical evidence is a study by Erzo Luttmer that demonstrates the existence of negative positional externalities. Luttmer matched data on subjective happiness to earnings by year and census locality. He found that "higher ... [community] earnings are associated with lower levels of happiness, controlling for a host of individual characteristics including [one's own] income. This effect is large, robust to changes in specification and highly statistically significant. An increase in neighbors' earnings and a similarly sized decrease in own income each lead to a reduction in happiness of about the same order of magnitude."[34] In other words, persons are equally happy whether their own incomes rise or the incomes of other persons in their community fall by an equivalent amount. Further empirical evidence that points to the existence of positional concerns comes from survey studies. In Sweden, Fredrik Carlsson and colleagues polled a random sample of adults aged 18–66 in May 2002 and found that car value and car safety are both significantly positional. That is, survey respondents valued their car's price and safety features relative to the price and safety features of cars possessed by others in Sweden, and not only in terms of their intrinsic value.[35]

Several empirical studies have investigated *which* consumers have positional concerns. Luttmer's study of U.S. consumers found that positional concerns were held by both sexes, persons of all age groups, persons of all education levels, both homeowners and renters, and both parents and

---

32. Hirsch, *Social Limits to Growth*, 28–29, 53; Frank, *Choosing the Right Pond*, 50, 130–33.

33. Frank, "Demand for Nonpositional Goods," 112.

34. Luttmer, "Neighbors as Negatives," 3–4. Luttmer does not use the term "neighbor" in the ordinary sense of a person with whom one interacts directly because of geographical proximity. Rather, the reference group that Luttmer finds capable of imposing a negative externality on individual happiness is a Census Bureau Public Use Microdata Area, a community or region of over 100,000 persons.

35. Carlsson et al., "Do You Enjoy Having More Than Others?," 587–96.

persons without children. However, Luttmer did find that positional concerns were more common for married persons than unmarried persons, perhaps because of their greater rootedness in their communities. A survey study by Francisco Alpizar and colleagues explored positional concerns by examining the fraction of respondents' utility gain from the last dollar spent that could be attributed to increased relative consumption. The degree of positionality in the consumption of cars, housing, insurance, and vacations was bipolar. The respondents either had a very high or a very low degree of positional concerns in each of these categories. This bipolar distribution suggests two distinct forms of life, one that engages in positional competition and one that does not. However, the fact that this result appeared in a survey study may also mean that these results point to two distinct moral judgments regarding positional competition rather than actual differences in behavior.[36]

As evidence for reference groups, Luttmer cites the phenomenon in which persons sort themselves geographically by income. Such sorting reduces opportunities for unfavorable comparisons if one's neighbors serve as a reference group. Luttmer also found that persons who socialize frequently with neighbors rank more highly in positional concerns than persons who socialize more frequently with family members, coworkers, or friends outside their neighborhood. This result makes sense if neighbors serve as a reference group for those who interact with them more frequently. In comparison to the evidence for neighbors as reference groups, the evidence for co-workers as reference groups is weaker. Amos Tversky and Dale Griffen conducted a survey of U.S. undergraduate students in which respondents were asked to choose between a workplace where they would be a higher paid but lower ranking employee and a workplace where they would be lower paid but higher ranking. Eighty-four percent of respondents preferred the job with the higher salary and lower position, but 62 percent believed that they would have higher satisfaction in the job with lower salary and higher rank. This suggests that the absolute utility of income and the positional utility of comparisons to reference groups outside the workplace were more important to the respondents than the positional utility of comparisons to coworkers.[37]

36. Luttmer, "Neighbors as Negatives," 25–26; Alpizar et al., "Absolute versus Relative Income and Consumption," 412–14.

37. Luttmer, "Neighbors as Negatives," 2, 27–28; Tversky and Griffen, "Judgments of Well-Being," 313. Since Luttmer identifies "persons who socialize with neighbors" by a survey response, he is using "neighbor" in the ordinary sense that people assign this

An Empirical Evaluation of Current Consumerism Theories

The empirical evidence suggests that more goods are at least partly positional than might be expected on the basis of Veblen's description of conspicuous consumption. Veblen reasoned that consumption must be visible to others in order to put one's pecuniary prowess into evidence. As expected, a survey study of U.S. university students, faculty and staff by Sara Solnick and David Hemenway found that respondents expressed positional concerns with respect to education level, since education level is clearly visible in an academic context. Also as expected, the study by Carlsson and colleagues found that car value is both visible and positional, and leisure, which is less visible, could not be shown to be positional. However they also found that car safety was significantly positional, even though it is not clearly visible. Similarly, the study by Alpizar and colleagues found that less visible goods like insurance and vacations were positional, in addition to visible goods like cars and housing. However, it should be noted that these results may be attributable to the methodological difficulty of representing actual life choices with survey responses. Alpizar and colleagues acknowledge that *all* goods may become visible in the context of a survey question that inquires how one's goods relate to others' goods. In effect, the survey discloses the values of others' goods which would ordinarily be concealed.[38] Therefore, no definitive conclusion is possible with respect to how well the consumerism theories identify goods subject to positional competition.

The empirical evidence for the existence of positional competition for consumer goods strongly contradicts the greed and imaginative hedonism theories, which claim that consumer desires arise autonomously. This evidence also contradicts Galbraith's manipulation theory, since Galbraith assigns emulation a relatively minor role compared to marketers' efforts to manufacture consumer wants. However, it is potentially consistent with Baudrillard's manipulation theory, since Baudrillard sees positional competition as the product of producers' manipulations. The status signaling theories and the parental concern theory are consistent with the existence of positional competition, but this does not mean that these theories are fully validated by the empirical evidence. In particular, Luttmer's findings that positional concerns were held by renters as well as homeowners and by persons without children as well as persons with children contradict

---

term, i.e., a person with whom one interacts directly because of geographical proximity.

38. Solnick and Hemenway, "Is More Always Better?" 378–79; Carlsson et al., "Do You Enjoy Having More Than Others?" 595–96; Alpizar et al., "Absolute versus Relative Income and Consumption," 412–15.

Warren and Tyagi's parental concern theory. Their theory attributes positional competition to concern for children's well-being and locates positional competition primarily in the market for owner-occupied homes. This leaves Veblen and the other status signaling theorists in the strongest position with respect to the evidence for positional competition, although it may be that these theorists fail to explain adequately which goods are the objects of positional competition.

The Influence of Unconscious Motives, Advertising, and Marketing

It is difficult to conceive of the possibility of an unconscious decision because, to the extent that unconscious decision processes exist, they cannot be the object of memory or reflection. Contemporary psychological research that addresses the longstanding question of whether human behavior is triggered unconsciously by the environment or determined by the conscious individual will has reached a new consensus. As John Bargh and Tanya Chartrand observe, "contemporary psychology . . . has moved away from doctrinaire either-or positions . . . to an acknowledgment that they are determined jointly by processes set into motion directly by one's environment and by processes instigated by acts of conscious choice and will. . . . The mainstream of psychology accepts both the fact of conscious or willed causation of mental and behavioral processes and the fact of automatic or environmentally triggered processes."[39] Chartrand offers an important clarification to the concept of an unconscious decision. To say that some human behavior is automatically triggered by unconscious processes does not mean that either the environmental events that trigger the action or the action taken are unknown to the individual. Rather, it is precisely the decision process that links the environmental trigger to the action that is unavailable to the individual's conscious reflection. Chartrand adds that it is precisely this type of decision process that is typically found in consumer behavior.[40] A consumer's motivation is unknown to her or him to the degree that it drives unconscious environmentally-triggered behaviors rather than reflective decisions.

---

39. Bargh and Chartrand, "Unbearable Automaticity of Being," 463.
40. Chartrand, "Conscious Awareness in Consumer Behavior," 203–4.

An Empirical Evaluation of Current Consumerism Theories

The psychological models of human agency used to describe the current consensus are known as dual process or two-system models. Roy Baumeister and colleagues observe that the two decision processes roughly correspond to what are known as intuition and reason.[41] They are defined more precisely by Keith Stanovich and Richard West. Stanovich and West assign the two decision processes the names System 1 and System 2 to remove prior connotations. They define System 1 processes as "automatic, largely unconscious, and relatively undemanding of computational capacity," while System 2 processes are characterized by "controlled processing" and "analytic intelligence." System 1 contextualizes, personalizes and socializes problems, infers intentions, and seeks conversational relevance. System 2 decontextualizes and depersonalizes problems, frames them in terms of underlying principles and rules, and is not preoccupied with social context, intentions, or conversational relevance.[42]

Daniel Kahneman observes that System 1 processes occupy a midpoint between perception and reason. Like perception, System 1 processes operate spontaneously, unreflectively, and effortlessly. They are often governed by emotion and habit. Like System 2, System 1 processes do not just respond to current stimuli but may also respond to language and concepts. However, unlike System 2, System 1 processes cannot form judgments—i.e., they cannot entertain doubt as to the correct choice, weigh alternative courses of action, or exercise impulse control. Judgments are always intentional and explicit, and therefore fall under System 2. Baumeister and colleagues emphasize the distinction between effortless System 1 processes and effortful System 2 reasoning, judgment, and self-control. The psychological capacity for System 2 is finite, and using this finite resource may temporarily deplete it. Depletion may result from cognitive load, multitasking, or making frequent, aversive, or complex choices. The consequences of ego-depletion is less intelligent, less compromising, more emotional, and more impulsive decision making—i.e., decision making dominated by System 1.[43]

Psychological experimentation has identified three types of System 1 decision processes in consumer choices. The first System 1 process is called the perception-behavior link. One way in which the perception-behavior

---

41. Baumeister, et al., "Free Will in Consumer Behavior," 7.

42. Stanovich and West, "Individual Differences in Reasoning," 658–59.

43. Kahneman, "Judgment and Choice," 698–99; Baumeister et al., "Free Will in Consumer Behavior," 4, 10–11.

link works is to drive decisions through the context that frames the perceived choice. In one experiment, Adrian North and colleagues played either French or German music in a wine store. When French music was played, customers were more likely to buy French wine, and when German music was played customers were more likely to buy German wine. Almost none of the customers reported being influenced by the music in their choice of wine. In another example of the perception-behavior link, Dan Ariely found that a decoy—a choice clearly inferior to one alternative—biased customers to choose the option similar to the decoy. Given the options of an Internet-only magazine subscription for $59, a print-only subscription for $125 (the decoy), and a print and Internet subscription for $125, respondents are more likely to choose the print and Internet option than respondents in a control group who were not offered the decoy. Habituation is a second form of the perception-behavior link. Ariely uses the example of buying coffee at a particular shop. Once this decision has been made and reinforced by repetition, the reasons for the decision are bypassed when the situation is encountered again, and the consumer will choose the same shop again and again without thinking about why he or she is doing so or whether he or she should do so.[44]

A third form of the perception-behavior link is unconscious mimicry. In an experiment by Lucy Johnston, participants were asked to judge the taste of an ice cream sample after an undisclosed confederate of the experimenter had taken either a large or small sample of ice cream. Participants consumed significantly more ice cream in the presence of the confederate who took a large sample than in the presence of the confederate who took a small sample, without knowing that their behavior had been influenced by the confederate. Stereotyping is a fourth form of the perception-behavior link. Both conduct and social attitudes are affected by stereotypes. In an experiment designed by Bargh and Chartrand, participants primed with words associated with a stereotype of the elderly subsequently walked more slowly and were more forgetful. In a separate study by Kerry Kawakami and colleagues, participants primed with the elderly stereotype expressed greater concern about sex on TV and greater support for health care spending than control participants.[45]

 44. North et al., "Music Affects Product Choice," 132; Ariely, *Predictably Irrational*, 1–9, 37–38.
 45. Johnston, "Behavioral Mimicry and Stigmatization," 24–28; Bargh and Chartrand, "Unbearable Automaticity of Being," 466; Kawakami et al., "Effects of Social Category Priming," 316–18.

An Empirical Evaluation of Current Consumerism Theories

A second type of System 1 decision process is known as unconscious goal-oriented activity. In this process, environmental stimuli serve to set goals in motion to produce behavior. Bargh and Chartrand observe that "goals do not require an act of will to operate and guide information processing and behavior. They can be activated instead by external, environmental information and events. Once they are put into motion they operate just as if they had been consciously intended, even to the point of producing changes in mood and in self-efficacy beliefs depending on one's degree of success or failure at reaching the goal."[46] An experiment by Chartrand demonstrated a feedback effect between the achievement of unconscious goals and self-efficacy beliefs. Participants primed for achievement who had succeeded at an easy verbal task subsequently performed better on a verbal section of the Graduate Record Examination (GRE) than participants primed for achievement who had failed at a difficult verbal task. For participants who had not been primed, there was no difference in GRE performance between the groups given the easy or difficult verbal task. The primed participants did not report having a goal on the verbal task. In a second experiment, Chartrand demonstrated that unconscious goals, like conscious goals, are characterized by satiation when met and increased intensity when unmet. Participants were primed with words associated with a value goal or an image goal and then were presented with a purchase decision between a lower priced "value product" and a higher priced "image product." The choice of the image product was significantly higher for the image-primed participants than for the value-primed participants. None of the participants reported that the word task had affected their consumption choice. When this study was repeated with a delay between the priming task and the consumption decision, the difference between the image- and value-primed customers was even greater, indicating that an unsatiated goal increases in effect over time.[47]

A third type of System 1 decision process is unconscious affective or moral evaluation. According to Bargh and Chartrand, "evaluations of objects or events come to be components of their perceptual representations and so become activated immediately in the course of perception of the object or event, without one consciously considering or intending to evaluate it."[48] In one experiment, Bargh and associates had participants pronounce

---

46. Bargh and Chartrand, "Unbearable Automaticity of Being," 473.
47. Ibid., 472; Chartrand, "Conscious Awareness in Consumer Behavior," 207.
48. Bargh and Chartrand, "Unbearable Automaticity of Being," 474.

the names of words with either strong or weak moral associations without being asked to make a value judgment. They found strong evidence that participants made value judgment for both strongly- and weakly-normative objects, without any conscious intent to evaluate.[49]

The strong experimental evidence for unconscious System 1 processes in consumer decision making contradicts the claim of the greed and imaginative hedonism theories that consumer decisions are driven by the conscious, autonomous pursuit of pleasure. This evidence also contradicts the parental concern theory, which holds that consumerism is driven by the conscious, rational pursuit of children's well-being. This evidence is consistent, however, with the manipulation theories, since these theories claim that persons engaged in a consumeristic form of life are not autonomous in their decision making. This evidence is also consistent with the status signaling theories since, in Veblen's argument, habit and social institutions can ensure that conventional means to achieve instinctive ends may be widely observed in society long after the original motives behind these conventions have been forgotten.

The empirical research investigating advertising's effectiveness is broad, systematic, and longstanding. This research unanimously contradicts Galbraith's claim that advertising dominates consumers to the extent that their consumption is effectively controlled by economic producers. Demetrios Vakratsas and Tim Ambler review over 250 journal articles and books and conclude that "Advertising elasticities consistently were found to be low, typically in the range 0 to 0.20."[50] Advertising elasticity is the ratio of the percentage change in sales to the percentage change in advertising quantity. Furthermore, the earlier literature may overstate the effect of advertising. Prior to the availability of scanner data, advertising effectiveness studies relied upon aggregate advertising and sales data, but the new technology permits disaggregation of individual consumers' advertising exposure and purchase behavior. Gerard Tellis and Doyle Weiss demonstrate that aggregating the advertising and sales data introduces a systematic upward bias in the estimated effects of advertising, and that the effects measured at their most disaggregated level "are not significantly different from zero."[51] Vakratsas and Ambler conclude from the empirical research literature that "product usage experience has a greater impact on

---

49. Bargh, et al., "Automatic Evaluation Effect," 113–17.
50. Vakratsas and Ambler, "How Advertising Works," 29.
51. Tellis and Weiss, "Does TV Advertising Really Affect Sales?," 8–9.

beliefs, attitude formation, and choice than advertising."[52] Tellis, in an empirical study of scanner records, identifies several factors that exert greater influence on consumer purchase decisions than advertising. "Without question, loyalty [i.e., past behavior] is the strongest determinant of purchase behavior.... The other marketing variables [price, coupons, displays, and features], especially price, are also more effective than advertising."[53] Habit—i.e., the influence of past behavior—price, and product features do not constitute consumer manipulation in the sense that Galbraith intends. Given that habit and price are the most significant factors that Tellis observes, all of the "manipulation" variables in Tellis's model have at most a minor influence that falls far short of Galbraith's claim of effective control.

Another way to examine Galbraith's manipulation hypothesis is to determine whether or not there are limits on the range of advertising quantity and expense over which they exert some influence. This is the question implicit in Galbraith's argument that producers wouldn't advertise if they didn't believe that it changes consumer behavior: if producers believe they can *control* consumer behavior, and not merely exert limited influence over a limited range of advertising expenses and sales, why do they not spend more on advertising to increase their sales above their present levels? Or, as Julian Simon and Johan Arndt express this point, "One would hardly expect the largest advertisers to stop advertising at a point of increasing returns, if such a point exists."[54] Simon and Arndt review more than 100 empirical studies of the advertising response function—the relationship between advertising quantity and sales—and conclude that these studies overwhelmingly show diminishing returns to advertising over the normal range of producers' advertising budgets.[55] In other words, the more a firm advertises its products, the less influence each additional advertisement has. These empirical results further contradict Galbraith's manipulation hypothesis since they prove that whatever influence advertising exerts falls far short of control.

---

52. Vakratsas and Ambler, "How Advertising Works," 33.
53. Tellis, "Advertising Exposure, Loyalty, and Brand Purchase," 142.
54. Simon and Arndt, "Shape of the Advertising Response Function," 20.
55. Ibid., 17, 22.

Consumerism in Housing Expenditures

If Warren and Tyagi's parental concern theory is correct, housing expenditure data for U.S. households should show continuous growth in real housing expenditures for households with minor children, but not for households that lack minor children. The U.S. Department of Labor has collected data on household expenditures by household type since 1984 in its Consumer Expenditure Surveys. Figure 15 plots real (inflation-adjusted) annual household housing expenditures for six household categories identified in the Consumer Expenditure Surveys.

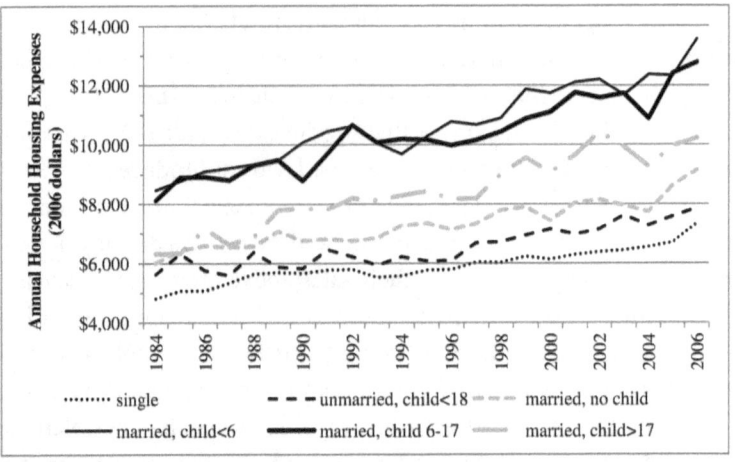

FIGURE 15: U.S. real annual household housing expenses by household type, 1984–2006. *Sources*: U.S. Department of Labor, Consumer Expenditures Survey; U.S. Department of Labor, Consumer Price Index.

Using the Consumer Expenditure Survey data shown in Figure 15, I constructed a regression model to estimate the relative change in real annual household housing expenditures as a function of year, whether the household includes a married couple, and whether the household includes minor children. The details of this regression are presented in Appendix 1. The t-statistics show that all three predictor variables in this model are statistically significant, including the variable for minor children. Therefore, the presence of minor children is one meaningful predictor of whether or not a household's real housing expenditures grew during the 1984–2006 time period. However, the sequential sum of squares statistics show that the

An Empirical Evaluation of Current Consumerism Theories

presence or absence of minor children accounts for only 21 percent of the regression model's explained variance. The other 79 percent is accounted for by the historical trend and the presence or absence of a married couple. If the presence of minor children only predicts a small share of the growth in real housing expenditures, then concern for the quality of one's children's public schools can at most account for a small share of consumers' housing spending growth.

I made a second evaluation of Warren and Tyagi's hypothesis by dividing the Consumer Expenditure Survey data into two sets based on the presence or absence of minor children and then repeating the previous regression for each set with the remaining two predictor variables. The results of these regressions are shown in Appendix 2. Holding the marriage variable constant and looking at the coefficients for the trend variable, these regressions show that from 1984 to 2006 U.S. real annual household housing expenditures rose an estimated 1.5 percent per year for households without minor children and 1.6 percent per year for households with minor children. This analysis confirms that the presence of minor children—and thus concern for the quality of children's public schools—can explain only a small fraction of the growth in U.S. consumer spending on housing during the 1984–2006 period.

In order further to test Warren and Tyagi's parental concern theory of consumerism, I evaluated U.S. households' real housing expenditure growth by income quintile. Figure 16 plots real (inflation-adjusted) household expenditures on housing by household income quintile, as reported in the U.S. Department of Labor's Consumer Expenditure Surveys.

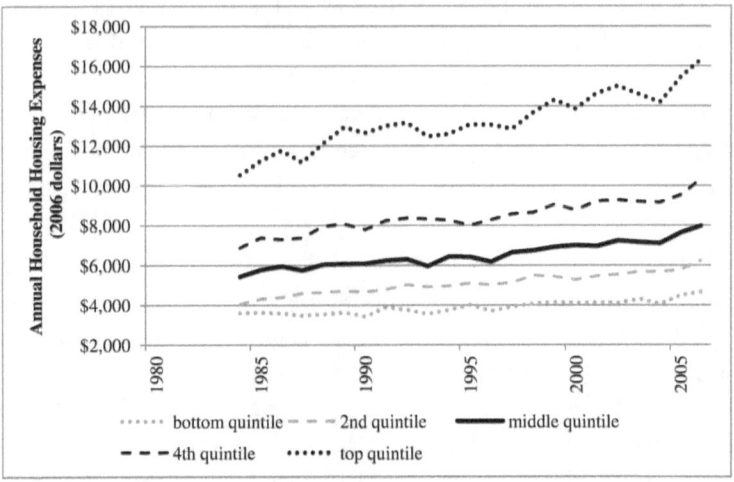

FIGURE 16: U.S. real annual household housing expenditures by household income quintile, 1984–2006. *Sources*: U.S. Department of Labor, Consumer Expenditures Survey; U.S. Department of Labor, Consumer Price Index.

Figure 16 shows that between 1984 and 2006 U.S. real household expenditures on housing grew across all income groups, not just the upper-middle income households that are the focus of Warren and Tyagi's theory. To quantify this observation, I divided the Consumer Expenditure Survey data into five sets, one for each household income quintile. For each income quintile, I performed a regression of the relative change in real household housing expenditures as a function of year. The results of these regressions are presented in Appendix 3. Comparing the regressions' trend variable coefficients shows that U.S. real (inflation-adjusted) household expenditures on housing grew an average of 1.5 percent per year for the second and fifth income quintiles, 1.4 percent per year for the third and fourth income quintiles, and 1.1 percent per year for the lowest income quintile. Housing spending growth was significant for all five income quintiles, and, except for the lowest quintile, the rate of housing spending growth was very nearly the same. This calls into question any explanation for consumption growth that only applies to upper-middle and middle class homeowners, since the pattern of housing consumption growth for the lower-middle and working classes is substantially the same.

Warren and Tyagi exclude upper class households from their theory about the pattern of unrestricted housing consumption. As I argued in chapter 3, their theory *must* do so: first, because the law of diminishing

An Empirical Evaluation of Current Consumerism Theories

marginal utility suggests that households who are already spending a great deal on education receive limited additional benefit from spending more, and second, because at some point in the process of increasing education spending it becomes cheaper to purchase high quality education directly through enrollment in private schools rather than indirectly through purchasing homes in more and more exclusive public school districts. Therefore, if the unrestricted housing consumption growth observed for lower and middle class households is duplicated among upper class households, it would call into question the proposition that public school district shopping is driving unrestricted growth in housing consumption.

The sample frame for the Federal Reserve Board's Survey of Consumer Finances is more useful for evaluating housing consumption for upper class households than the sample frame for the Department of Labor's Consumer Expenditure Survey because it intentionally oversamples high-income households. Although the Survey of Consumer Finances does not specifically collect data on housing-related expenditures, it does track outstanding mortgage debt and home equity loans secured by a household's primary residence. Since both mortgage and home equity loan debt correspond to liabilities incurred for future housing expenditures, they serve as useful proxies for evaluating trends in current housing expenditures. This can be seen by comparing the trend for real (inflation-adjusted) mortgage and home equity loan debt, by income quintile, in Figure 17 to the corresponding trends for real housing expenditures in Figure 16.

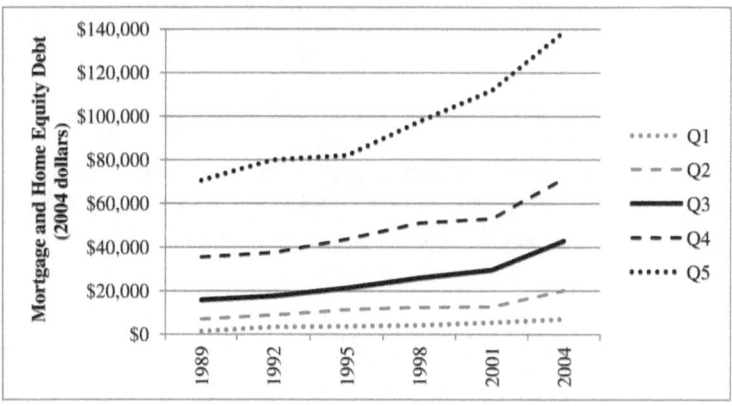

FIGURE 17: U.S. real household mortgage and home equity loan debt by income quintile, 1989–2004. *Sources*: U.S. Federal Reserve Board, Survey of Consumer Finances; U.S. Department of Labor, Consumer Price Index.

Figure 18 plots U.S. real (inflation-adjusted) household mortgage and home equity loan debt for upper-income groups. As Figure 18 shows, there is no income level above which housing consumption levels off. In fact, between 1989 and 2004 U.S. housing consumption grew faster among the highest income households than among the upper-middle class households that are the focus of Warren and Tyagi's theory. Between 1989 and 2004 the top forty percent of U.S. households by income increased their real (inflation-adjusted) mortgage and home equity debts by 7.6 percent per year, but the top five percent of households increased these debts by 8.1 percent per year and the top one percent by 9.9 percent per year. Warren and Tyagi's theory cannot explain why unrestricted growth in housing consumption is just as prevalent—or more prevalent—among upper-class households as among middle-class households. It would be highly implausible to suppose that the same trends in spending are found among all income groups, but that their causes are different for the different classes.

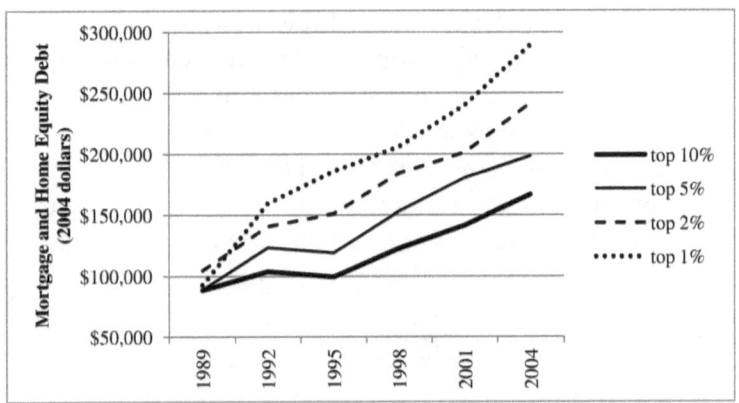

FIGURE 18: U.S. real household mortgage and home equity loan debt for upper-income households, 1989–2004. *Sources*: U.S. Federal Reserve Board, Survey of Consumer Finances; U.S. Department of Labor, Consumer Price Index.

THE FAILURE OF CURRENT THEORIES TO EXPLAIN THE BEHAVIOR OF WESTERN CONSUMERS

The greed theories of consumer motivation are poorly supported in my empirical evaluations. They are contradicted by the evidence of a historical emergence of contemporary Western consumerism in the 1970s and

1980s, by the evidence of consumerism in the lower classes, by the failure to demonstrate a time-series relationship between consumption and happiness in developed Western nations, by the evidence for positional competition, and by the evidence that much consumer behavior is driven by unconscious decision processes.

The imaginative hedonism theories suffer from all of the empirical shortcomings of the greed theories, except that they recognize that consumerism emerges in the postmodern era. In addition, the imaginative hedonism theories are also contradicted by the empirical evidence for consumerism in the upper classes.

The manipulation theories are definitively contradicted by the evidence from the marketing literature that the influence of advertising and marketing falls far short of effective control over consumers. They are also contradicted by the presence of consumerism in the upper and lower classes.

The parental concern theory of Warren and Tyagi is strongly contradicted by my analyses in this chapter. I have shown that the presence of children is only a minor factor driving housing consumption. I have also shown that housing consumption growth in upper-middle-class households has differed little from housing consumption growth in lower-middle-class, working-class, and upper-class households.

The status signaling theories are the least problematic of the theories I evaluate, but they are also partly contradicted by the empirical evidence. The status signaling theories explain positional competition, unconscious motivations, and upper class consumerism, but they are contradicted by the presence of consumerism in the lower-middle and working classes. Their failure to explain this behavior is attributable to the fact that in the status signaling theories status is the only good sought through positional competition and the only meaning signified by consumer goods. When I turn to my constructive proposal for a theory of the motivation of consumerism in chapter 5, I will draw on the empirically-validated features of the status signaling theories—including positional competition and unconscious motivation—but I will reject these theories' claim that the scope of positional competition and the meanings assigned to consumer goods are universal.

5

The Religious Motive of Consumerism and How It May Be Redirected

IN THIS CHAPTER I have two aims. First, I will show that that consumerism's motivation may best be understood as religious. By religious, I mean that consumerism answers a question posed by the nature of human existence. Consumerism offers one possible answer to the existential question of the meaning of an individual life. A consumeristic culture institutionalizes a practical form of life through which an individual can make a claim that his or her life is meaningful, and it establishes social norms through which he or she may expect others to validate this claim to individual significance. The correlation between consumerism and the existential question of meaning can be shown independently from any particular theological standpoint. To demonstrate this correlation, I will describe how an existential meaning strategy functions in Paul Tillich's existential philosophy and then apply this description to consumerism using evidence from psychology, the social sciences, and marketing research. I will then evaluate the empirical validity of the claim that consumerism is religiously motivated using the same socioeconomic findings that I identified in chapter 4 to test the competing consumerism theories.

Since consumerism's motivation is existential and religious, it is a matter of ultimate concern, in Tillich's expression.[1] It supersedes all other claims upon an individual's decision-making. No one can escape the demands of their ultimate concern unless it fails to fulfill its purpose of grounding a sense of personal meaning. If it fails, one must replace it with a different solution to the existential problem of meaning or suffer the despair of

---

1. See Tillich, "Aspects of a Religious Analysis of Culture," 40.

meaninglessness. Therefore my second aim in this chapter is to identify the solution to the existential problem of meaning that should replace consumerism. I will argue that Christian faith, understood as existential trust in the promise of the Christian message, offers an answer to the problem of individual meaning that is existentially more secure and morally less troubling than consumerism. In chapter 1, I detailed the moral and religious failings of consumerism. This is sufficient to demonstrate that consumerism is a form of life that should be replaced. My conclusion that existential Christian faith answers these problems will not be accepted by everyone, however, but only by those who already acknowledge the substance of the Christian message as a matter of ultimate concern. To demonstrate the correlation between the existential question of meaning and the answer of existential Christian faith is a task that Tillich has already undertaken in his *Systematic Theology*. In my argument, I will critically appropriate Tillich's correlation, evaluating it according to criteria from my own theological standpoint within the Pauline-Augustinian-Lutheran tradition in Christian theology.

Existential Strategies to Ground Individual Meaning

How does a consumeristic form of life secure an individual against the existential threat of meaninglessness? To begin to answer this question, I draw on Tillich's philosophy to describe why persons need an existential meaning strategy, what is meant by meaningful individual life, how meaningful individual life can be validated, and what barriers exist to fully understanding or changing one's existential meaning strategy.

To have assurance of the meaningfulness of one's individual life is an existential necessity. Tillich calls this assurance "spiritual self-affirmation." He describes it in this way: "Spiritual self-affirmation occurs in every moment in which man lives creatively in the various spheres of meaning. . . . Everyone who lives creatively in meanings affirms himself as a participant in these meanings. He affirms himself as receiving and transforming reality creatively. He loves himself as participating in the spiritual life and as loving its contents. He loves them because they are his own fulfillment and because they are actualized through him."[2] The existential need for

2. Tillich, *Courage to Be*, 46.

spiritual self-affirmation is continuous. Søren Kierkegaard observes that unless a person at every moment destroys the possibility of being able to despair he will be in despair. Tillich argues that the individual who cannot maintain existential courage in the face of doubt and anxiety about meaninglessness faces the disintegration of his or her existence, actions, and personal responsibility. According to Tillich, the threat of meaninglessness to spiritual self-affirmation is the dominant anxiety of the modern age. This implies that, in this era, the existential need for meaningful existence is the most important determinant of human motivation. The need for a secure ground of meaning cannot be met by the self, Tillich contends, because of human finitude and estrangement. In order for an individual to be assured of meaningful individual life and resist the threat of meaninglessness to spiritual self-affirmation, the individual's claim to meaningful life must be validated by something or someone outside the self. Even when the individual subjectively asserts his or her self as meaningful, this claim must be validated externally in order for the self to maintain assurance and courage in the face of the threat of meaninglessness.[3]

What does it mean for one's self to have meaning? By "self," I am referring to the self as experienced by the particular individual, that is, the particular individual's subjective interior experience of reflexivity. Tillich recognizes the practical unity between the human experience of self-awareness, which he calls the "psychological self," and the human experience of freedom regulated by morality, the "personal" or "spiritual" self.[4] Both are made possible by the reflexive structure of human consciousness. The experience of reflexivity is the individual's capacity to objectify his or her past, present, and future experience and identity. Reflexivity gives the individual the capacity to evaluate and choose among potential directions of the will in a manner that establishes and preserves a relative stability of character, values, and purposes. It is precisely the subjectivity with which the individual experiences her or his own reflexivity that gives it primary value in her or his self-evaluation.

The individual can hold his or her unique subjectively-experienced self to be meaningful when he or she has primary value that is both irreplaceable and irreducible. These conditions are met when the individual is related to a meaningful system or whole in an essential or necessary manner. Tillich calls the relationship of an individual self to a meaningful

3. Kierkegaard, *Sickness Unto Death*, 15–18; Tillich, *Courage to Be*, 48–49, 61, 174.
4. Tillich, *Systematic Theology*, vol. 3, 36–39.

The Religious Motive of Consumerism and How It May Be Redirected

whole "intentionality." He defines intentionality as "living in tension with (and toward) something objectively valid."[5] The finite self needs an essential or necessary relation to a system as a whole because of human finitude within the ontological category of causality. Tillich describes this finitude as the inability of any finite creativity to depend on itself without a causal nexus.[6] Tillich's understanding is affirmed independently by semioticians Charles Ogden and Ivor Richards, who provide a more general definition of meaning, understood as significance. "When Meaning is equated with 'Significance'... the meaning of anything is said to have been grasped when it has been understood as related to other things or as having its place in some system as a whole."[7] Thus every successful strategy to assure oneself of the meaningfulness of one's life requires a whole system of meaning and a secure relationship between the self and the whole.

The structure of reality in Tillich's ontology suggests three ways in which the meaningfulness of an individual self can be validated. These three approaches to validation correspond to Tillich's three pairs of ontological elements in the self-world structure of being: individuation and participation, dynamics and form, and freedom and destiny.[8] In the polarity of individuation and participation, the self can be validated in relation to the whole of society. The unique reflexive self corresponds to individuation and the self's relationship to society corresponds to the element of participation. In this relationship, the society functions as a meaningful whole, and the individual's relationship to society is validated as essential or necessary when his or her asserted self-valuation is recognized by other persons in society. In socially-validated meaning systems, the individual's motivation is driven by the need to secure other persons' recognition of his or her asserted self-valuation.

In the polarity of dynamics and form, the self can be validated in relation to human history. The individual's potentiality and creative vitality correspond to the element of dynamics and the creations of the individual spirit that have lasting significance in the history of human culture correspond to the element of form. In this type of validation, human history functions as the meaningful whole, and the individual's relationship to history is validated as essential or necessary when future generations recognize

---

5. Tillich, *Systematic Theology*, vol. 1, 180.
6. Ibid., 196.
7. Ogden and Richards, *Meaning of Meaning*, 196.
8. See Tillich, *Systematic Theology*, vol. 1, 164–65, 174–86.

the significance of her or his cultural legacy. In historically-validated meaning systems, the individual's motivation is driven by the imperative to create cultural artifacts that she or he believes will procure future generations' validation of her or his significance. This type of validation is retrospective. The individual's assurance of her or his meaningfulness is based on trust in a future validation.

In the polarity of freedom and destiny, the self can be validated in relation to a metaphysical whole. The reflexive capacities of the individual human spirit for deliberation, decision, and responsibility correspond to freedom, and the ground of meaning toward which the self conditions his or her free acts corresponds to destiny. In this type of validation, the meaningful whole is the whole of reality, and the individual is essentially related to the whole of reality when the nature of God or the universe ensures an essential relationship. This type of validation also rests on trust. The individual trusts in God or the universe, or in his or her understanding of them. In metaphysically-grounded meaning systems, the individual's motivation depends upon how he or she understands the relationship between his or her agency and the whole of reality.

The key characteristic of the social, historical, and metaphysical "wholes" that gives all three types of relationship the potential to ground individual significance is their absolute or relative permanence in comparison with finite individual human life. Even if individual biological life must end, a person may have assurance that his or her life has meaning if it is semiotically linked in an essential, non-arbitrary manner to that which endures. The meanings signified by one's life can be immortal even if one's biological life cannot. If the sign of one's unique individual self and its associated meanings can be essentially or necessarily linked to an enduring system of meaning, it ensures that the sign and its meanings will transcend one's biological mortality.

Each of the three types of existential meaning strategy is potentially fragile. Socially-validated meaning systems are secured only by social affirmation, which may be ephemeral. Historically- and metaphysically-validated meaning systems rest on trust, but that trust is necessarily accompanied by doubt that arises from the lack of ultimate certainty with respect to the expected validation of one's individual significance. Yet every person desires absolute certainty in her or his meaning strategy because one's existential ground of meaning is a matter of ultimate concern. Tillich observes that an existential commitment is always a risk. The individual cannot escape doubt because doubt "is aware of the element of insecurity in every existential truth."[9] Every individual responds to this risk by attempting to impose certitude on his or her meaning system, even at the cost of significant harm to self and others. "Man tries to escape despair," Tillich observes, by making "absolute a finite security or a finite certainty. The threat of a breakdown leads to the establishment of defenses, some of which are brutal, some fanatical, some dishonest, and all insufficient and destructive; for there is no security and certainty within finitude. The destructive force may be directed against those who represent the threat to false security and certainty, especially against those who compete or contradict."[10] Full consciousness of one's meaning strategy poses the risk of heightening existential anxiety, since it draws attention to the fragility of the meaning strategy that stands alone between the individual and existential anxiety and despair. This threat is particularly acute for socially-validated meaning strategies because general social affirmation makes it easier to maintain the assurance of one's own significance without reflecting on the strategy upon which one's assurance is based. By contrast, the individual whose meaning strategy is not socially validated is already compelled to engage in introspection to maintain assurance of the meaningfulness of her or his life, despite general social disapprobation.

An individual cannot fully desire to be aware of the strategy upon which his or her assurance of meaningful life is based. Nor can the individual desire to change meaning strategies so long as his or her meaning strategy remains viable. The price that one must pay to acknowledge the inadequacy of one's current meaning strategy and to choose another is existential despair. That is a price one cannot choose to pay except by necessity. Tillich affirms Kierkegaard's description of existential despair in *The Sickness Unto Death*. In existential despair, Tillich observes, the individual experiences meaninglessness, responsibility for his or her meaninglessness, and hopelessness to escape it.[11] Kierkegaard explains that the individual "must go through the despair of the self to the self."[12] In other words, it is existential despair over the failure of a culturally-received strategy to secure meaningful life that breaks apart the personality organized around the culturally-received meaning strategy and frees one to develop a new

---

9. Tillich, *Dynamics of Faith*, 20.
10. Tillich, *Systematic Theology*, vol. 2, 73.
11. Ibid., 75.
12. Kierkegaard, *Sickness Unto Death*, 65.

personality, organized around a freely-chosen and more secure ground of meaning.

The Semiotic Culture of Consumerism

Every existential strategy can be understood in terms of Tillich's basic self-world ontological structure. To interpret consumerism as an existential strategy is to recognize that there exists a dialectical relationship between the consumeristic individual and the consumeristic culture that he or she inhabits, a relationship in which each implies and conditions the other. Since human beings are only potentially and teleologically individualized selves at birth, while the culture into which they are thrown is already a partly realized community,[13] the influence of culture on self precedes the influence of self on culture. Therefore, the institutions and processes that inculcate the prevailing signs, meanings, values, worldviews, and existential forms of life in Western consumer cultures provide the context through which consumerism may develop in particular individuals. Accordingly, I will describe the culture of consumerism before I demonstrate how Tillich's description of an existential strategy may be applied to consumerism as it is expressed in individual selves.

Every person who comes to be an individual in a given culture learns the culture's dominant system of signs and meanings through which he or she perceives his or her social reality and, reflexively, his or her self. It is characteristic of modern thought to recognize, as Tillich does, that human beings have no direct access to reality apart from the self, but only world interpretations that are mediated by language and cultural symbols. According to Tillich, every self transcends his or her environment "by grasping and shaping it according to universal norms and ideas [into a coherent system of meanings, a world].... Language, as the power of universals, is the basic expression of man's transcending his environment, of having a world."[14] This process of interpretation is never simply one's own, because one's symbols, language, and concepts are not one's own. As Ogden and Richards point out, every interpretation is refracted through a "common inherited scheme of conception which ... being inherent in the very lan-

---

13. Tillich calls the full actualization of human society "communion," a community in which one completely centered and individual self participates in another completely centered and individual self. Tillich, *Systematic Theology*, vol. 1, 176.

14. Tillich, *Systematic Theology*, vol. 1, 170.

guage we must use to express the simplest meaning . . . is adopted and assimilated before we can so much as begin to think for ourselves at all."[15] Anthropologist Grant McCracken observes that even those persons and groups who seek to dissent from a culture's values and worldview must express their critique through the culture's set of shared signs and meanings in order to render their critique comprehensible to others. In so doing, they participate in and reinforce the values and worldview encoded in the semiotic system that they seek to undermine.[16]

Psychologists Sheldon Solomon, Jeff Greenberg, and Thomas Pyszczynski observe that a cultural worldview is sustained by general social consensus. "When everyone around us believes the same thing, we can be confident of the veracity of our beliefs."[17] Thus there is an incentive for parents, teachers, and others members of a culture who contribute to individual formation to reproduce the same worldviews that they themselves hold. Social psychologist Ernest Becker expresses a comparable insight regarding a culture's predominant existential meaning strategy. He contends that culture reflects "the particular style that a society adopts to deny despair," that is, to deny the threat of personal meaninglessness. Stated positively, the "crucial function of culture is to make *continued* self-esteem possible. Its task, in other words, is to provide the individual with the conviction that he is *an object of primary value in a world of meaningful action*."[18] Becker's observations correspond to Tillich's insight that the substantive meaning of culture is religion.[19] Given that culture provides the forms through which the existential meaning strategy of consumerism comes to be expressed, what are the features of Western cultures that help to form and sustain a consumeristic form of life in the members of these cultures?

Two characteristics of contemporary affluent Western cultures that have significance for the enculturation of consumerism are the dominant influences of mass media communication and commercial speech, in comparison with cultures and epochs that are, or were, still significantly influenced by traditional cultural forms. Psychologist Tim Kasser and colleagues suggest that mass media advertising performs a mythic function in

---

15. Ogden and Richards, *Meaning of Meaning*, 25–26, quoting Cornford, *From Religion to Philosophy*, 45.

16. McCracken, *Culture and Consumption*, 133–34.

17. Solomon, Greenberg, and Pyszczynski, "Lethal Consumption," 132.

18. E. Becker, *Birth and Death of Meaning*, 79, 148.

19. Tillich, "Aspects of a Religious Analysis of Culture," 42.

the contemporary United States. Marketing researcher Russell Belk argues that mass media advertising has replaced folklore in Western cultures as the form through which meanings are sustained and reproduced. One reason for the dominance of mass media advertising and marketing is the scale of commercial broadcasting and the corresponding increase in the time that persons spend watching or listening to commercial broadcasts. Advertising researchers William Leiss, Stephen Kline, and Sut Jhally contend that the scale and complexity of the meaning system that links commercial products to individuals' self-realization distinguish contemporary Western cultures no less than the scale and number of consumer products available in these cultures.[20]

Another reason that mass media advertising and marketing now exercise disproportionate influence in Western cultures is the decline of social relationships and noncommercial institutions as channels to establish, communicate, and validate meaning. Psychologist Philip Cushman argues that "an absence of communal forms and beliefs [leaves] individuals in the postwar era... particularly vulnerable to influence from cultural forms such as advertising that emanate authority and certainty."[21] Cushman's observation concerning the erosion of community echoes the findings of sociologist Robert Putnam that I described in chapter 2. Mass media advertising and marketing also have disproportionate influence because broadcasting technology is particularly suited to propagating pre-rational, affective forms of communication. Leiss, Kline, and Jhally report that "research shows that iconic [i.e., visual] representation has a relatively greater impact on the 'affective-opinion' components of attitude.... Iconic representation can be absorbed in a sort of 'parallel process' without full conscious awareness, and thus it can register an impact without being translated into explicit verbal formulations."[22] Television advertising and marketing thus provide environmental stimuli that can prompt individuals' uncritical appropriation of meanings and trigger unconscious goal-oriented activity, such as I described in chapter 4 in connection with the research of psychologists John Bargh and Tanya Chartrand.

The consequence of the cultural dominance of mass media is a shift of the power to encode meanings in signs toward commercial institutions.

---

20. Kasser et al., "Materialistic Values," 12; Belk, "Changing Consumer," 155; Leiss et al., *Social Communication in Advertising*, 237–38.

21. Cushman, "Why the Self is Empty," 605.

22. Leiss, Kline, and Jhally, *Social Communication in Advertising*, 244.

Because "the modern world has been dominated by mass media and other powerful top-down communication and power systems," argue Søren Askegaard and A. Fuat Firat, "the individual . . . has been rendered secondary and unimportant in the semiotic system."[23] Askegaard and Firat's claim is too absolute, since it ignores the role of individuals in refining and completing meanings proposed by commercial institutions through mass media communications. Nevertheless, as social psychologist Helga Dittmar argues, there is no question that meaning creation is a social process that reflects social power relationships, and that this applies to the meanings associated with consumer goods that function as signs.[24] One consequence of the relationship in Western cultures between economic power and access to mass media communications, then, is the dominant influence of commercial institutions in the process of constructing the culture's meaning system and associating it with the domain of consumer goods.

The function of commercial advertising is to make consumer goods into signs. Charles Sanders Peirce describes a sign as part of a triadic meaning structure between a sign or signifier, its object or referent, and its interpretant or signified meaning. Marketing researcher David Glen Mick observes that, because the signified meaning is also a sign or a complex of signs, there is an infinite regress of meanings associated with any sign. Advertisers seek to turn consumer goods into signs by establishing associations between consumer goods and meanings that exist independently in the culture. While these meaning associations are not validated until they are accepted by consumers, advertisers propose meaning associations through the contiguity of the product-sign and the signified meaning in the advertisement. Leiss, Kline, and Jhally explain that the signified meaning is represented through the selection, arrangement, and relationships among characters, activities, and scenes that are themselves a complex of signs already associated with particular cultural meanings.[25] McCracken suggests that contiguity posits an essential connection between the product and meaning that are juxtaposed. "Advertising works as a potential method of meaning transfer by bringing the consumer good and a representation [i.e., a sign or sign complex] of the culturally constituted world together within the frame of a particular advertisement. The creative director of an

---

23. Askegaard and Firat, "Critique of Material Culture," 123.

24. Dittmar, *Social Psychology of Material Possessions*, 92.

25. Peirce, *Collected Papers*, 5.484; Mick, "Consumer Research and Semiotics," 199; Leiss et al., *Social Communication in Advertising*, 153, 169.

agency seeks to conjoin these two elements in such a way that the viewer/reader glimpses an essential similarity between them."[26] This juxtaposition of good-sign and meaning is repeated with the aim of leading the viewer to infer inductively an associative rule between them.

Leiss, Kline, and Jhally observe that, to the extent that the product-sign and cultural meanings are represented nonverbally through visual and auditory signs, meaning associations may be conveyed subconsciously. Mick distinguishes two types of relationships in advertising between the product-sign and cultural meanings. The relationship is *metaphor* when advertisers place goods side by side with people, activities, and scenes that are wholly unrelated to the product except by contiguity. It is *metonymy* when the advertiser uses a part to represent the whole, for example a product that is suggested as part of an experience or lifestyle. A metonym has particular power to establish meanings because it is an indexical sign, a sign that relates to its referent by some factual correspondence.[27]

Marketing researchers William Baker, Walter Nord, and J. Paul Peter identify five techniques that marketers have drawn from experimental psychology to influence consumer behavior. The first technique, *mere exposure*, repeatedly exposes consumers to a brand or product, without any additional information, in order to habituate consumers unconsciously to its presence as a sign and to reduce the perceived risk associated with it. The second technique, *respondent conditioning*, aims to produce responses to the product-sign that are comparable to the responses to the stimuli (i.e., the cultural meanings) associated with it, particularly unconscious affective responses. The third technique, *operant conditioning*, differs from respondent conditioning in that the stimuli follow the consumption behavior, and the association between stimuli and behavior is generally conscious. The fourth technique, *vicarious learning*, shows the potential consumer the consumption behavior of another person (the "model," who is typically an actor in an advertisement) and the supposed consequences of that consumption behavior for the other person. The fifth technique, *ecological design*, refers to the design of sales environments to suggest meanings in association with goods. Advertising tends to employ mere exposure, respondent conditioning, and vicarious learning, while operant conditioning

---

26. McCracken, *Culture and Consumption*, 77.

27. Leiss, Kline, and Jhally, *Social Communication in Advertising*, 159; Mick, "Consumer Research and Semiotics," 199, 206.

is more likely to be employed in sales promotions and ecological design is a key tactic in store layout, ambience, and sales displays.[28]

Thus far I have explored the *forms* of enculturation in Western consumer culture, and particularly mass media advertising. What, then, is the *substance* of commercial mass media communication, in the sense in which Tillich distinguishes religious substance from cultural form? In other words, what meanings are proposed by commercial institutions through mass media advertising that have religious-existential significance? Marketing researcher Theodore Levitt suggests that advertisers deliberately seek to foster associations between particular products and existential meanings of personal significance and security. He writes:

> Everyone in the world is trying in his special personal fashion to solve a primal problem of life—the problem of rising above his own negligibility, of escaping from nature's confining, hostile, and unpredictable reality, of finding significance, security, and comfort in the things he must do to survive. Many of the so-called distortions of advertising, product design, and packaging may be viewed as a paradigm of the many responses that man makes to the conditions of survival in the environment. Without distortion, embellishment, and elaboration, life would be drab, dull, anguished, and at its existential worst.[29]

Levitt further claims that, in offering these meaning associations, advertisers and marketers are only responding to consumers' demand for existential reassurance. Cushman makes a similar argument with reference to the advertising technique of vicarious learning. According to Cushman, advertisers suggest that the life of the model will magically be transferred to the consumer who purchases the product.[30] This suggests that identity and selfhood are at stake in this transaction. The model is represented as having a meaningful individual life, and the model's existential significance is a commodity that can be transferred with the appropriate purchase.

Linguist Ferdinand de Saussure first recognized that meanings were not conveyed by individual signs, but by the relationship among signs in a system. Mick applies this insight to the relationship between signs in advertising and marketing communication, arguing that distinctions between

---

28. Baker, "Affective Conditioning and Mere Exposure," 32–33; Nord and Peter, "Behavior Modification Perspective," 37–43.
29. Levitt, "Morality (?) of Advertising," 90.
30. Ibid., 91; Cushman, "Why the Self is Empty," 605.

signs are intended to signify distinctions between persons, that is, relative social positions. Sociologists Steven Miles, Kevin Meethan, and Alison Anderson make a comparable argument that the intended meaning association is a positional or status relationship.[31] In conjunction with Levitt and Cushman's observations about the relationship between advertising and individual existential meaning, this suggests that advertisements' positional significations are bound up with significations of who does and who does not have individually meaningful lives.

While every individual who inhabits a particular culture does not necessarily maintain the dominant existential meaning system of his or her culture, it is impossible to challenge a meaning system at the time that it is learned in early childhood, and difficult to will to change meaning systems later in life. Psychologist Alfred Adler observes that "every individual acts and suffers in accordance with his peculiar teleology, which has all the inevitability of fate, so long as he does not understand it [that is, so long as it remains unconscious]. Its springs may be traced to his earliest childhood, and nearly always we find that they have been diverted into false channels by the pressure of the earliest situations in the child's life."[32] Adler uses "teleology" in the same sense that I use "moral motivation" to refer to the ultimate spring that gives direction to the will and shapes a form of life. Motivation in this sense is determined by one's ultimate concern, that is, the system through which an individual seeks to ground the meaning of her or his life. Therefore the difficulty of changing one's received moral motivation is precisely the difficulty of changing one's received existential meaning strategy. In Western consumer cultures, Dittmar argues, what an individual tends to be taught in childhood are "the meanings of possessions as symbols of identity . . . and individuals gradually internalize them in interaction with other people and from social institutions, such as the mass media."[33] Because such socialization begins before children are capable of conceptual reflexive thought, the learned meaning system is acquired unconsciously, at least initially.

When socialized into a consumer culture's proposed meaning associations between product-signs and meanings of personal identity, the individual in that culture does not merely absorb the proposed meaning

---

31. Saussure, *Course in General Linguistics*; Mick, "Consumer Research and Semiotics," 197, 202; Miles et al., "Meaning of Consumption," 2.

32. Adler, *Individual Psychology of Alfred Adler*, 93.

33. Dittmar, *Social Psychology of Material Possessions*, 90.

associations but completes them. McCracken notes that it is an advertisement's "observer who is the final agent of the process of transference. ... The individual's mind is not merely drawing information from the ad, which it will then store in memory and variously grade and manipulate at the moment of decision. It is participating in the assignation of meaning to consumer goods."[34] Marketing researchers James Hunt, Jerome Kernan, and Deborah Mitchell argue that, to the extent that the system of meaning associations proposed by advertisers is accepted, this meaning system not only affects how an individual interprets products but also how he or she or he understands other persons and even himself or herself.[35] When these consumeristic interpretations of persons are internalized, the reproduction of the consumer culture's meaning system occurs in interaction between individuals, and not only in communication between commercial institutions and their potential customers.

Philosopher John Waide describes the social enforcement of the meaning associations between products and social identity. "In the most effective cases of associative advertising, people begin to talk like ad copy. We begin to sneer at those who own the wrong things. We all become enforcers for the advertisers. In general, if the advertising images are effective enough and reach enough people, even preposterous marketing claims can become at least partially self-fulfilling."[36] Ernest Becker argues that persons do not engage in practices of social enforcement because they are manipulated by marketers but because they need to legitimate a system for validating personal meaning claims that they themselves are relying upon for existential courage.[37]

In reviewing research on materialistic values, Kasser finds that the influence of negative social enforcement is not as significant as processes of parental socialization and modeling by persons seen as worthy of emulation.[38] Dittmar describes this process: "Initially, meaning is inferred from observing the conduct of others towards an object. By imaginatively adopting their perspectives, an individual gradually comes to understand and thus internalize their 'attitudes' or, in other words, to learn the meaning of that particular symbol or object. This is not a process of simple imitation

---

34. McCracken, *Culture and Consumption* II, 167.
35. Hunt et al., "Materialism as Social Cognition," 67–68.
36. Waide, "Making of Self and World in Advertising," 74.
37. E. Becker, *Birth and Death of Meaning*, 101.
38. Kasser, *High Price of Materialism*, 13.

but involves making others' perspectives one's own."[39] Given these processes for the social transmission of meaning systems, it is now time to explore how the consumeristic meaning system is appropriated by individuals as a strategy to secure the meaning of their lives.

Consumerism as an Existential Strategy

Tillich's claim that the existential problem of meaninglessness is the dominant anxiety of the modern age and thus the principal determinant of modern persons' motivation, is affirmed by two secular psychologists, Alfred Adler and Erich Fromm. Adler and Fromm contend that the existential need to assert and defend the meaningfulness of one's life is the root of *all* human motivation. According to Adler, the supreme law of human life is that "the sense of worth of the self shall not be allowed to be diminished."[40] Fromm contends that "all passions and strivings of man are attempts to find an answer to his existence."[41] This existential motivation underlies a natural self-preoccupation or egoism. According to Ernest Becker, "the qualitative feeling of self-value is the basic predicate for human action, precisely because it epitomizes the whole development of the ego."[42] Becker points to empirical evidence from psychoanalytical observations that affirms Tillich's characterization of the existential threat of meaninglessness. He notes that loss of self esteem—the ability to assert the meaningfulness of the self—is correlated with cases of clinical depression and schizophrenia.[43]

Alfred Adler and Ernest Becker suggest that the existential strategy for asserting the meaningfulness of one's individual self is expressed through one's character and form of life.[44] How does a form of life establish a claim of a meaningful self? The answer is specific to the form of life. In consumerism, however, the individual asserts his or her self-valuation semiotically and the signs that he or she deploys are consumer goods. The consumeristic form of life entails a strategic presentation of a system of good-signs that employs the meaning associations of the consumer culture's semiotic

39. Dittmar, *Social Psychology of Material Possessions*, 78.
40. Adler, *Individual Psychology of Alfred Adler*, 358.
41. Fromm, *Sane Society*, 29.
42. E. Becker, *Birth and Death of Meaning*, 67.
43. Ibid., 75.
44. Adler, *Individual Psychology of Alfred Adler*, 99–100; E. Becker, *Birth and Death of Meaning*, 148.

system for the purpose of securing other persons' recognition of one's self as a self. The consumeristic individual has no choice but to employ the goods-based semiotic system predominant in her or his culture to assert a meaningful identity if the system of signs that she or he puts into evidence is to be comprehensible to others.

It is not simply taste, character, or categorical identity that must be asserted through a consumeristic form of life, but selfhood itself. Russell Belk, Grant McCracken, Scott Lash, John Urry, and Robert Wuthnow all associate consumerism with identity-construction but fail to acknowledge its existential dimension.[45] Ernest Becker observes that "the human animal can be symbolically located *wherever* he feels a part of him really exists or belongs."[46] Accordingly, the consumeristic individual's selfhood exists symbolically in the system of good-signs that she or he places into public evidence for social validation. This leads to unlimited consumption for two reasons. First, the goods that the consumeristic individual must put into evidence to be judged meaningful are at least partly positional. The economic costs associated with these positional goods are potentially unlimited. Second, the consumer culture's system of signs and meanings, through which the individual must communicate, is in constant flux. Therefore the individual who lives a consumeristic form of life must continually consume new good-signs in order to update his or her deployment of signs to present the most advantageous system of signs possible, given the constraints of his or her economic means and the current state of the culture's semiotic system. At the same time, he or she must also strive to maximize his or her economic means for purchasing new good-signs.

Empirical psychological research demonstrates the existential function of consumerism. Kasser identifies several studies in which study participants who are primed with thoughts of death, guilt, or meaninglessness are more likely to display consumeristic values and desires. "Experimental manipulations . . . show that people become more materialistic and more desirous of consuming when they confront the fact of their own mortality . . . when they are made aware that they have failed to live up to important ideals . . . and when feelings of isolation or meaninglessness are primed."[47] Kasser also identifies research that shows higher levels of consumeristic

45. Belk, "Changing Consumer: Changing Disciplinarity," 148; McCracken, *Culture and Consumption II*, 3–4; Lash and Urry, *Economies of Signs and Space*, 58; Wuthnow, *After Heaven*, 10.

46. E. Becker, *Birth and Death of Meaning*, 32.

47. Kasser, "Good Life or the Goods Life?," 59.

values to be associated with children of divorced parents and children of parents who devalue their self-worth.[48]

While my argument focuses specifically on the threat of meaninglessness, the studies cited by Kasser demonstrate the interrelatedness of existential anxieties. Thoughts of death do not only raise the anxiety of nonbeing but also the anxiety of meaninglessness, since one is aware that one's own unique reflexive self will be extinguished and one's unique name and deeds will be left to others, among whom they may be forgotten and undone. Likewise, the anxiety of meaninglessness is linked to the anxiety of guilt since the individual must transgress familial and cultural norms to the extent that these norms reflect culturally conventional meaning systems that the individual cannot affirm because they are not completely or universally effective. The guilt of violating familial and cultural norms is tied to a heightened anxiety of meaninglessness since those whose meaning strategies one rejects will seek to undermine one's chosen meaning strategy in defense of their own.

How does a meaning system associated with good-signs enables an individual to assert his or her selfhood? First, the modern Western understanding of private property facilitates the identification of property with its owner, and likewise the identification of the owner with her or his property. Central to this identification, Dittmar argues, are the traits of exclusive association and control in the relationship between owner and property. Many thinkers, including Dittmar, Ernest Becker, Mary Douglas and Baron Isherwood, Lash and Urry, Leiss, Klein, and Jhally, McCracken, and Mick, also identify material goods' concreteness and relative stability as features that facilitate their use as signs for identity. Concreteness corresponds to the individual's desire to posit her or his meaning as real, tangible, irreducible, essential, and necessary. Stability corresponds to the individual's desire to posit her or his meaning as fixed, irreplaceable, and enduring, even beyond her or his own biological mortality. The other characteristic that these thinkers generally agree is central to the ability of good-signs to signal individual identity is the distribution of signifying goods and, more particularly, their scarcity.[49]

48. Kasser, *High Price of Materialism*, 31–32.

49. Dittmar, *Social Psychology of Material Possessions*, 8–9, 93; E. Becker, *Birth and Death of Meaning*, 149–50; Douglas and Isherwood, *World of Goods*, 59–61; Lash and Urry, *Economies of Signs and Space*, 132; Leiss et al., *Social Communication in Advertising*, 166, 250; McCracken, *Culture and Consumption*, 113–14; Mick, "Consumer Research and Semiotics," 205.

To understand the relevance of good-signs' scarcity to individual identity it is necessary to examine the relationship between good-signs' categorical and individual meanings. Dittmar observes that consumer goods signify both types of meanings. "Possessions symbolize not only the personal qualities of individuals, but also the groups they belong to and their social standing generally."[50] Dittmar notes that this dual signification was observed empirically in studies by Sidney Levy, G. P. Stone, and Erving Goffman.[51] There is a relationship between categorical and individual recognition that explains why positional concerns are relevant to the social recognition of an individual self. Dittmar explains that when one person interprets another person's system of good-signs, categorical judgments precede individual judgments. "Sets of material possession are used initially to locate another person in a social-material hierarchy, before considering their personal qualities and attitudes."[52] There is, in general, a motive for persons belonging to one's own social group to affirm one's claim to individual meaning as a means of bolstering their own claim to significance. This explains why, in contrast to the status signaling theories, it is one's own social group and not society as a whole that is the principal audience to whom the individual seeks to communicate a claim to meaningful identity by displaying a system of good-signs.

The strategy of seeking intra-group recognition is only effective in practice for high- to moderate-status groups. Dittmar reports that "studies of actual groups in the 'real world' highlight that we live in a society where group relations invariably involve unequal status, and where ingroup favoritism is often limited, particularly for people who belong to underprivileged groups.... Social categories which are viewed negatively cannot easily provide their members with a positive social identity. [Low-status] minority group members may internalize the negative representations held about them and come to identify with majority evaluations."[53] Thus persons belonging to low-status social categories are excluded from social recognition even by members of their own group. The categorical interpretations that other persons make toward them—whether members of other social

50. Dittmar, *Social Psychology of Material Possessions*, 10–11.

51. Dittmar, *Social Psychology of Material Possessions*, 96–99; Levy, "Symbols for Sale," 117–24; Stone, "Appearance and the Self," 86–118; Goffman, "Symbols of Class Status," 294–304.

52. Dittmar, *Social Psychology of Material Possessions*, 155.

53. Ibid., 172.

groups or of their own group—identify them as undeserving of individual evaluation. More generally, observers' categorical interpretations of a person's good-sign system determine the degree to which the observers are willing to expend the effort to interpret that person's good-sign system individually. A person must be validated categorically in order to be judged worthy of the effort to be assessed as an individual, and he or she must be assessed as an individual to be recognized individually, that is, to have his or her self validated as a meaningful self.

The impetus for a consumeristic individual to compete for positional good-signs arises from the screening function of categorical interpretation. An individual can gain social validation as an individual only if she or he presents a system of good-signs that asserts membership in a group in which members recognize one another's individuality, and only if other persons validate this categorical claim. Therefore the most significant categorical meanings associated with a consumeristic individual's display of good-signs are positional and defensive. That is, the consumeristic individual must claim a status sufficiently high that intra-group recognition is likely, and it is intra-group recognition rather than recognition by members of higher status groups that is the primary aim for the individual's positional claims. As I explained in chapter 4 in connection with the research of Fred Hirsch and Robert Frank, positional goods must be scarce in order to function as positional signifiers, and this scarcity is established by high price, market barriers, or social limits on the goods' conditions of use. The combination of inelastic demand and fixed supply for positional goods means that the consumeristic individual who must assert a status claim using positional good-signs is committed to positional competition and insatiable consumption. As with any sort of sign, the positional meaning of good-signs does not correspond to individual signifiers (i.e., goods) but to a system of good-signs. When signifying positional meanings, it is the relationship between good-signs that corresponds to the positional or categorical relationship between individuals.[54]

Just as meanings proposed by advertisers must be completed by consumers who interpret the signs in advertisements, so too the identity that an individual asserts through his or her display of good-signs must be completed by others. Without validation by others, a subjectively asserted meaning is not secure enough to stave off the threat of meaninglessness. Ernest Becker echoes this assessment when he contends that "man's best

---

54. Leiss et al., *Social Communication in Advertising*, 295.

efforts seem utterly fallible without appeal to something higher for justification, some conceptual support for the meaning of one's life from a transcendental dimension of some kind. As this belief has to absorb man's basic terror, it cannot be merely abstract but must be rooted in . . . an inner feeling that one is secure in something stronger, larger, more important than one's owns strength and life."[55] As I observed earlier, an individual can be assured that his or her life has significance if he or she can be meaningfully and essentially related to a meaning system or whole that is social, historical, or metaphysical. These three systems or wholes correspond to the three ways in which an individual can be validated by something beyond himself or herself. The individual may be validated as meaningfully and essentially related to society through social recognition. He or she may be validated as meaningfully and essentially related to history through the firm expectation of posthumous recognition of his or her uniquely significant creative expressions. Or he or she may be validated through trust in his or her essential relationship to a metaphysical ground of meaning that establishes and guarantees the meaningfulness of the whole of reality.

Psychologist Otto Rank identifies the path of historical validation with the creative genius, whose work sacrifices conventional existential meaning strategies and "creates, as it were, a private religion for itself, that not only expresses the collective spirit of the epoch, but produces a new ideology," that is, a uniquely significant body of creative work that the genius trusts will be validated by posterity, despite its rejection by the artist's contemporaries.[56] Ernest Becker describes the metaphysical validation of meaning as a surrender of the problem of meaning to a cosmic guarantor. "By making your hero-system [i.e., your existential meaning strategy] the service of your Creator, you have the distinction of making a gift of your life no matter what the special quality of that gift is: as you last out your life with courage, forbearance, and dignity you affirm your divine calling by simply living it out. Your Creator will make good [i.e., make meaningful] your service."[57] Of course, this does not mean that everyone who professes religion is seeking metaphysical rather than social validation of her or his life's meaning. I will return to this point later in this chapter. Consumerism, however, is an existential meaning strategy that aims for the most common form of validation, validation through social recognition.

55. Becker, *Denial of Death*, 120.
56. Rank, *Art and Artist*, 86.
57. E. Becker, *Birth and Death of Meaning*, 189.

In consumerism, as with every other strategy to obtain social recognition, every assertion of the meaningfulness of one's self is a claim for an other or others to recognize one's self-valuation as a self and thereby validate that valuation. According to sociologist Erving Goffman, this claim depends upon social norms of mutual recognition. Goffman writes, "Society is organized on the principle that any individual who possesses certain social characteristics has a moral right to expect that others will value and treat him in an appropriate way. . . . When an individual projects a definition of the situation and thereby makes an implicit or explicit claim to be a person of a particular kind, he automatically exerts a moral demand upon the others, obliging them to value and treat him in the manner that persons of his kind have a right to expect."[58] However, the observer is not compelled to honor the social norm of mutual recognition in all cases. The observer must evaluate the claimant's system of good-signs in light of her or his own need to uphold the meaningfulness of the cultural system that undergirds her or his claim to personal significance. Thus, Solomon, Greenberg, and Pyszczynski observe, "people's actions are directed toward sustaining a dual component cultural anxiety-buffer: faith in their [cultural] worldviews and a sense that they are valued components of that meaningful reality."[59] Unless the observer knows the claimant well, the form of reasoning that the observer follows in evaluating a meaning claim is generally abductive. Abduction means, according to Peirce, that a person infers a particular case probabilistically from a general rule and an observed result or fact.[60] For example, if the rule is "elite status persons drive expensive cars" and the observed fact is "Veronica drives an expensive car," the inferred case would be "Veronica is an elite status person."[61] In practice, many abductive inferences are necessary for the observer to assign the case a high probability, which is why the claimant must assert her or his selfhood through a comprehensive and coherent good-sign system rather than through a single good-sign.

Ernest Becker confirms my earlier observation that the social validation of a self requires recognition from at least some others, but this recognition need not be universal. In childhood, Becker observes, the individual *"learns that there are certain reactions to his cues that he can discount. . . . The child leans thereby to sustain his own valued self in the face of negative*

---

58. Goffman, *Presentation of Self in Everyday Life*, 13.
59. Solomon et al., "Lethal Consumption," 132.
60. Peirce, *Collected Papers*, 5.317.
61. This example is from Holbrook and Hirschman, *Semiotics of Consumption*, 28.

responses: there are those, he finds, whose evaluation he can ignore."[62] In order to facilitate mutual recognition, consumeristic individuals tend to associate with others who have similar systems of good-signs. However recognition needs to be repeated if it is to keep the consumeristic individual secure in her or his subjective belief in her or his personal significance. Social validation does not demonstrate once and for all that a claim to meaningful selfhood is true, in Tillich's sense that it is grounded in a universal system of meanings.[63] It merely defends the person who asserts a selfhood claim from challenge in his or her social world for the present.

The aim of the individual who seeks social recognition is nothing less than the continuation of the individual's existence as a self. "If we uphold our part in the performance, we are rewarded with social affirmation of our identity," Ernest Becker writes, but "if we bungle the performance, show that we do not merit the part, we are destroyed—not figuratively, but literally."[64] The individual who can sustain a claim to meaningful identity is able to suppress his or her existential anxiety of meaninglessness and to get on with the more mundane activities of life. The individual who cannot sustain such a claim suffers personal disintegration as he or she is overwhelmed with existential despair.

As I argued for socially-validated meaning strategies in general, it is difficult for consumeristic individuals to understand their meaning strategy fully and impossible for them to desire to do so. The first obstacle between the consumeristic individual and a fully conscious understanding of her or his existential meaning strategy is that most individuals who employ this strategy do so because they learned it in early childhood from their family and culture. Ernest Becker observes that the individual's received meaning strategy is, in part, pre-conceptual and thus pre-conscious. "We ourselves are largely ignorant of our own life-style, our way of seeking and earning self-esteem. Each of us has a . . . life-style, formed during our early training. And this formation is largely a process of conditioning that begins even before we learn symbols, it is pre-symbolic."[65] To the extent that one's meaning strategy is learned pre-consciously, it cannot be recalled and described if one seeks to make it an object of reflection later in life. The individual's received meaning strategy is also learned pre-critically. Becker observes

62. E. Becker, *Birth and Death of Meaning*, 93.
63. See Tillich, *Systematic Theology*, vol. 1, 14.
64. E. Becker, *Birth and Death of Meaning*, 99.
65. Ibid., 72.

that "we take large parts of our parents' images and commands into our own self—without . . . 'digesting' them, making them an integral part of ourselves that responds to our honest control."[66] The individual's received meaning system becomes a lens through which he or she perceives experience, so that he or she is never aware that this meaning system is potentially inadequate unless and until it fails. Rank observes that "in order to be able to accept for himself any of the conventionally sanctioned illusions, through which it loses for him the character of illusion . . . [the individual] must first create in himself the presupposition required for it. This consists of finding an inner level of illusion of his own on which all experiencing as it were plays itself out potentially, like the shadows in Plato's cave without actually occurring."[67] Therefore, individuals do not necessarily consciously understand that they are living one possible meaning system among many. In general, they believe that they live according to what is real and true because that is what they were first taught to understand as real and true, and because that is what the culture surrounding them maintains.

Although it is possible in part for the meaning strategy one learns in childhood to be brought to conscious understanding through sustained philosophical reflection or psychoanalysis, there is a second obstacle that prevents the consumeristic individual from attaining full conscious understanding of his or her existential meaning strategy. A conscious self-understanding poses the risk of heightening existential anxiety by drawing attention to the fragility of the meaning strategy that stands alone between the individual and existential anxiety and despair. Therefore the individual cannot fully desire such self-awareness. Adler contends that the self creates an arbitrary goal as a strategy to secure self-esteem. He views this as a necessary fiction that requires self-deception. Adler explains:

> The healthy individual as well as the neurotic would have to forego orientation in the world if he did not organize the picture of the world and his experiences according to fictions. In hours of insecurity, these fictions become more prominent. They become imperatives of belief, of the ideal, of free will, but beyond this they are effective in secret, in the unconscious, like all psychological mechanisms. The final goal [i.e., the moral motivation determined by the individual's existential meaning strategy] emerges

66. Ibid.
67. Rank, *Will Therapy*, 244.

for everyone, consciously or unconsciously, but its significance is never understood [by the individual himself].[68]

Becker affirms Adler's judgment that the individual's need to defend his or her meaning system overrides any conscious desire for self-understanding. He writes that "self-knowledge is the hardest human task because it risks revealing to the person how his self-esteem was built: on the powers of others in order to deny his own creatureliness and death."[69] Becker's insight applies to the existential threat of meaninglessness because self-esteem is not threatened by finitude as such but by the effect that consciousness of one's finitude has on the ability to assert the meaningfulness of one's life. To the extent that an individual becomes conscious of the fragility and non-necessity of the social recognition that upholds her or his assurance of personal meaningfulness, the existential threat of meaninglessness is brought closer to consciousness and the individual is exposed to debilitating existential anxiety. To prevent this, Becker observes, "modern man is closed off, tightly, against dimensions of reality and perceptions of the world that would threaten or upset his standardized reactions: he will have it his way if he has to strangle the segment of reality that he has equipped himself to cope with."[70] Faced with a choice between self-awareness and the capacity to function in the world, we necessarily choose the latter.

As Tillich recognizes, the fragility of a socially-validated meaning strategy like consumerism does not merely compel the individual to be unaware of his or her meaning strategy, it compels the individual to defend his or her meaning strategy and his or her unconsciousness of it. Ernest Becker observes that this defense may take the form of scapegoating or aggression towards those individuals who cannot be fit meaningfully into the worldview arising from one's own meaning system.[71] Solomon, Greenberg, and Pyszczynski likewise observe that because "people with different beliefs . . . [pose] a challenge to our death-denying belief system . . . we . . . typically respond . . . by berating them, trying to convert them to our system of beliefs, or just killing them and in so doing asserting that 'my God (or political-economic system) is better than yours and we'll kick your ass to prove it.'"[72] In situations of religious and cultural pluralism, Becker

68. Adler, *Individual Psychology of Alfred Adler*, 93.
69. E. Becker, *Escape from Evil*, 163.
70. E. Becker, *Birth and Death of Meaning*, 150–51.
71. Ibid., 164, 170–71.
72. Solomon et al., "Lethal Consumption," 132.

observes, aggression is frequently directed towards persons who employ different meaning systems because the encounter with such persons confronts those who adhere to a socially-validated meaning system with an awareness of meaning systems' plurality that undermines the social assurance that their meaning system has unquestioned validity.[73]

The existential threat to the consumeristic individual that arises from becoming fully conscious of her or his meaning strategy underlies the difficulty of changing to a different meaning strategy. Because they are typically adopted in early childhood, most individuals' existential meaning systems are not only unconscious, they are not freely chosen. Ernest Becker explains:

> Since ... [a child's] choice of mechanisms of defense, of a style of life, is the child's adaptation to superior powers, this choice does not reflect his own real feelings, his own true perceptions. In fact, it would be difficult to determine what these might be since, in large part, the child was not given the chance to have them. This means that the child's denial of his burdens is "dishonest," not fully under his control, unknown to him: his character, in a word, is an *urgent lie* about the nature of reality. His whole life is an attempt to "be cool" about his lie, to try to appear as though what de did made good, logical sense, and was the authentic expression of himself.[74]

In order to adopt a more self-conscious and self-chosen meaning system, Becker argues, the individual "needs to renounce precisely that form of comfort and salvation that have become inseparable from his deepest values.... The person has to renounce precisely that which he feels ... least able to renounce—that which is as dear as life itself because it has become the indispensable condition for his life."[75] Becker thus affirms Kierkegaard's characterization of a change in one's ground of meaning as a kind of death, an experience of facing fully the existential threat of one's own meaninglessness. Becker argues that "one cannot even begin to be an adult"—that is, an individual who has chosen his or her own meaning strategy—"unless one has gone through ... the disintegration of the self-esteem that sustains one's character."[76] He elaborates: "The self must be destroyed, brought down to nothing, in order for self-transcendence to begin. Then the self

---

73. E. Becker, *Birth and Death of Meaning*, 140.
74. Ibid., 148.
75. Ibid., 145.
76. Ibid., 146.

can begin to relate itself to powers beyond itself. It has to thrash around in its finitude, it has to 'die,' in order to question that finitude, in order to see beyond it."[77] Western cultures define the failure to maintain the assurance of one's own importance as mental illness, and yet it is precisely the individual who suffers an involuntary breakdown of his or her culturally-given meaning strategy who is able to leave this perceptual system behind and enter into a new one.[78]

Empirical Validation of the Religious-Existential Motivation Theory

I argued in chapter 4 that theological ethical proposals are subject to empirical validation or falsification insofar as they rest upon descriptions of the observable world that overlap the scientific community's objects of empirical observation and interpretation. Accordingly, I will now consider the empirical validity of my theory that consumerism is motivated by a strategy to secure the existential meaning of individuals' lives. To perform this validation, I use the same socioeconomic criteria that I used in chapter 4 to evaluate and empirically falsify the greed, status signaling, manipulation, imaginative hedonism, and parental concern theories.

My empirical finding of a historical emergence of consumerism in the 1970s and 1980s is consistent with my proposed theory. I explained in chapter 2 why the historical failure of competing meaning systems made consumerism relatively more attractive in the contemporary situation of affluent Western nations. Since *some* meaning strategy is existentially necessary for every person, consumerism has gained in relative favor by process of elimination. I am not suggesting that consumerism has become a universal form of life in Western societies, only that it is a particularly prevalent answer to a universal question in human existence.

My claim that consumerism is a form of life oriented by an existential meaning strategy is consistent with my empirical finding that consumerism is found across all social classes, with the exception of the very poor who are excluded by definition. This is because the existential question that persons seek to answer through a consumeristic life is universal. Moreover, the dependence of consumeristic individuals upon the meaning-creating

---

77. E. Becker, *Denial of Death*, 89.
78. E. Becker, *Birth and Death of Meaning*, 151.

function of mass media advertising to render their meaning claims intelligible to others makes this existential strategy equally available to all social classes exposed to the same media. For the same reasons, an existential motivation of consumerism is consistent with my empirical findings that consumeristic behavior in housing consumption is not restricted to particular income classes or to particular household types.

My theory that consumerism is an existentially motivated form of life is consistent with the empirical evidence that consumerism is not motivated by subjective happiness. Existential motives are clearly distinct from happiness. Happiness is a conscious, affective state accompanying the satisfaction of subjective desires and goals. An existential motive, on the other hand, is driven not by contingent desires and experiences but by necessity in the face of the inescapable estrangement of the individual's existence from her or his essential humanity. Unlike happiness, this motive is generally unconscious, but that does not diminish its force. The existential need for meaningful individual life, in particular, is the individual's ontological need to unite freedom and destiny, which are separated under the conditions of existence.[79] Unless an individual's freedom is united with something larger and more enduring than himself or herself, deliberation, decision, and action lose their meaning, and the individual suffers the anxiety of meaninglessness.

As I argued earlier in this chapter, the motive for a particular existential strategy is generally not consciously understood because it is typically learned in early childhood and because individuals with socially-validated meaning strategies need to preserve their meaning strategy from challenge. An existential motivation for consumerism therefore conforms to the empirical evidence that consumers' decision processes are frequently unconscious.

An existential motivation for consumerism is consistent with the empirical evidence of consumer goods' social utilities and positional competition because consumerism is an existential strategy that relies on social validation. Other persons' validation of the individual as a meaningful self is conditioned upon the other persons' prior categorical validation of the individual as belonging to a group with sufficiently high status to justify individual evaluation. That categorical validation depends upon how observers interpret the meaning of the individual's system of good-signs, which must includes positional good-signs in order to support the observers' positive

---

79. Tillich, *Systematic Theology*, vol. 2, 25–26, 36–38, 62–63.

status judgments. Therefore, the consumeristic individual must engage in positional competition to seek to secure categorical validation. Wherever consumerism is widespread, this positional competition will lead a market economy to assign values to some goods—those culturally acknowledged as positional—that are based in part on their social utilities.

An existential motivation for consumerism is consistent with the empirical evidence that advertising has limited effectiveness in determining consumer behavior. Recall that this criterion specifically stands in opposition to the manipulation theories' claim that advertisers' influence is sufficient to override consumers' freedom and control their consumption decisions. The studies of advertising effectiveness that I cited in chapter 4 measure the ability of advertisers to move consumers to purchase specific products and specific brands, rather than to provide a general context for consumers' consumption decisions. In contrast, my existential motivation theory recognizes that consumers pick and choose among the meaning associations offered by advertisers, complete these meaning associations, and use them for their own ends. Even if these ends are known to marketing researchers like Levitt but not generally known to the consumers themselves, the ends arise from the consumers in response to their existential situation. These ends may be more or less successfully exploited by advertisers that offer meaning associations between their goods and the consumers' existential ends, but they are not created by advertisers. An existential strategy that relies on social recognition needs *some* semiotic system that can be used to represent social distinctions, and advertisers supply this demand for consumeristic individuals by associating social distinctions with distinctions among good-signs. If they did not, however, individuals would necessarily construct some other system of semiotic distinction so long as they remain dependent on social validation of the meanings that they claim for their selves.

Redirecting Consumerism to Existential Christian Faith

From a Christian theological standpoint, every strategy to ground the meaning of one's individual life through one's own efforts, including consumerism, is doomed to failure. It fails because it lacks a ground of meaning that can sustain the meaning of a finite human life beyond the scope of its finitude. As Tillich expresses this point, "no act within the context of existential estrangement can overcome existential estrangement."[80] Every human being experiences the existential estrangement of freedom from destiny, which is the alienation of human deliberation, decision, and action from ultimate concern with an unconditioned ground of meaning. This leads to the loss of a deciding center. Decisions become meaningless, mechanistic responses to internal compulsions and external causes. The estranged human being loses both freedom and destiny.[81] Every meaning for personal existence that is not grounded in an essential ground of meaning is merely posited or conventional. It cannot provide the lasting certainty necessary for an individual to stake the meaningfulness of his or her life on it with confidence. It lacks any ultimate significance or security. Thus, Tillich argues, "if no essential relation between a free agent and his objects exists, no choice is objectively preferable to any other; no commitment to a cause or a person is meaningful; no dominant purpose can be established."[82] Indeed, Alfred Adler, Ernest Becker, and Otto Rank's characterizations of human beings' autonomous meaning systems as illusory or fictitious demonstrate that socially- or historically-validated meaning systems' lack of ultimate substance or import is evident even without reference to theological claims.[83]

Every strategy to ground the meaning of an individual life by relying on human authority is also doomed to failure. This is because every heteronomy demands the surrender of individual identity and freedom to a group. But a person can only truly secure meaningful individual identity through an essential relationship to a meaningful whole if it is, in fact, a whole. A group—whether nation, race, class, political party, or religious organization—that demands absolute submission in return for absolute meaning is promising what it cannot deliver. No group is a whole meaning system, an unconditioned ground of meaning. Since every meaning strategy based on group identity is not universal, it cannot be necessary. A system that is recognized as unnecessary cannot ground individual meaning or justify the surrender of the self. Thus, heteronomy is not a viable meaning system in any culture in which persons enjoy freedom of inquiry or awareness of alternate meaning systems. An entire population cannot

---

80. Ibid., 80.

81. Tillich, *Systematic Theology*, vol. 2, 63; Tillich, *Courage to Be*, 47.

82. Tillich, *Systematic Theology*, vol. 2, 63.

83. See Adler, *Individual Psychology of Alfred Adler*, 93–97; E. Becker, *Birth and Death of Meaning*, 126; E. Becker, *Denial of Death*, 56; Rank, *Will Therapy*, 243–45.

simultaneously forget or refuse to perceive a heteronomous meaning system's non-universality and non-necessity. Strategies to ground meaning in group identity cannot be sustained in societies in which the evidence of religious and cultural pluralism is plain.

For those who acknowledge the substance of the Christian message as their ultimate concern, the answer to the existential problem of meaning can be summarized by Tillich's material norm of theology: "New Being in Jesus as the Christ as our ultimate concern."[84] Tillich correlates the existential question of meaning with the answer to the question of meaning provided by the Christian message. In the remainder of this chapter, I will examine the substance of Tillich's symbolic expression and describe how the power represented through these symbols creates the possibility of conversion from the consumeristic form of life to that of existential Christian faith.

The symbol of "New Being" indicates a deliverance from the tragic universal destiny of individual human beings and social structures. Human existence is tragic, Tillich observes, because in the individual's exercise of freedom she or he contradicts her or his essential nature and this self-contradiction leads toward self-destruction. Human existence is destiny because self-contradiction and self-destruction are the universal predicament of every individual from earliest childhood, and cannot be escaped by an individual's own power.[85] "New reality presupposes an old reality," Tillich writes, where the "old reality . . . is the state of the estrangement of man and his world from God."[86] Estrangement is the universal human predicament described by existentialist philosophy in which the individual has finite freedom, and because he or she has the capacity to reflect on his or her finitude, is beset by the anxieties of death, meaninglessness, and guilt.[87] The anxiety of meaninglessness, in particular, is the threat of despair—of "being responsible for the loss of the meaning of one's existence and of being unable to recover it."[88] The threat of despair is magnified by human beings' attempts to escape despair. When human beings employ strategies like consumerism to attempt to secure their individual meaning through their

---

84. Tillich, *Systematic Theology*, vol. 1, 50.
85. Tillich, *Systematic Theology*, vol. 2, 56–63.
86. Ibid., 27.
87. Ibid., 34–36, 66–73.
88. Ibid., 75.

own agency, they undermine their moral centeredness and bind themselves to the pursuit of arbitrary, meaningless, and destructive desires.

Defined negatively, then, New Being is the deliverance by a power beyond oneself from estrangement from the unconditioned ground of meaning (God), the anxiety and despair of meaninglessness, and self-destruction through vain attempts to secure one's own meaning. Defined positively, New Being is an individual's coming into being as a true self, empowered by and centered in God, the unconditioned ground of meaning, within a community of centered selves.[89] New Being entails all three movements that Tillich describes as belonging to self actualization: the movement of self-integration that actualizes the self's moral center, the movement of self-creation that realizes the self's potentiality, and the movement of self-transcendence in which "life drives beyond itself as finite life."[90] In the individual human spirit, self-integration is morality, self-creation is culture, and self-transcendence is religion. In the relationship of the centered self to community, self-integration is the moral encounter with an other in which the other is fully recognized as a person simply by virtue of being a person, self-creation is creative action (praxis) aimed at growth toward just and virtuous community, and self-transcendence is the depth dimension of interpersonal morality and praxis, i.e., their relation to the unconditioned ground of meaning.[91] New Being thus contrasts with the consequences of seeking to secure personal meaning through social or historical validation: namely, the loss of a deciding center and the loss of one's potential for self-creation and self-transcendence.

The symbol of "the Christ" signifies the agent of New Being and of the *metanoia*, or reversal of purpose, by which a self is brought from existential estrangement to New Being. It is a foundational claim of Christian doctrine and belief, especially as it is expressed in the Pauline-Augustinian-Lutheran theological tradition, that New Being—represented in traditional theological language by the symbols salvation, redemption, justification, and reconciliation—cannot be effected by human beings for themselves, but is the work of God in the Christ. This claim is expressed by the traditional symbol "grace" in the classic formulation of St. Paul in Rom 3:23–24 (NRSV): "Since all have sinned and fall short of the glory of God; they are now justified by his grace as a gift, through the redemption that is in

---

89. See Tillich, *Morality and Beyond*, 19.
90. Tillich, *Systematic Theology*, vol. 3, 30–31.
91. Ibid., 38–40, 57–67, 95–97.

Christ Jesus." The Christ is the mediator who overcomes the infinite gap between finite human existence and the unconditioned ground of meaning represented by the symbol "God." The Christ reconciles human beings to God. As mediator, the Christ represents God to human beings, the God for whom love overcomes estrangement. As mediator, the Christ also represents human beings to God, as the human being who suffers the consequences of humanity's tragic destiny of existential estrangement without surrendering his essential relationship to God. The Christ is the Incarnate One, the one in whom, paradoxically, God becomes human and yet remains God. The Christ enters historical existence and yet overcomes existential estrangement by remaining essential human being.[92] In so doing, the Christ "creates the meaning of human history ... the eternal relation of God to man,"[93] which is the essential relationship of an infinite and eternal ground of meaning to the meaning of each finite individual human being.

The symbolic formula "New Being in Jesus as the Christ" represents the paradoxical and distinctively Christian claim that the agent of New Being is a particular historical human being, Jesus of Nazareth. This claim is paradoxical because it offends human beings' reliance on their own attempts to secure the meaning of their existence by asserting that one, and only one, human being who participated in the conditions of existence was not bound by them, as other human beings are, but conquered them and transcended humanity's estrangement from God. This claim is distinctively Christian because Christian identity is defined by an individual's confession of the historical human being Jesus of Nazareth as the Christ.[94] As the incarnate Christ, Christians confess, New Being enters human historical existence in the person of Jesus of Nazareth. The particular historical individual, Jesus, overcame the threat of human finitude to his personal meaning through the power of his relationship to the unconditioned ground of meaning, a relationship that transcended his death. As the mediating Christ, the reception of Jesus as the Christ through existential faith establishes New Being in the life of the Christian.

I argued earlier in this chapter that it is impossible for an individual to will to depart from his or her meaning system so long as it continues to function adequately to sustain the individual's assurance of meaningful individual life. However, a socially-validated meaning strategy like

---

92. Tillich, *Systematic Theology*, vol. 2, 93–95.
93. Ibid., 96.
94. Ibid., 92, 97.

consumerism is subject to involuntary falsification. A consumeristic individual may suffer a catastrophic financial loss that makes it impossible to "keep up appearances," that is, to continue to present a system of good-signs adequate to signify the categorical status of a group that offers mutual recognition of individual meaningfulness. Or a consumeristic individual may fail to be socially validated as a meaningful self for reasons apart from the system of good-signs that he or she presents—for example, disability, loss of health, or a failure to master and sustain the culturally accepted rituals for asserting a claim to meaningful selfhood. In any of these circumstances, the observer may withhold recognition as a defensive measure to secure the meaning system that grounds his or her own claims to personal significance. A socially-validated meaning strategy may also fail involuntarily if an individual fails to escape, suppress, or discredit a cognitive confrontation with his or her meaning system's non-necessity.

The consumeristic individual who suffers a loss of self-certainty, either through interior dissonance or failure to secure social validation, faces catastrophic existential failure. She or he loses self-esteem, loses the self-assurance to function in the world in everyday matters, and experiences despair and self-destruction. Yet precisely this failure is the condition for possible entry into the meaning system of existential Christian faith. Therefore this self-destruction and the circumstances that produce it can be understood as the first movement of grace, even though they are subjectively experienced as suffering and as evil. It is grace, understood as a necessary part of the process of turning an individual away from existential estrangement that the individual is unable or unwilling to undertake by his or her own power.

The second movement of grace, in Tillich's expression, is the experience of "being grasped by the power of the New Being,"[95] which transcends the individual self. Even though this experience happens within a human being, Tillich writes, it is not the work of that human being, but the work of the Christ.[96] This is a restatement of the traditional Pauline-Augustinian-Lutheran doctrine of justification by grace alone. It is this experience that establishes existential faith in which "New Being in Jesus as the Christ" is one's ultimate concern. The existential significance of faith, in Ernest Becker's words, is that it trusts "that one's very creatureliness has some meaning to a Creator; that despite one's true insignificance, weakness, death, one's

---

95. Ibid., 155.
96. Ibid., 178.

existence has meaning in some ultimate sense because it exists within an eternal and infinite scheme of things."[97] This faith is existential because it is an absolute trust in something or someone, upon which or upon whom the individual stakes his or her entire self. This faith is Christian because it is an absolute trust that one's existence has meaning in an ultimate sense because Jesus as the Christ overcame for himself and overcomes for other human beings the meaninglessness of finite human existence, that is, its estrangement from the unconditioned ground of meaning, God. In Tillich's words, this movement of grace is the acceptance that one is accepted in spite of one's unacceptability.[98] It is trust that the significance of one's relationship with God, the unconditioned ground of meaning, is established unshakably by God in spite of one's own estranged condition.

Tillich distinguishes faith, understood existentially, from a variety of ways in which the word faith is commonly used. Understood existentially, faith "is not an act of cognitive affirmation"; it is not "the acceptance of factual statements or valuations taken on authority, even if the authority is divine"; it is not obedience or the aim of a will to believe; it is not feeling.[99] Beyond this, existential faith must be distinguished from conventional religion. Existential faith and conventional religion are distinct existential strategies and forms of life that use the symbols and forms of the Christian religious tradition in distinct ways. Existential faith is a direct relationship of the individual to the unconditioned ground of meaning disclosed beneath the symbols of the Christian message. The individual trusts that her or his life has significance because, and only because, the infinite and eternal ground of meaning, God, guarantees the meaningfulness of the individual in relationship to God, and she or he stakes the meaningfulness of her or his life upon this trust. By contrast, in conventional religion, the individual is sustained in the belief that his or her life has meaning because he or she receives social recognition within a particular religious community that validates his or her claim to meaningful life on the basis of membership, participation, and standing in that community. Kierkegaard classifies the person of conventional religion as a "man of immediacy," that is, a person who has not become a self because he or she accepts social conventions

---

97. E. Becker, *Denial of Death*, 90.
98. Tillich, *Systematic Theology*, vol. 2, 179.
99. Tillich, *Systematic Theology*, vol. 3, 131–32.

passively. He or she identifies himself or herself through external possessions, not as a self but as part of a social whole.[100]

The moral motivation of the person of existential faith is freed from incessant striving for existential security precisely because he or she trusts that there is nothing that can be done or needs to be done by his or her own efforts to secure meaningful existence. He or she is thereby enabled to be redirected in love, through union with the divine life, towards the well being of other persons, other generations, and other life. New Being is characterized by freedom from striving to secure the meaning of one's self. In contrast, the moral motivation of the person of conventional religion—like the moral motivation of the consumeristic individual—is necessarily directed towards self-securing. Therefore, an individual who relies upon conventional religion for personal meaning may only serve the well being of other persons, other generations, and other life insofar as such service contributes to a system of signs that he or she displays to achieve social recognition of his or her meaningfulness within a particular religious community.

New Being in Jesus as the Christ is a transformed existence, and yet it is not an existence that removes an individual from the human predicament. As Ernest Becker observes, "there is simply no way to transcend the limits of the human condition or to change the psychological structural conditions that make humanity possible."[101] The same structure of reflexivity in the human spirit that enables human freedom makes the anxiety of meaninglessness ever available to human consciousness. Existential faith does not remove anxiety; it enables an individual to live with anxiety by each moment facing it with courage and renouncing it. Thus Kierkegaard states that the "courage to renounce anxiety without anxiety . . . [is something] only faith can do; faith does not thereby annihilate anxiety, but, itself eternally young, it extricates itself from anxiety's moment of death."[102] The inescapability of anxiety creates the possibility of doubt and of being torn between trust in God and trust in oneself to secure meaning. As Tillich recognizes, doubt is always an element in existential faith: "Faith is certain in so far as it is an experience of the holy. But faith is uncertain in so far as the infinite to which it is related is received by a finite being."[103] Because the

---

100. Kierkegaard, *Sickness Unto Death*, 51–53.
101. E. Becker, *Denial of Death*, 277.
102. Kierkegaard, *Concept of Anxiety*, 117.
103. Tillich, *Dynamics of Faith*, 16.

The Religious Motive of Consumerism and How It May Be Redirected

self is finite and reflexive, faith entails existential risk. Indeed, every commitment to a particular existential strategy is a risk in which the finite self is wagered by affirming one ground of meaning among many, even though this plurality of meaning systems may be hidden. The risk is that "a wrong faith can destroy the meaning of one's life."[104] Every person whose meaning is grounded through existential Christian faith lives in a dialectical tension between faith and doubt. Her or his realization of New Being is fragmentary and ambiguous. To the extent that an existential Christian responds to the threat of meaninglessness with existential faith, he or she actively renounces the anxiety of meaningless, actively trusts in the divine establishment of his or her meaning through the agency of Jesus as the Christ, and exercises a centered moral freedom motivated by love of God, his or her fellow human beings, and other life, present and future. To the extent that an existential Christian responds to the threat of meaninglessness with doubt, he or she is driven by the threat of meaninglessness to strive to secure himself or herself through some self-securing meaning strategy, his or her will is bound to prioritize that strategy at the expense of the moral demands of his or her essential nature, and he or she fails to act as a centered self, and instead acts to disintegrate the self. Since all realization of New Being under the conditions of human existence is ambiguous,[105] these dialectical movements are simultaneous, although at any given moment in time one or the other may be relatively more influential.

In Christian communal life, as Tillich recognizes, New Being is similarly ambiguous. To the extent that those in the church respond to the threat of meaninglessness with existential Christian faith, the church participates in the essential character of the Spiritual Community in which the Holy Spirit, which bears the power of the unconditioned ground of meaning, grasps individuals ecstatically in faith and overcomes their estrangement. In this participation, existential Christians are united in love with God and one another, producing a divinely-attuned morality and a morally serious, creative culture. To the extent that those in the church respond to the threat of meaninglessness with doubt, the church responds with efforts to secure the meaning of its members and its institutions with all of the distorting, disintegrating, and personally destructive consequences entailed by such efforts towards self-securing.[106]

---

104. Tillich, *Systematic Theology*, vol. 2, 116–17.
105. Ibid., 178–79.
106. Tillich, *Systematic Theology*, vol. 3, 115, 129, 155–65.

Theological Validation of the Proposed Alternative to Consumerism

Now that I have elaborated the claim that existential Christian faith provides an answer to the problem of individual meaning that is existentially more secure and morally less troubling than consumerism, I evaluate this claim's consistency with the Pauline-Augustinian-Lutheran tradition in Christian theology. The first criterion from this theological tradition that I consider is the Augustinian insight—affirmed by the Protestant Reformers—that moral forms of life and religious-existential orientations are inextricably bound together. Martin Luther labeled this insight "the bondage of the will."[107] As Tillich interprets it, "the bondage of the will . . . is the inability of man to break through his estrangement. . . . Attempts to overcome estrangement within the power of one's estranged existence lead to hard toil and tragic failure."[108] This may be understood as a particular case of Adler's insight into the relationship between existential concern and moral motivation. The doctrine of the bondage of the will is affirmed in my claim that the moral motivation of consumerism is bound to the need to secure one's subjective claim to meaning through social validation. Indeed, every existential strategy by which an individual seeks to secure his or her own meaningfulness is similarly bound, as I argued in the case of conventional religion. I have argued that only the moral motivation of the person of existential faith is free from the need to secure individual meaning by her or his own efforts, but this person's freedom is not therefore independent of her or his meaning system. Rather, precisely because she or he is united with God, the unconditioned ground of meaning, she or he participates in the activity of the divine life whose essence is love, and this participation directs her or his moral motivation towards love of God, other persons, other generations, and other life.

My second theological criterion for evaluating the correlation between the existential question of meaning and existential Christian faith is human beings' naturally self-referential will. This position is recognized in the traditional doctrine of "original sin." It coincides with Fromm's observation concerning human beings' natural narcissism. Following Augustine's injunction that the self is something that a person is to use, not enjoy,

---

107. Augustine, *City of God*, 14.13, 14.28; Luther, "Bondage of the Will." See also Calvin, *Institutes*, 2.7.1.

108. Tillich, *Systematic Theology*, vol. 2, 79-80.

The Religious Motive of Consumerism and How It May Be Redirected

Luther described the nature of human beings after the Fall as "curved in upon itself."[109] Tillich prefers to describe this situation in terms of universal estrangement. By estrangement, Tillich means that "man as he exists is not what he essentially is and ought to be."[110] This implies that the natural direction of the human will towards the self cannot be altered apart from a change in a person's basic religious-existential orientation. I have affirmed the doctrine of original sin, in the first place, by my argument that social and historical meaning strategies are strategies by which an individual seeks to secure himself or herself through his or her own agency. Therefore, the moral motivation of persons who employ these strategies is self-referential. In the second place, among possible metaphysical grounds of meaning, I have argued that Christian faith is distinctive in that individual meaning is secured by another agency, that of the Christ. This frees an individual's moral motivation from the need to secure his or her own meaning.

My third theological criterion for evaluating the correlation between the existential question of meaning and existential Christian faith is the recognition that subjective reporting cannot fully account for persons' motives. Not only may individuals' motives be unconscious without sustained and rigorous introspection but, because of their existential need for justification, human beings naturally avoid any such introspection that might present their conduct in a morally unfavorable light. Furthermore, persons tend to affirm one another in their morally sanguine self-assessments. This theological insight is found in the Protestant doctrine of the noetic effect of sin.[111] Tillich argues that this theological insight has been affirmed by existentialist philosophy and modern psychoanalysis. "One of the most striking facts about the dynamics of the human personality is the intentional ignorance concerning one's real motives. The motives themselves are bodily and psychic strivings, often far removed from what appears as conscious reason in a centered decision."[112] These unconscious motives, Tillich maintains, are ethically significant because they are impervious to the influence of the moral law.[113] I have affirmed the doctrine of the noetic effect of sin by arguing that unconsciousness of one's existential meaning strategy contrib-

---

109. Augustine, *On Christine Teaching*, 1.22; Luther, "Lectures on Romans," 291. See also Calvin, *Institutes*, 2.1.2.

110. Tillich, *Systematic Theology*, vol. 2, 45.

111. See Luther, "Heidelberg Disputation," 39; Luther, "Smalcald Articles," 311; Calvin, *Institutes*, 2.1.2, 2.7.6.

112. Tillich, *Systematic Theology*, vol. 2, 42.

113. Tillich, *Systematic Theology*, vol. 3, 49.

utes to the success of that strategy when an individual's meaning strategy rests upon social validation. Given that moral motivation is bound to an individual's existential meaning strategy, unconsciousness of one's meaning strategy dictates unconsciousness of one's moral motivation.

My fourth theological criterion for evaluating the correlation between the existential question of meaning and existential Christian faith is the Protestant tradition's explanation of religious-existential, and therefore moral, fragmentation and self-contradiction. Protestant theology, at least in the predominant Reformation traditions, does not suppose that persons of Christian faith are either wholly Christian and wholly moral or wholly unchristian and wholly immoral. This doctrine is traditionally formulated in the expression *simul justus et peccator*, at the same time justified and sinner, which follows St. Paul's description of the divided will in Rom 7:15–23. The expression *simul justus et peccator* indicates that existential Christians hold contradictory religious-existential ends that are at war with one another.[114] Tillich affirms that "the paradoxical formula, *simul peccator, simul justus* . . . is decisive for the whole Christian message as the salvation from despair about one's guilt. It is actually the only way to overcome the anxiety of guilt; it enables man to look away from himself and his state of estrangement and self-destruction to the justifying act of God."[115] This formula explains the fragmentary and ambiguous fulfillment of Christian morality in the Spiritual Community. The *simul justus et peccator* doctrine is affirmed in my description of the ambiguous dialectic of faith and doubt that characterizes New Being in lived experience. This affirmation leads me to describe the movements of faith and doubt as simultaneous, despite the fact that one or the other may exert greater influence over the will at any particular moment in time.

In addition to these four theological criteria, I affirm Tillich's description of the religious functionality of existential questions and forms of life, and his claim that there is a correspondence between the existential question of meaning and the answer offered by the Christian message. Finally, I situate my proposal within Christian theology generally by identifying Jesus as the Christ, the agent of religious-existential transformation.

In this chapter I have demonstrated that consumerism is a religious-existential form of life that serves as a strategy to secure the meaning of the self against the existential threat of meaninglessness. I have argued that

---

114. See Luther, "Lectures on Galatians," 235; Calvin, *Institutes*, 3.3.10.
115. Tillich, *Systematic Theology*, vol. 2, 178.

the moral harms of consumerism may be avoided by conversion to existential Christian faith, which frees persons from bondage to self-securing pursuits and moves them to seek the well being of other persons, other generations, and other life. The dilemma of a religious answer to a moral problem, when the religious answer depends on grace, is that persons cannot escape the moral harms of consumerism simply by seeking to do so. This is because persons who ground the meanings of their lives through consumerism must act to maintain that meaning system in order to avoid existential failure and the despair of meaninglessness. Therefore, they must participate in the moral harms that consumerism engenders, even though they may deplore consumerism's moral harms, considered in abstraction from the meaning strategy that produces them, and even though they may deny their own consumeristic meaning strategy and contribution to those harms. This is a specific instance of a problem that Augustine identifies: the inability to seek a morality for oneself that one does not already possess.[116] However, the knowledge that consumerism is an existential meaning strategy may contribute to the failure of consumerism as an existential strategy for some persons if they cannot avoid recognizing their own meaning strategy in this description. Since self-concealment contributes to the viability of consumerism as a meaning strategy, the disclosure of consumerism as an individual's existential meaning strategy may be a means of existential failure. Therefore it may be a means of grace, given that existential failure is the precondition for conversion to another meaning system and the first movement of grace in the *metanoia* that leads to existential faith.

Existential failure is encountered as grace only if the self is immediately grasped by the power of New Being in faith. Otherwise, the individual in existential failure will grasp at whatever alternate self-securing strategy presents itself in order to avoid remaining in the despair of meaninglessness. Therefore, the promise in the Christian message of New Being through Jesus as the Christ must be present along with the disclosure of consumerism's moral cost and inadequacy as a meaning strategy if consumerism is to be superseded by existential faith. Only then will the individual be able, through participation in the activity of the divine life whose essence is love, to direct his or her moral motivation to the well being of other persons, other generations, and other life without concern for his or her own significance. If she or he fails to do so, she or he must grasp at another self-securing strategy and thereby bind herself or himself to another self-referential moral motivation.

116. Augustine, "Morals of the Catholic Church," 6.

6

Conclusion

IN THIS BOOK, I have shown, first, that consumerism is a significant problem in the contemporary world. In chapter 1, I described the scope of consumerism's negative personal, social, and environmental consequences. In chapter 4 I provided evidence for my initial assumption that consumerism is widespread enough in Western nations to produce measurable effects on national economic statistics. Given the interdependence of the contemporary global economy, if consumerism is widespread enough to influence Western economic statistics, its negative social and environmental consequences are widespread enough to undermine economic justice and environmental sustainability worldwide.

Despite the moral pluralism of contemporary Western societies, I illustrated in chapter 1 how the consequences of consumerism are morally unacceptable across many possible forms of ethical understanding and ethical commitment, from egoism to Kantian universalism. However, because consumerism is rarely confessed among those persons for whom it functions as an existential meaning strategy, most moral judgments with respect to consumerism are directed only towards its most egregious practitioners—for example, spendthrift corporate bosses, social climbers, compulsive shoppers, or "yuppies" (young urban professionals)—rather than the full population of those who participate to some degree in this form of life. An honest moral accounting would have to acknowledge that it is very difficult for any of us who live in Western cultures to avoid participating in consumerism to some degree.

Second, I have substantiated my claim that consumerism has been poorly understood. In chapter 3, I reviewed the major thinkers who have addressed consumerism and classified their theories into a typology according to their explanation of consumerism's motivation. In chapter 4, I developed empirical findings that falsified all of the theories belonging to these five types, to greater or lesser degree. Consumerism is not hedonistic. It is not a loss of control to advertisers. It is not confined to one social class or household type. It is not generally conscious in decision-making. It is not simply a relationship between a person and his or her goods, but something social as well. Historically, it has become widespread only in the past few decades. The consequence of consumerism being poorly understood is that too little has been done or even proposed that could effectively limit its destructive consequences. Without knowing why persons are motivated to lead consumeristic lives, it is impossible to know how they could be motivated to change.

Third, I have demonstrated that consumerism's motivation is religious. It is religious in the sense that consumerism is a strategy aimed at answering the existential question of meaning. In chapter 5, I show how the consumeristic individual seeks to secure her or his claim to a meaningful life. Since consumerism functions as an existential strategy to secure meaning and since the existential imperative to secure one's personal meaning is absolute, consumerism overrides a person's other goals and norms when conflicts arise. This existential imperative shapes a form of life organized according to the consumer culture's institutions and norms of social validation. The desired social validation takes the form of other persons' categorical recognition of the individual's life as sufficiently important to be evaluated and responded to as an individual subject, a meaningful self. Recognition is sought primarily from persons within the individual's own social group, since they share an interest in upholding a norm of mutual recognition within the group. To maximize the likelihood of recognition, the individual must endlessly consume—and produce the means of consumption for—those good-signs most likely to elicit others' recognition. In chapter 5, I validated my religious-existential interpretation of consumerism empirically. This interpretation is consistent with all of the empirical findings that I developed in chapter 4.

In chapter 2, I proposed that consumerism has become so prevalent in contemporary Western cultures because of the historical failure of the answers that these cultures previously offered to the existential problem of meaningful individual life. In recent decades, many formerly widespread meaning strategies have been empirically falsified or diminished in plausibility. This corresponds to the period in which consumerism emerges as a dominant form of life in the West, according to my findings in chapter 4. Of course, human creativity is capable of generating new existential strategies when faced with the existential need for meaningful individual life and the failure of previous meaning systems. Nevertheless, Western cultures have largely failed to institutionalize any new answers to the existential problem of meaning that are less destructive than consumerism. In chapter 2, I suggested three reasons why environmentalism is failing to fulfill this role: it offers a collective rather than an individual meaning, it is readily co-opted by consumerism, and it is vulnerable to historical refutation.

Fourth, I have shown—at least to those who acknowledge the substance of the Christian message as ultimate concern—that, rightly understood, Christian faith is an existentially and morally superior answer to the problem of meaning that consumerism seeks to answer. This is not an affirmation of Christian religion as it generally exists in the West today. Traditional religious meaning strategies that rely on trust in religious authority or social validation have lost ground to secularization in Europe and to syntheses with consumerism in North America. By secularization, I do not mean that religious substance has disappeared in European cultures but that it is increasingly found outside the explicitly religious sphere of culture. Since they are not explicitly and intentionally religious, meaning systems in secularized cultures are less likely to be understood as religious.

Fifth, for those who claim the substance of the Christian message as ultimate concern, I have shown that consumerism is a religious problem. The disclosure that consumerism functions as a religion reveals an inescapable contradiction between the consumeristic form of life and existential Christian faith. Stated in terms of the norms of the Christian scripture, a form of life which intrinsically violates the command "You shall love your neighbor as yourself" (Matt 22:39, NRSV) reveals the logically prior sin of idolatry, that is, the violation of the First Commandment, "You shall love the Lord your God with all your heart, and with all your soul, and with all your mind" (Matt 22:37, NRSV).[1] The disclosure that one has failed to keep God's commandments and is therefore not reconciled to God is the necessary precursor to the possibility of repentance and conversion to existential Christian faith, whether this transformation is the initial movement

---

1. While my standpoint here is explicitly Christian, these passages quote Levitcus 19:18 and Deuteronomy 6:5 respectively, giving this insight validity for persons of Jewish religious identification as well.

to existential faith or part of a process of ongoing conversion within the ambiguity of faith and doubt.

Christians cannot claim that consumerism is only a religious and moral problem for non-Christians. The research of Robert Wuthnow that I cited in chapter 2 demonstrates the prevalence of consumeristic behaviors and dispositions among self-identified Christians. Since consumerism functions religiously as an answer to the question of meaning, Wuthnow's research suggests that idolatry is prevalent among self-professed Christians. This does not necessarily imply simple hypocrisy, since, as I observed in chapter 5, Protestant theology recognizes that the Christian is at the same time justified and sinner. However, the dialectical opposition between faith and doubt cannot be resolved into a stable synthesis of faith and consumerism. The person of existential Christian faith remains divided and in conflict. While the disclosure of self-contradiction can and should lead to further conversion towards existential faith, this faith always retains some measure of doubt and religious ambiguity.

On the other hand, Wuthnow's research may point to hypocrisy as well as ambiguity. Persons who self-identify as Christians in research surveys include those who seek to secure meaning through conventional religion, not just persons of existential faith. Søren Kierkegaard's description of the man of immediacy, which I quoted in chapter 5, illustrates the compatibility between different socially-validated meaning systems. There is no inherent contradiction in a stable synthesis of consumerism and conventional Christian religion since they are both socially-validated forms of life. Whether the idolatry implied by Wuthnow's research represents ambiguity or hypocrisy, the answer disclosed by the Christian message is the imperative of repentance and conversion to existential Christian faith. The implication for the Christian churches is that they cannot transcend the problem of consumerism by advocating moral striving. The churches can only transcend consumerism through their normative function: the mediation of the means of grace, that is, the means of conversion to existential Christian faith and of ongoing conversion within ambiguous existential Christian faith. These means include the disclosure that the consumeristic individual is not fully reconciled to God, and the promise that the unacceptable individual is nevertheless accepted and reconciled to God by the agency of Jesus as the Christ.

What do my findings mean for those who seek to counteract the problem of consumerism, individually and socially? Without appealing to any particular theological standpoint, my research shows that the roots of consumerism lie in a problem of the human condition, the threat that human finitude poses to the meaning of an individual life. Because it is rooted in a problem of the human condition, some credible alternative existential strategy is needed if the moral harms of consumerism are to be overcome. Secular Western cultures can only ameliorate consumerism's moral harms if they can create widely plausible and effective alternate meaning strategies within which the existential imperative to secure a meaningful life does not conflict with striving to secure the good of other persons, other generations, and other life. Whether secular cultures are capable of providing viable alternate meaning strategies that are fully compatible with concern for other persons, other generations, and other life, and what those strategies might be, are questions beyond the scope of this book. I claim only that existential Christian faith does provide such an alternative, and that secular Western cultures have not thus far provided one.

While consumerism has functionally religious roots, its prevalence in Western cultures and consumerism's repression of self-understanding make these roots difficult for many to acknowledge. To the extent that persons in a society rely on consumerism to validate their personal meaning while holding conscious values that conflict with consumerism, that society may seek to treat the symptoms of consumerism without treating its causes. However, unless and until Western cultures move toward another meaning system or systems, political efforts to achieve social goals like poverty reduction or climate change mitigation will be resisted by consumeristic persons. Consumeristic persons cannot choose to limit their consumption for the sake of social goals, since that would be to act contrary to their need for existential meaning.

For persons who confess Christian faith, my findings offer the possibility of a deeper level of self-awareness and self-critique according to the moral and religious norms of their own tradition. For example, wherever there is evidence of syncretism between consumerism and Christianity, this indicates the presence of both consumerism and conventional Christian religion, both of which reflect trust in social validation rather than divine validation of personal meaningfulness. In traditional theological language, both consumerism and conventional religion are forms of idolatry. Likewise, any attempt by the churches to condemn consumerism in their cultures that fails to recognize their own implication in this form of life is an exercise in scapegoating, which is a sign of socially-validated conventional religion rather than existential Christian faith. Without the self-awareness and self-critique that I propose here, the churches will fail to identify consumerism for what it is—a rival to existential Christian faith at the level of religious function. If they fail to name consumerism for what it is, the churches will also fail to fulfill their normative function: to mediate the means of conversion to—and ongoing conversion within—existential Christian faith.

In this conclusion, I have offered some preliminary observations on consumerism's interaction with the meaning systems of existential and conventional Christian religion. Wuthnow's research, which I cited in chapter 2, suggests a situational polytheism between consumerism and conventional Christian religion. Recalling Tillich's distinction between the form, content, and substance of cultural creations, it is useful to distinguish between syncretism at the level of religious forms and content and situational polytheism at the level of religious-existential function. This question is complicated by the distinction that must be maintained between conventional Christian religion and existential Christian faith. In a culture like the contemporary United States in which the profession of Christianity and the practice of consumerism are both widespread, there is a threefold relationship of meaning systems that encompasses consumerism, conventional Christian religion, and existential Christian faith. While a thorough exploration of this threefold relationship is beyond the scope of this book, it deserves further investigation at the communal as well as the individual level. Since existential Christian faith is normative within the churches, the question of how this norm may be fostered in communal forms that are permeated by a competing functional religion has great urgency for contemporary Christian ethics.

While consumerism has been described in many ways, I have demonstrated in this book that it has not been well understood. My disclosure of consumerism as an existential meaning strategy represents a possibility. It is the possibility that participation in consumerism by those who rightly condemn its moral consequences may be undermined by greater self-understanding. It is the possibility that this self-understanding may daily free those who participate in consumerism to be given the power to live new lives, freed through trust in a meaning that is already given from the need to strive to secure meaningful lives, free to reject consumerism's imperatives and to seek the well being of other persons, other generations, and other life.

Appendix 1

Regression model for U.S. real annual household housing expenditures, 1984–2006

Regression Analysis:

LGHSEXP versus YEAR, MARRIED, MINCHILD
Weighted analysis using weights in CONSUNIT

The regression equation is:

LGHSEXP = - 21.3 + 0.0150 YEAR + 0.296 MARRIED + 0.249 MINCHILD

Predictor	Coef	SE Coef	T	P	VIF
Constant	-21.264	1.709	12.44	0.000	
YEAR	0.0149981	0.0008563	17.52	0.000	1.002
MARRIED	0.29642	0.01193	24.85	0.000	1.106
MINCHILD	0.24869	0.01344	18.50	0.000	1.105

S = 8.58067   R-Sq = 92.4%   R-Sq(adj) = 92.2%

Analysis of Variance

Source	DF	SS	MS	F	P
Regression	3	119630	39877	541.60	0.000
Residual Error	134	9866	74		
Total	137	129496			

Shopping for Meaningful Lives

Source	DF	Seq SS
YEAR	1	18655
MARRIED	1	75779
MINCHILD	1	25196

LGHSEXP = natural log of real annual household housing expenditures

YEAR = year

MARRIED = 1 if the household includes a married couple, else 0

MINCHILD = 1 if the household includes children 17 years of age or less, else 0

The regression is weighted by the number of U.S. consumer units (households) in thousands.

Sources: U.S. Department of Labor, Consumer Expenditures Survey; U.S. Department of Labor, Consumer Price Index.

APPENDIX 2

Regression models for U.S. real annual household housing expenses, 1984–2006, for a) households without minor children, and b) households with minor children

a) Results for: MINCHILD = 0

Regression Analysis:

LGHSEXP versus YEAR, MARRIED
Weighted analysis using weights in CONSUNIT

The regression equation is:
LGHSEXP = - 20.4 + 0.0146 YEAR + 0.250 MARRIED

Predictor	Coef	SE Coef	T	P	VIF
Constant	-20.380	1.961	-10.39	0.000	
YEAR	0.0145650	0.0009827	14.82	0.000	1.001
MARRIED	0.24996	0.01322	18.90	0.000	1.001

S = 8.42553   R-Sq = 89.4%   R-Sq(adj) = 89.1%

Analysis of Variance

Source	DF	SS	MS	F	P
Regression	2	39683	19842	279.50	0.000
Residual Error	66	4685	71		
Total	68	44369			

Source	DF	Seq SS
YEAR	1	14320
MARRIED	1	25364

LGHSEXP = natural log of real annual household housing expenditures
YEAR = year
MARRIED = 1 if the household includes a married couple, else 0
MINCHILD = 1 if the household includes children 17 years of age or less, else 0

The regression is weighted by the number of U.S. consumer units (households) in thousands.

Sources: U.S. Department of Labor, Consumer Expenditures Survey; U.S. Department of Labor, Consumer Price Index

Appendix 2

b) Results for: MINCHILD = 1

Regression Analysis:

LGHSEXP versus YEAR, MARRIED
Weighted analysis using weights in CONSUNIT

The regression equation is:

LGHSEXP = -23.4 + 0.0161 YEAR + 0.465 MARRIED

Predictor	Coef	SE Coef	T	P	VIF
Constant	-23.415	1.571	-14.90	0.000	
YEAR	0.0161367	0.0007873	20.50	0.000	1.001
MARRIED	0.46504	0.01222	38.06	0.000	1.001

S = 4.08378 R-Sq = 96.5% R-Sq(adj) = 96.4%

Analysis of Variance

Source	DF	SS	MS	F	P
Regression	2	30542	15271	915.67	0.000
Residual Error	66	1101	17		
Total	68	31642			

Source	DF	Seq SS
YEAR	1	6383
MARRIED	1	24158

LGHSEXP	= natural log of real annual household housing expenditures
YEAR	= year
MARRIED	= 1 if the household includes a married couple, else 0
MINCHILD	= 1 if the household includes children 17 years of age or less, else 0

The regression is weighted by the number of U.S. consumer units (households) in thousands.

Sources: U.S. Department of Labor, Consumer Expenditures Survey; U.S. Department of Labor, Consumer Price Index.

APPENDIX 3

Regression models for U.S. real annual household housing expenses, 1984–2006, for:

a) bottom household income quintile,
b) second household income quintile,
c) middle household income quintile,
d) fourth household income quintile, and
e) top household income quintile

a) Results for: QUINTILE = 1

Regression Analysis:

LGHSEXP versus YEAR
Weighted analysis using weights in CONSUNIT

The regression equation is:

LGHSEXP = -14.0 + 0.0112 YEAR

Predictor	Coef	SE Coef	T	P	VIF
Constant	-14.021	2.403	-5.84	0.000	
YEAR	0.011171	0.001204	9.28	0.000	1.000

S = 5.23837   R-Sq = 80.4%   R-Sq(adj) = 79.5%

Analysis of Variance

Source	DF	SS	MS	F	P
Regression	1	2362.2	2362.2	86.08	0.000
Residual Error	21	576.3	27.4		
Total	22	2938.4			

LGHSEXP = natural log of real annual household housing expenses
YEAR = year
QUINTILE = U.S. household income quintile

The regression is weighted by the number of U.S. consumer units (households) in thousands.

Sources: U.S. Department of Labor, Consumer Expenditures Survey, U.S. Department of Labor, Consumer Price Index.

b) Results for: QUINTILE = 2

Regression Analysis:

LGHSEXP versus YEAR
Weighted analysis using weights in CONSUNIT

The regression equation is:

LGHSEXP = -21.6 + 0.0151 YEAR

Predictor	Coef	SE Coef	T	P	VIF
Constant	-21.586	1.522	-14.18	0.000	
YEAR	0.0150947	0.0007682	19.79	0.000	1.000

S = 3.32228   R-Sq = 94.9%   R-Sq(adj) = 94.7%

Analysis of Variance

Source	DF	SS	MS	F	P
Regression	1	4322.0	4322.0	391.57	0.000
Residual Error	21	231.8	11.0		
Total	22	4553.8			

LGHSEXP = natural log of real annual household housing expenses
YEAR   = year
QUINTILE = U.S. household income quintile

The regression is weighted by the number of U.S. consumer units (households) in thousands.

Sources: U.S. Department of Labor, Consumer Expenditures Survey, U.S. Department of Labor, Consumer Price Index.

Appendix 3

c) Results for: QUINTILE = 3

Regression Analysis:

LGHSEXP versus YEAR
Weighted analysis using weights in CONSUNIT

The regression equation is:

LGHSEXP = - 19.0 + 0.0139 YEAR

Predictor	Coef	SE Coef	T	P	VIF
Constant	-19.043	1.757	-10.84	0.000	
YEAR	0.0139454	0.0008803	15.84	0.000	1.000

S = 3.83271   R-Sq = 92.3%   R-Sq(adj) = 91.9%

Analysis of Variance

Source	DF	SS	MS	F	P
Regression	1	3686.5	3686.5	250.96	0.000
Residual Error	21	308.5	14.7		
Total	22	3395.0			

LGHSEXP   = natural log of real annual household housing expenses
YEAR   = year
QUINTILE = U.S. household income quintile

The regression is weighted by the number of U.S. consumer units (households) in thousands.

Sources: U.S. Department of Labor, Consumer Expenditures Survey, U.S. Department of Labor, Consumer Price Index.

d) Results for: QUINTILE = 4

Regression Analysis:

LGHSEXP versus YEAR
Weighted analysis using weights in CONSUNIT

The regression equation is:

LGHSEXP = - 18.3 + 0.0137 YEAR

Predictor	Coef	SE Coef	T	P	VIF
Constant	-18.339	1.873	-9.79	0.000	
YEAR	0.0137213	0.0009386	14.62	0.000	1.000

S = 4.08795   R-Sq = 91.1%   R-Sq(adj) = 90.6%

Analysis of Variance

Source	DF	SS	MS	F	P
Regression	1	3571.2	3571.2	213.70	0.000
Residual Error	21	350.9	16.7		
Total	22	3922.1			

LGHSEXP = natural log of real annual household housing expenses
YEAR = year
QUINTILE = U.S. household income quintile

The regression is weighted by the number of U.S. consumer units (households) in thousands.

Sources: U.S. Department of Labor, Consumer Expenditures Survey, U.S. Department of Labor, Consumer Price Index.

Appendix 3

e) Results for: QUINTILE = 5

Regression Analysis:

LGHSEXP versus YEAR
Weighted analysis using weights in CONSUNIT

The regression equation is:

LGHSEXP = - 20.3 + 0.0149 YEAR

Predictor	Coef	SE Coef	T	P	VIF
Constant	-20.291	2.362	-8.59	0.000	
YEAR	0.014926	0.001184	12.61	0.000	1.000

S = 5.15877   R-Sq = 88.3%   R-Sq(adj) = 87.8%

Analysis of Variance

Source	DF	SS	MS	F	P
Regression	1	4231.1	4231.1	158.99	0.000
Residual Error	21	558.9	26.6		
Total	22	4789.9			

LGHSEXP = natural log of real annual household housing expenses
YEAR = year
QUINTILE = U.S. household income quintile

The regression is weighted by the number of U.S. consumer units (households) in thousands.

Sources: U.S. Department of Labor, Consumer Expenditures Survey, U.S. Department of Labor, Consumer Price Index.

Bibliography

Adler, Alfred. *The Individual Psychology of Alfred Adler: A Systematic Presentation in Selections from His Writings*. Edited by Heinz L. Ansbacher and Rowena R. Ansbacher. New York: Basic, 1956.

Alpizar, Francisco, Fredrik Carlsson, and Olof Johansson-Stenman. "How Much Do We Care About Absolute versus Relative Income and Consumption?" *Journal of Economic Behavior and Organization* 56:3 (March 2005) 405–21.

Aquinas, Thomas. *Summa Theologica*. Vol. 2. Translated by Fathers of the English Dominican Province. New York: Benziger Brothers, 1947.

Ariely, Dan. *Predictably Irrational: The Hidden Forces That Shape Our Decisions*. New York: HarperCollins, 2008.

Askegaard, Søren, and A. Fuat Firat. "Towards a Critique of Material Culture, Consumption and Markets." In *Experiencing Material Culture in the Western World*, edited by Susan M. Pearce, 114–39. London: Leicester University Press, 1997.

Augustine. *City of God*. Translated by Henry Bettenson. New York: Penguin, 1984.

———. *On Christian Teaching*. Translated by R. P. H. Green. Oxford: Oxford University Press, 1997.

———. "On the Morals of the Catholic Church." In *Basic Writings of Saint Augustine*, vol. 1, edited by Whitney J. Oates, 319–57. Grand Rapids: Baker, 1948.

Baker, William E. "When Can Affective Conditioning and Mere Exposure Directly Influence Brand Choice?" *Journal of Advertising* 28:4 (Winter 1999) 31–46.

Bargh, John A., and Tanya L. Chartrand. "The Unbearable Automaticity of Being." *American Psychologist* 54:7 (July 1999) 462–79.

Bargh, John A., et al. "The Automatic Evaluation Effect: Unconditional Automatic Attitude Activation With a Pronunciation Task." *Journal of Experimental Social Psychology* 32:1 (January 1996) 104–28.

Baudrillard, Jean. *The Consumer Society: Myths and Structures*. London: Sage, 1998.

———. *For a Critique of the Political Economy of the Sign*. Translated by Charles Levin. St. Louis: Telos, 1981.

———. *The Mirror of Production*. Translated by Mark Poster. St. Louis: Telos, 1975.

———. "The System of Objects." In *Selected Writings*, translated and edited by Mark Poster, 13–31. Stanford, CA: Stanford University Press, 2001.

Baumeister, Roy F., et al. "Free Will in Consumer Behavior: Self-control, Ego Depletion, and Choice." *Journal of Consumer Psychology* 18:1 (January 2008) 4–13.

Beck, Ulrich. *Risk Society: Towards a New Modernity*. Translated by Mark Ritter. London: Sage, 1992.

Becker, Ernest. *The Birth and Death of Meaning*. New York: Free Press, 1971.

———. *The Denial of Death*. New York: Free Press, 1973.

———. *Escape from Evil*. New York: Free Press, 1975.

Becker, Gary S. *Accounting for Tastes*. Cambridge, MA: Harvard University Press, 1996.

Belk, Russell W. "Changing Consumer: Changing Disciplinarity." In *The Changing Consumer: Markets and Meanings*, edited by Steven Miles, Alison Anderson, and Kevin Meethan, 145–61. London: Routledge, 2002.

Bell, Daniel. *The Cultural Contradictions of Capitalism*. New York: Basic, 1976.

Bibliography

Boss, Shira. *Green With Envy: Why Keeping Up With the Joneses Is Keeping Us in Debt.* New York: Warner Business, 2006.

Bourdieu, Pierre. *Distinction: A Social Critique of the Judgment of Taste.* Translated by Richard Nice. Cambridge, MA: Harvard University Press, 1984.

Boyle, Nicholas. *Who Are We Now? Christian Humanism and the Global Market from Hegel to Heaney.* Notre Dame: University of Notre Dame Press, 1998.

Brown, Lester. *Plan B 2.0: Rescuing a Planet Under Stress and a Civilization in Trouble.* New York: Norton, 2006.

Browning, Don S. *Marriage and Modernization: How Globalization Threatens Marriage and What To Do About It.* Grand Rapids: Eerdmans, 2003.

Bunting, David. "The Saving Decline: Macro-facts, Micro-behavior." *Journal of Economic Behavior and Organization* 70:1–2 (May 2009) 282–95.

Calvin, John. *Institutes of the Christian Religion.* Edited by John T. McNeill. Translated by Ford Lewis Battles. 2 vols. Louisville: Westminster John Knox, 1960.

Campbell, Colin. "Character and Consumption: An Historical Action Theory Approach to the Understanding of Consumer Behavior." *Culture and History* 7 (1990) 37–48.

———. "Considering Others and Satisfying the Self: The Moral and Ethical Dimension of Modern Consumption." In *The Moralization of the Markets*, edited by Nico Stehr, Christoph Henning, and Bernd Weiler, 213–26. New Brunswick, NJ: Transaction, 2006.

———. "Consuming Goods and the Goods of Consuming." In *Ethics of Consumption: The Good Life, Justice, and Global Stewardship*, edited by David A. Crocker and Toby Linden, 139–54. Lanham, MD: Rowman & Littlefield, 1998.

———. *The Romantic Ethic and the Spirit of Modern Consumerism.* Oxford: Blackwell, 1987.

———. "*The Romantic Ethic and the Spirit of Modern Consumerism*: Reflections on the Reception of a Thesis Concerning the Origin of the Continuing Desire for Goods." In *Experiencing Material Culture in the Western World*, edited by Susan M. Pearce, 36–48. London: Leicester University Press, 1997.

Carlsson, Fredrik, Olof Johansson-Stenman, and Peter Martinsson. "Do You Enjoy Having More Than Others? Survey Evidence of Positional Goods." *Economica* 74:296 (November 2007) 586–98.

Cavanaugh, William T. *Being Consumed: Economics and Christian Desire.* Grand Rapids: Eerdmans, 2008.

Chartrand, Tanya L. "The Role of Conscious Awareness in Consumer Behavior." *Journal of Consumer Psychology* 15:3 (2005) 203–10.

Cohen, Patricia, and Jacob Cohen. *Life Values and Adolescent Mental Health.* Mahwah, NJ: Erlbaum, 1996.

Cornford, Francis M. *From Religion to Philosophy: A Study in the Origins of Western Speculation.* London: E. Arnold, 1912.

Cushman, Philip. "Why the Self is Empty: Toward a Historically Situated Psychology." *American Psychologist* 45:5 (May 1990) 599–611.

Deffeyes, Kenneth S. *Hubbert's Peak: The Impending World Oil Shortage.* Princeton: Princeton University Press, 2001.

DeNavas-Walt, Carmen, Bernadette D. Proctor, and Jessica C. Smith. U.S. Census Bureau, Current Population Reports, P60-235, *Income, Poverty, and Health Insurance Coverage in the United States: 2007.* U.S. Government Printing Office, Washington, DC, 2008. Online: http://www.census.gov/prod/2008pubs/p60-235.pdf.

Bibliography

Diamond, Jared M. *Collapse: How Societies Choose to Fail or Succeed.* New York: Viking, 2005.
Diggins, John P. *The Bard of Savagery: Thorstein Veblen and Modern Social Theory.* New York: Seabury, 1978.
Dittmar, Helga. *The Social Psychology of Material Possessions.* New York: St. Martin's, 1992.
Douglas, Mary, and Baron Isherwood. *The World of Goods.* New York: Basic, 1979.
Duesenberry, James S. *Income, Saving and the Theory of Consumer Behavior.* Cambridge, MA: Harvard University Press, 1949.
Duffy, Martyn H. "Advertising and the Inter-product Distribution of Demand: A Rotterdam Model Approach." *European Economic Review* 31:5 (July 1987) 1051–70.
Dunlap, Thomas R. *Faith in Nature: Environmentalism as Religious Quest.* Seattle: University of Washington Press, 2004.
Eagleton, Terry. *The Crisis of Contemporary Culture.* Oxford: Clarendon, 1993.
———. *The Idea of Culture.* Oxford: Blackwell, 2000.
Easterlin, Richard A. "Income and Happiness: Towards an Unified Theory." *Economic Journal* 111:473 (July 2001) 465–84.
———. "Will Raising the Incomes of All Increase the Happiness of All?" *Journal of Economic Behavior and Organization* 27:1 (June 1995) 35–47.
Emerson, Ralph Waldo. "Nature." In *The Selected Writings of Ralph Waldo Emerson*, edited by Brooks Atkinson, 3–42. New York: Modern Library, 1992.
European Union. "The History of the European Union: 1957." No pages. Online: http://europa.eu/abc/history/1945-1959/1957/index_en.htm.
———. "Member States of the EU." No pages. Online: http://europa.eu/abc/european_countries/index_en.htm.
Frank, Robert H. *Choosing the Right Pond: Human Behavior and the Quest for Status.* New York: Oxford University Press, 1985.
———. "The Demand for Unobservable and Other Nonpositional Goods." *American Economic Review* 75:1 (March 1985) 101–16.
———. "Frames of Reference and the Quality of Life." *American Economic Review* 79:2 (May 1989) 80–85.
Frank, Robert, and Philip Cook. *The Winner-Take-All Society: How More and More Americans Compete for Ever Fewer and Bigger Prizes, Encouraging Economic Waste, Income Inequality, and Impoverished Cultural Life.* New York: Free Press, 1995.
Frankfurt, Harry G. *The Importance of What We Care About: Philosophical Essays.* Cambridge, UK: Cambridge University Press, 1988.
Friedman, Milton. *A Theory of the Consumption Function.* Princeton: Princeton University Press, 1957.
Friedman, Thomas L. *The Lexus and the Olive Tree.* New York: Farrar, Straus & Giroux, 1999.
Fromm, Erich. *The Sane Society.* New York: Rinehart, 1955.
Fullerton, Howard N., Jr. "Labor Force Participation: 75 Years of Change, 1950–98 and 1998–2025." *Monthly Labor Review* 122:12 (December 1999): 3–12. Online: http://www.bls.gov/opub/mlr/1999/12/art1full.pdf.
Galbraith, John Kenneth. *The Affluent Society*, 3rd ed. New York: Houghton Mifflin, 1976.
———. *The Culture of Contentment.* Boston: Houghton Mifflin, 1992.
———. "Economics as a System of Belief." *American Economic Review* 60:2 (May 1970) 469–78.
———. *The Good Society: The Humane Agenda.* Boston: Houghton Mifflin, 1996.
———. *The New Industrial State.* Boston: Houghton Mifflin, 1967.

Bibliography

———. "Time and the New Industrial State." *American Economic Review* 78:2 (May 1988) 373–6.

Gilkey, Langdon. "The Religious Situation at the End of the Twentieth Century." In *Religion in the New Millennium: Theology in the Spirit of Paul Tillich*, edited by Raymond F. Bulman and Frederick J. Parella, 7–18. Macon, GA: Mercer University Press, 2001.

Goffman, Erving. *The Presentation of Self in Everyday Life*. New York: Doubleday, 1956.

———. "Symbols of Class Status." *British Journal of Sociology* 2:4 (Dec. 1951) 294–304.

Gronow, Jukka. "What is 'Good Taste'?" *Social Science Information* 32:2 (June 1993) 279–301.

Gustafson, James. *Intersections: Science, Theology, and Ethics*. Cleveland: Pilgrim, 1996.

Habermas, Jürgen. *Moral Consciousness and Communicative Action*. Translated by Christian Lenhardt and Shierry Weber Nicholsen. Cambridge, MA: MIT Press, 1999.

Hicks, Douglas A. *Inequality and Christian Ethics*. Cambridge, UK: Cambridge University Press, 2000.

Hirsch, Fred. *Social Limits to Growth*. London: Routledge, 1976.

Hodgson, Geoffrey M. "The Hidden Persuaders: Institutions and Individuals in Economic Theory." *Cambridge Journal of Economics* 27:2 (March 2003) 159–75.

Holbrook, Morris B., and Elizabeth C. Hirschman. *The Semiotics of Consumption: Interpreting Symbolic Consumer Behavior in Popular Culture and Works of Art*. Berlin: Gruyter, 1993.

Horkheimer, Max, and Theodor W. Adorno. *Dialectic of Enlightenment*. Translated by John Cumming. New York: Continuum, 1997.

Hunt, James M., Jerome B. Kernan, and Deborah J. Mitchell. "Materialism as Social Cognition: People, Possessions, and Perception." *Journal of Consumer Psychology* 5:1 (1996) 65–83.

Huntington, Samuel P. *The Clash of Civilizations and the Remaking of World Order*. New York: Touchstone, 1997.

John Paul II. "Address of John Paul II to the Bishops of Japan on their Ad Limina Visit." Vatican City, March 31, 2001. Online: http://www.vatican.va/holy_father/john_paul_ii/speeches/2001/documents/hf_jp-ii_spe_20010331_japan-ad-limina_en.html.

———. "Address of John Paul II to the Bishops of the Episcopal Conference Of Italy." Vatican City, May 20, 1999. Online: http://www.vatican.va/holy_father/john_paul_ii/speeches/1999/may/documents/hf_jp-ii_spe_19990520_ad-limina-italia_en.html.

———. "Address of John Paul II to the New Ambassador of the United Kingdom to the Holy See." Vatican City, September 7, 2002. No pages. Online: http://www.vatican.va/holy_father/john_paul_ii/speeches/2002/september/documents/hf_jp-ii_spe_20020907_ambassador-great-britain_en.html.

———. "Address of John Paul II to the Sixth Public Session of the Pontifical Academies of Theology and of St Thomas Aquinas." Vatican City, November 8, 2001. Online: http://www.vatican.va/holy_father/john_paul_ii/speeches/2001/november/documents/hf_jp-ii_spe_20011108_pontificie-accademie_en.html.

———. "Address of John Paul II to the Tribunal of the Roman Rota." Vatican City, January 28, 1991. Online: http://www.vatican.va/holy_father/john_paul_ii/speeches/1991/documents/hf_jp-ii_spe_19910128_roman-rota_en.html.

———. "Address of Pope John Paul II to H.E. Mr. Margus Laidre, Ambassador of Estonia to the Holy See." Vatican City, January 11, 1997. No pages. Online: http://www.vatican.va/holy_father/john_paul_ii/speeches/1997/january/documents/hf_jp-ii_spe_19970111_ambassador-estonia_en.html.

---. "Address of Pope John Paul II to the Bishops Of Angola and São Tomé on their Ad Limina Apostolorum Visit." Vatican City, May 27, 1997. Online: http://www.vatican.va/holy_father/john_paul_ii/speeches/1997/may/documents/hf_jp-ii_spe_19970527_ad-limina-angola_en.html.

---. *Centesimus Annus*. Encyclical letter, Vatican City, May 1, 1991. Online: http://www.vatican.va/holy_father/john_paul_ii/encyclicals/documents/hf_jp-ii_enc_01051991_centesimus-annus_en.html.

---. *Dilecti Amici*. Apostolic letter, Vatican City, March 31, 1985. Online: http://www.vatican.va/holy_father/john_paul_ii/apost_letters/documents/hf_jp-ii_apl_31031985_dilecti-amici_en.html.

---. *Ecclesia in Oceania*. Post-synodal apostolic exhortation, Vatican City, November 22, 2001. Online: http://www.vatican.va/holy_father/john_paul_ii/apost_exhortations/documents/hf_jp-ii_exh_20011122_ecclesia-in-oceania_en.html.

---. *Evangelium Vitae*. Encyclical letter, Vatican City, March 25, 1995. Online: http://www.vatican.va/holy_father/john_paul_ii/encyclicals/documents/hf_jp-ii_enc_25031995_evangelium-vitae_en.html.

---. "The Holy Father's Message for World Mission Sunday 1998." Vatican City, May 31, 1998. Online: http://www.vatican.va/holy_father/john_paul_ii/messages/missions/documents/hf_jp-ii_mes_31051998_world-day-for-missions-1998_en.html.

---. "Jubilee of the Agricultural World: Address of John Paul II." Vatican City, November 11, 2000. Online: http://www.vatican.va/holy_father/john_paul_ii/speeches/2000/oct-dec/documents/hf_jp-ii_spe_20001111_jubilagric_en.html.

---. "Letter to Families from Pope John Paul II." Vatican City, February 2, 1994. Online: http://www.vatican.va/holy_father/john_paul_ii/letters/documents/hf_jp-ii_let_02021994_families_en.html.

---. *Memory and Identity: Conversations at the Dawn of a New Millennium*. Translated by Theresa Sandok. New York: Rizzoli, 2005.

---. "Message for the XXVII World Day of Peace." Vatican City, December 8, 1993. Online: http://www.vatican.va/holy_father/john_paul_ii/messages/peace/documents/hf_jp-ii_mes_08121993_xxvii-world-day-for-peace_en.html.

---. "Message of His Holiness Pope John Paul II for the Celebration of the World Day of Peace." Vatican City, December 8, 1989. Online: http://www.vatican.va/holy_father/john_paul_ii/messages/peace/documents/hf_jp-ii_mes_19891208_xxiii-world-day-for-peace_en.html.

---. *Pastores Dabo Vobis*. Post-synodal apostolic exhortation, Vatican City, March 25, 1992. Online: http://www.vatican.va/holy_father/john_paul_ii/apost_exhortations/documents/ hf_jp-ii_exh_25031992_pastores-dabo-vobis_en.html.

---. "The Problem of the Constitution of Culture through Human Praxis." In *Person and Community: Selected Essays*, translated by Theresa Sandok, 263–78. New York: Peter Lang, 1993.

---. *Reconciliation and Penance*. Post-synodal apostolic exhortation, Vatican City, December 2, 1984. Online: http://www.vatican.va/holy_father/john_paul_ii/apost_exhortations/documents/hf_jp-ii_exh_02121984_reconciliatio-et-paenitentia_en.html.

---. *Redemptoris Missio*. Encyclical letter, Vatican City, December 7, 1990. Online: http://www.vatican.va/holy_father/john_paul_ii/encyclicals/documents/hf_jp-ii_enc_07121990_redemptoris-missio_en.html.

---. *Sollicitudo Rei Socialis*. Encyclical letter, Vatican City, December 30, 1987. Online: http://www.vatican.va/holy_father/john_paul_ii/encyclicals/documents/hf_jp-ii_enc_30121987_sollicitudo-rei-socialis_en.html.

Bibliography

———. "Thomistic Personalism." In *Person and Community: Selected Essays*, translated by Theresa Sandok, 165–76. New York: Peter Lang, 1993.

———. *Veritatis Splendor*. Encyclical letter, Vatican City, August 6, 1993. Online: http://www.vatican.va/holy_father/john_paul_ii/encyclicals/documents/hf_jp-ii_enc_06081993_veritatis-splendor_en.html#$1L.

Johnston, Lucy. "Behavioral Mimicry and Stigmatization." *Social Cognition* 20:1 (February 2002) 18–35.

Kahneman, Daniel. "A Perspective on Judgment and Choice: Mapping Bounded Rationality." *American Psychologist* 58:9 (September 2003) 697–720.

Kant, Immanuel. *Groundwork of the Metaphysics of Morals*. Translated by H. J. Paton. New York: Harper & Row, 1964.

Kasser, Tim. "The Good Life or the Goods Life? Positive Psychology and Personal Well-Being in the Culture of Consumption." In *Positive Psychology in Practice*, edited by P. Alex Linley and Stephen Joseph, 55–67. Hoboken, NJ: Wiley, 2004.

———. *The High Price of Materialism*. Cambridge, MA: MIT Press, 2002.

Kasser, Tim, et al. "Materialistic Values: Their Causes and Consequences." In *Psychology and Consumer Culture: The Struggle for a Good Life in a Materialistic World*, edited by Tim Kasser and Allen D. Kanner, 11–28. Washington, DC: American Psychological Association, 2004.

Kawakami, Kerry, John F. Dovidio, and Ap Dijksterhuis. "Effects of Social Category Priming on Personal Attitudes." *Psychological Science* 14:4 (July 2003) 315–19.

Kennickell, Arthur B. *The Role of Over-Sampling of the Wealthy in the Survey of Consumer Finances*. U.S. Federal Reserve Board, March 28, 2008. No pages. Online: http://www.federalreserve.gov/pubs/oss/oss2/papers/isi2007/index.html.

Keynes, John Maynard. "Economic Possibilities for Our Grandchildren." In *Essays in Persuasion*, 358–73. New York: Norton, 1963.

Kierkegaard, Søren. *The Concept of Anxiety*. Edited and translated by Reidar Thomte and Albert B. Anderson. Princeton: Princeton University Press, 1980.

———. *The Sickness Unto Death*. Edited and translated by Howard V. Hong and Edna H. Hong. Princeton: Princeton University Press, 1980.

Lane, Robert E. "The Road Not Taken: Friendship, Consumerism, and Happiness." In *Ethics of Consumption: The Good Life, Justice, and Global Stewardship*, edited by David A. Crocker and Toby Linden, 218–48. Lanham, MD: Rowman & Littlefield, 1998.

Lash, Scott, and John Urry. *Economies of Sign and Space*. London: Sage, 1994.

Leiss, William, Stephen Kline, and Sut Jhally. *Social Communication in Advertising: Persons, Products, and Images of Well-Being*. New York: Macmillan, 1986.

Levinson, Sanford. *Constitutional Faith*. Princeton: Princeton University Press, 1988.

Levitt, Theodore. "The Morality (?) of Advertising." *Harvard Business Review* 48:4 (July-August 1970) 84–92.

Levy, Sidney J. "Symbols for Sale." *Harvard Business Review* 37:4 (July-August 1959) 117–24.

Luther, Martin. "The Bondage of the Will." In *Luther's Works*, vol. 33, edited and translated by Philip S. Watson, 15–295. Philadelphia: Fortress, 1972.

———. "Heidelberg Disputation." In *Luther's Works*, vol. 31, edited by Harold J. Grimm, 39–69. Philadelphia: Fortress, 1957.

———. "Lectures on Galatians." In *Luther's Works*, vol. 26, edited and translated by Jaroslav Pelikan, 3–461. St. Louis: Concordia, 1963.

———. "Lectures on Romans." In *Luther's Works*, vol. 25, edited by Hilton C. Oswald, translated by Walter G. Tillmanns and Jacob A. O. Preus, 3–524. St. Louis: Concordia, 1972.

———. "Smalcald Articles." In *The Book of Concord: The Confessions of the Evangelical Lutheran Church*, 2nd ed., edited by Robert Kolb and Timothy J. Wengert, 297–328. Minneapolis: Fortress, 2000.

Luttmer, Erzo F. P. "Neighbors as Negatives: Relative Earnings and Well-Being." National Bureau of Economic Research Working Paper 10667, Cambridge, MA, August 2004.

Malthus, Thomas. *An Essay on the Principle of Population.* 1798. Reprint, Amherst, NY: Prometheus, 1998.

Marcuse, Herbert. *One Dimensional Man: Studies in the Ideology of Advanced Industrial Society.* Boston: Beacon, 1964.

Marshall, Gordon. "The Culture of Capitalism." *Work, Employment & Society* 2:2 (June 1988) 247–60.

McCracken, Grant. *Culture and Consumption: New Approaches to the Symbolic Character of Consumer Goods and Activities.* Bloomington: Indiana University Press, 1988.

———. *Culture And Consumption II: Markets, Meaning, And Brand Management.* Bloomington: Indiana University Press, 2005.

Meadows, Donella H., et al. *The Limits to Growth: A Report for the Club of Rome's Project on the Predicament of Mankind.* New York: Universe, 1972.

Mick, David Glen. "Are Studies of Dark Side Variables Confounded by Socially Desirable Responding? The Case of Materialism." *Journal of Consumer Research* 23:2 (September 1996) 106–19.

———. "Consumer Research and Semiotics: Exploring the Morphology of Signs, Symbols, and Significance." *Journal of Consumer Research* 13:2 (September 1986) 196–213.

Miles, Steven, Kevin Meethan, and Alison Anderson. "Introduction: The Meaning of Consumption; the Meaning of Change?" In *The Changing Consumer: Markets and Meanings*, edited by Steven Miles, Alison Anderson, and Kevin Meethan, 1–9. London: Routledge, 2002.

Miller, Vincent J. *Consuming Religion: Christian Faith and Practice in a Consumer Culture.* New York, Continuum, 2005.

Munier, Francis and Zhao Wang. "Consumer Sovereign and Consumption Routine: A Reexamination of the Galbraithian Concept of the Dependence Effect." *Journal of Post Keynesian Economics* 28:1 (Fall 2005) 65–82.

National Opinion Research Center. General Social Surveys. No pages. Online: http://publicdata.norc.org/webview/.

Nelson, Robert H. *Economics as Religion: From Samuelson to Chicago and Beyond.* University Park: Pennsylvania State University Press, 2001.

Niebuhr, H. Richard. "Translator's Preface." In *The Religious Situation*, by Paul Tillich, translated by H. Richard Niebuhr, vii–xxv. New York: Holt, 1932.

Nord, Walter R., and J. Paul Peter. "A Behavior Modification Perspective on Marketing." *Journal of Marketing* 44:2 (Spring 1980) 36–47.

North, Adrian C., David J. Hargreaves, and Jennifer McKendrick. "In-store Music Affects Product Choice." *Nature* 390:6656 (November 13, 1997) 132.

Ogden, Charles K., and Ivor A. Richards. *The Meaning of Meaning: A Study of the Influence of Language Upon Thought and of the Science of Symbolism.* San Diego: Harcourt Brace Jovanovich, 1989.

Bibliography

Oppenheimer, Paul. *Infinite Desire: A Guide to Modern Guilt*. Lanham, MD: Madison, 2001.

Palmer, Michael. "Paul Tillich's Theology of Culture." In *Paul Tillich: Main Works*, vol. 2, *Paul Tillich: Writings in the Philosophy of Culture*, by Paul Tillich, 1–31. Berlin: De Gruyter-Evangelisches Verlagswerk, 1990.

Peirce, Charles Sanders. *Collected Papers*. Vol. 5. Edited by Charles Hartshorne and Paul Weiss. Cambridge, MA: Harvard University Press, 1934.

Postrel, Virginia. *The Substance of Style: How the Rise of Aesthetic Value Is Remaking Commerce, Culture and Consciousness*. New York: HarperCollins, 2003.

Putnam, Robert. *Bowling Alone: The Collapse and Revival of American Community*. New York: Simon & Schuster, 2000.

———. *Making Democracy Work: Civic Traditions in Modern Italy*. Princeton: Princeton University Press, 1993.

Rank, Otto. *Art and Artist: Creative Urge and Personality Development*. New York: Tudor, 1932.

———. *Will Therapy: An Analysis of the Therapeutic Process in Terms of Relationship*. Translated by Jesse Taft. New York: Knopf, 1936.

Rawls, John. *A Theory of Justice*. Revised edition. Cambridge, MA: Belknap, 1999.

Reich, Robert. *The Work of Nations: Preparing Ourselves for 21st-Century Capitalism*. New York: Vintage, 1992.

Richins, Marsha, and Scott Dawson. "A Consumer Values Orientation for Materialism and its Measurement: Scale Development and Validation." *Journal of Consumer Research* 19:3 (December 1992) 303–16.

Rittenhouse, Bruce P. "Assessing the Developing World's Relationship with Global Governance Institutions in View of Paul Tillich's Proposals for Justice and Peace in an Economically Integrated World." *Bulletin of the North American Paul Tillich Society* 34:2 (Spring 2008) 38–48.

Roof, Wade Clark, and William McKinney. *American Mainline Religion: Its Changing Shape and Future*. New Brunswick, NJ: Rutgers University Press, 1987.

Rothenburg, Jerome. "Consumers' Sovereignty Revisited and the Hospitality of Freedom of Choice." *American Economic Review* 52:2 (May 1962) 269–83.

Samuelson, Paul, and William D. Nordhaus. *Economics*. 17th ed. New York: McGraw-Hill, 2001.

Saussure, Ferdinand de. *Course in General Linguistics*. Translated by Wade Baskin. New York: McGraw-Hill, 1966.

Schor, Juliet B. "The New Politics of Consumption." In *Do Americans Shop Too Much?*, edited by Joshua Cohen and Joel Rodgers, 3–33. Boston: Beacon, 2000.

———. *The Overspent American: Why We Want What We Don't Need*. New York: Basic, 1998.

———. *The Overworked American: The Unexpected Decline of Leisure*. New York: Basic, 1991.

Sciotovsky, Tibor. *Papers on Welfare and Growth*. London: Allen & Unwin, 1964.

Sedgwick, Peter H. *The Market Economy and Christian Ethics*. Cambridge, UK: Cambridge University Press, 1999.

Sen, Amartya K. "Poor, Relatively Speaking." *Oxford Economic Papers* 35:2 (July 1983) 153–69.

Sennett, Richard. *The Corrosion of Character: The Personal Consequences of Work in the New Capitalism*. New York: Norton, 1998.

———. *The Culture of the New Capitalism.* New Haven: Yale University Press, 2006.
Simmel, Georg. "Fashion." *International Quarterly* 10 (Oct. 1904) 130–55.
Simon, Julian L., and Johan Arndt. "The Shape of the Advertising Response Function." *Journal of Advertising Research* 20:4 (August 1980) 11–28.
Soetevent, Adriaan R. "Empirics of the Identification of Social Interactions: An Evaluation of the Approaches and Their Results." *Journal of Economic Surveys* 20:2 (April 2006) 193–228.
Solnick, Sara J., and David Hemenway. "Is More Always Better? A Survey of Positional Concerns." *Journal of Economic Behavior and Organization* 37:3 (November 1988) 373–83.
Solomon, Sheldon, Jeffrey L. Greenberg, and Thomas A. Pyszczynski. "Lethal Consumption: Death-Denying Materialism." In *Psychology and Consumer Culture: The Struggle for a Good Life in a Materialistic World*, edited by Tim Kasser and Allen D. Kanner, 127–46. Washington, DC: American Psychological Association, 2004.
Sombart, Werner. *Luxury and Capitalism.* Translated by W. R. Dittmar. 1913. Reprinted with an introduction by Philip Siegelman. Ann Arbor: University of Michigan Press, 1967.
Stanovich, Keith E., and Richard F. West. "Individual Differences in Reasoning: Implications for the Rationality Debate?" *Behavioral and Brain Sciences* 23:5 (October 2000) 645–726.
Stevenson, Betsey, and Justin Wolfers. "Economic Growth and Subjective Well-Being: Reassessing the Easterlin Paradox." *Brookings Papers on Economic Activity* (Spring 2008) 1–87.
———. "The Paradox of Declining Female Happiness." *American Economic Journal: Economic Policy* 1:2 (August 2009) 190–225.
Stiglitz, Joseph E. *Globalization and Its Discontents.* New York: Norton, 2002.
Stone, G. P. "Appearance and the Self." In *Human Behavior and Social Processes: An Interactionist Approach*, edited by Arnold M. Rose, 86–118. London: Routledge, 1962.
Taylor, Mark C. *Confidence Games: Money and Markets in a World Without Redemption.* Chicago: University of Chicago Press, 2004.
Tellis, Gerard J. "Advertising Exposure, Loyalty, and Brand Purchase: A Two-Stage Model of Choice." *Journal of Marketing Research* 25:2 (May 1988) 134–44.
Tellis, Gerard J., and Doyle L. Weiss. "Does TV Advertising Really Affect Sales? The Role of Measures, Models, and Data Aggregation." *Journal of Advertising* 24:3 (Fall 1995) 1–12.
Tillich, Paul. "Aspects of a Religious Analysis of Culture." In *Theology of Culture*, edited by Robert C. Kimball, 40–51. Oxford: Oxford University Press, 1959.
———. *Christianity and the Encounter of World Religions.* Minneapolis: Fortress, 1963.
———. "Church and Culture." In *The Interpretation of History*, translated by Elsa L. Talmey, 219–41. New York: Scribner's, 1936.
———. *The Courage to Be.* New Haven: Yale University Press, 1952.
———. "Das Dämonische, ein Beitrag zur Sinndeutung der Geschichte." In *Gesammelte Werke*, vol. 6, *Die Widerstreit von Raum und Zeit: Schriften zur Geschichtsphilosophie*, 42–71. Stuttgart: Evangelisches Verlagswerk, 1963.
———. "The Decline and the Validity of the Idea of Progress." In *The Spiritual Situation in Our Technical Society*, edited by J. Mark Thomas, 83–95. Macon, GA: Mercer University Press, 1988.

Bibliography

———. "The Demonic: A Contribution to the Interpretation of History." In *The Interpretation of History*, translated by Elsa L. Talmey, 77-122. New York: Scribner's, 1936.

———. *Dynamics of Faith*. New York: Harper & Row, 1957.

———. "The End of the Protestant Era?" In *The Protestant Era*, 222-33. Chicago: University of Chicago Press, 1948.

———. "How Has Science in the Last Century Changed Man's View of Himself?" In *The Spiritual Situation in Our Technical Society*, edited by J. Mark Thomas, 77-82. Macon, GA: Mercer University Press, 1988.

———. "The Lost Dimension in Religion." In *The Spiritual Situation in Our Technical Society*, edited by J. Mark Thomas, 41-48. Macon, GA: Mercer University Press, 1988.

———. *Morality and Beyond*. Louisville: Westminster John Knox, 1963.

———. "On the Boundary." In *The Interpretation of History*, translated by N. A. Rasetzki, 3-73. New York: Scribner's, 1936.

———. "On the Idea of a Theology of Culture." In *Visionary Science: A Translation of Tillich's "On the Idea of a Theology of Culture" with an Interpretive Essay*, edited by Victor Nuovo, 19-39. Detroit: Wayne State University Press, 1987.

———. "Paul Tillich in Conversation: Culture and Religion." *Foundations* 14:1 (Jan.-Mar., 1971) 6-17.

———. "The Present Theological Situation in the Light of the Continental European Development." *Theology Today* 6:3 (Oct. 1949) 299-310.

———. "Realism and Faith." In *The Protestant Era*, translated by James Luther Adams, 66-82. Chicago: University of Chicago Press, 1948.

———. "The Relationship Today between Science and Religion." In *The Spiritual Situation in Our Technical Society*, edited by J. Mark Thomas, 151-58. Macon, GA: Mercer University Press, 1988.

———. "Religion and Secular Culture." In *The Protestant Era*, translated by James Luther Adams, 55-65. Chicago: University of Chicago Press, 1948.

———. "Die Religiöse Lage der Gegenwart." In *Gesammelte Werke*, vol. 10, *Die Religiöse Deutung der Gegenwart: Schriften zur Zeitkritik*, 21-93. Stuttgart: Evangelisches Verlagswerk, 1968.

———. *The Religious Situation*. Translated by H. Richard Niebuhr. New York: Holt, 1932.

———. "The Religious Situation in Germany Today." *Religion in Life* 47:3 (Autumn 1978) 361-70.

———. "Spiritual Problems of Postwar Reconstruction." In *The Protestant Era*, 261-69. Chicago: University of Chicago Press, 1948.

———. "Storms of Our Times." In *The Protestant Era*, 237-52. Chicago: University of Chicago Press, 1948.

———. *The System of the Sciences According to Objects and Methods*. Translated by Paul Wiebe. Lewisburg, PA: Bucknell University Press, 1981.

———. *Systematic Theology*. 3 vols. Chicago: University of Chicago Press, 1951-63.

Tilman, Rick. *The Intellectual Legacy of Thorstein Veblen: Unresolved Issues*. Westport, CT: Greenwood, 1996.

Tversky, Amos, and Dale Griffen. "Endowment and Contrast in Judgments of Well-Being." In *Strategy and Choice*, edited by R.J. Zeckhauser, 297-319. Cambridge, MA: MIT Press, 1991.

Bibliography

United Nations Secretariat, Department of Economic and Social Affairs, Population Division. *The World Population Prospects: The 2004 Revision*. New York: United Nations, 2005. Online: http://www.un.org/esa/population/publications/WPP2004/2004EnglishES.pdf.

U.S. Census Bureau. Current Population Survey, Annual Social and Economic Supplements, Historical Income Tables—Families. No pages. Online: http://www.census.gov/hhes/www/income/histinc/h04.html.

U.S. Department of Commerce. Bureau of Economic Analysis. *Concepts and Methods of the U.S. National Income and Product Accounts*. Washington, DC, July 2008. Online: http://www.bea.gov/national/pdf/NIPAhandbookch1-4.pdf.

———. National Income and Product Accounts, Selected NIPA Tables. No pages. Online: http://www.bea.gov/national/nipaweb/SelectTable.asp?Selected=Y.

U.S. Department of Labor. Bureau of Labor Statistics. Consumer Expenditures Survey, CE Database. No pages. Online: http://www.bls.gov/cex/data.htm.

———. Consumer Price Index: All Urban Consumers (CPI-U). No pages. Online: ftp://ftp.bls.gov/pub/special.requests/cpi/cpiai.txt.

———. Labor Force Statistics from the Current Population Survey. No pages. Online: http://www.bls.gov/cps/tables.htm#empstat.

U.S. Federal Reserve Board. Survey of Consumer Finances. No pages. Online: http://www.federalreserve.gov/pubs/oss/oss2/scfindex.html.

Vakratsas, Demetrios, and Tim Ambler. "How Advertising Works: What Do We Really Know?" *Journal of Marketing* 63 (January 1999) 26–43.

Veblen, Thorstein. *Absentee Ownership and Business Enterprise in Recent Times: The Case of America*. Reprinted with an introduction by Marion J. Levy, Jr. New Brunswick, NJ: Transaction, 1997.

———. "The Economic Theory of Woman's Dress." In *Essays in Our Changing Order*, edited by Leon Ardzrooni, 65–77. New York: Viking, 1945.

———. "The Instinct of Workmanship and the Irksomeness of Labor." In *Essays in Our Changing Order*, edited by Leon Ardzrooni, 78–96. New York: Viking, 1945.

———. *The Instinct of Workmanship and the State of the Industrial Arts*. New York: Macmillan, 1914.

———. "Mr. Cummings's Strictures on 'The Theory of the Leisure Class.'" In *Essays in Our Changing Order*, edited by Leon Ardzrooni, 16–31. New York: Viking, 1945.

———. *The Theory of Business Enterprise*. Reprinted with an introduction by Douglas Dowd. New Brunswick, NJ: Transaction, 1978.

———. *The Theory of the Leisure Class: An Economic Study of Institutions*. Reprinted with an introduction by C. Wright Mills. New York: Mentor, 1953.

Waide, John. "The Making of Self and World in Advertising." *Journal of Business Ethics* 6:2 (February 1987) 73–79.

Warren, Elizabeth, and Amelia Warren Tyagi. *The Two-Income Trap: Why Middle-Class Mothers and Fathers Are Going Broke*. New York: Basic, 2003.

Weber, Max. *The Protestant Ethic and the Spirit of Capitalism*. 2nd ed. Translated by Talcott Parsons. Los Angeles: Roxbury, 1998.

Whybrow, Peter C. *American Mania: When More Is Not Enough*. New York: Norton, 2005.

Whyte, William H., Jr. *The Organization Man*. New York: Simon & Schuster, 1956.

World Trade Organization, "Members and Observers." No pages. Online: http://www.wto.org/english/thewto_e/whatis_e/tif_e/org6_e.htm.

Bibliography

Wuthnow, Robert. *After Heaven: Spirituality in America Since the 1950s.* Berkeley: University of California Press, 1998.

———. *God and Mammon in America.* New York: Free Press, 1994.

Index

Adler, Alfred, 144, 146, 154–55, 160, 168
Adorno, Theodor, 67–68, 74–75
advertising, 15, 45, 52, 55–56, 67–68, 71–72, 75, 77, 81–82, 86, 90, 110, 139–45, 150, 158, 173
    effectiveness, 124–25, 131, 159
affluence, 19, 23, 51, 56, 64, 68, 70–71, 75, 84, 97, 113, 116
    ideology of, 68, 74
affluent society, 32, 51, 68, 70–71, 74–75, 116
Alpizar, Francisco, 118–19
ambiguity, 19, 21–22, 167, 170, 175
Ambler, Tim, 124
Anderson, Alison, 144
anthropology, 2, 20, 35, 53, 79, 95
anxiety, existential. See existential anxiety
Aquinas, Thomas, 50–51
Ariely, Dan, 122
Arndt, Johan, 125
Askegaard, Søren, 141
assets, 32, 103–9
Augustine, 4, 50–51, 168, 171
autonomy, 7, 27, 33, 39, 79–80, 83, 114, 119, 124, 160
avarice, 51

Baker, William, 142
Bargh, John, 120, 122–23, 140
Baudrillard, Jean, 67–68, 75–77, 119
Baumeister, Roy, 121
Becker, Ernest, 139, 145–48, 150–57, 160, 164, 166

Belk, Russell, 9, 140, 147
Bell, Daniel, 49, 55–56
bondage of the will, 15, 167–68, 171
Boss, Shira, 57, 67
Bourdieu, Pierre, 57, 65, 77
Boyle, Nicholas, 25, 32, 34–35, 44–45
Browning, Don, 30
business cycle, 96, 103, 105, 113

Calvinism, 79, 82
Campbell, Colin, 2, 14, 48, 77–86, 89, 95, 109
capitalism, 19, 22–23, 33, 50, 76
    corporate, 68
    industrial, 27, 44, 54, 61, 69, 84
    late, 74
    network, 33, 39, 44
capitalist culture, 19
Carlsson, Fredrik, 117, 119
Cavanaugh, William, 48
Chartrand, Tanya, 120, 122–23, 140
children, 7, 15, 30–31, 89–90, 124, 126–27, 131, 179–83
    concern for. See parental concern
Christ, 3, 53, 161–67, 169–71, 175
Christian
    ethics. See theological ethics
    faith. See existential faith
    theology. See theology
church, 16, 19, 30, 39–40, 43, 45, 48, 167, 175–77
clash of civilizations, 9
class, 15, 41, 56–57, 60–62, 64–68, 70, 72, 76, 82, 87–90, 95–96,

Index

class (*cont.*) 103–11, 115, 128–31, 157–58, 173, 184–89
  leisure. *See* leisure class
  mobility, 113
climate change, 176
Cohen, Jacob, 6
Cohen, Patricia, 6
common good, 53, 73, 84, 95
community, 12, 22, 30, 33, 60, 97, 117, 138, 165–66
  Christian, 162, 167, 170, 177
  loss of, 23, 31, 39, 44, 56, 66, 140
concupiscence, 53
conditioning
  operant, 142–43
  respondent, 142
consumerism, 2–5, 7–9, 16, 41, 44–49, 51–52, 54–58, 64, 66, 68, 71, 74–78, 81–82, 84, 86–87, 92–93, 96–97, 100–101, 110–13, 115, 124, 127, 131–33, 138–39, 146–47, 159, 172–76
  existential-religious, 3, 11, 16, 19, 32, 36, 38, 132, 146–47, 151–52, 155, 157–58, 161, 164, 166, 168, 170–77
  historical emergence, 36, 57, 66, 76–78, 101–2, 109, 130–31, 157, 173–74
  moral harms, 5–9, 171–72, 175–76
  motivation, 1–2, 11, 13–15, 48, 51, 53, 57–58, 65, 67, 76, 85, 87, 90, 96, 131, 173
  new, 66
  prevalence, 3, 50, 157, 173, 175
  religious problem, 9–10, 174–75
  Western, 3, 78, 82, 96, 130, 172
consumeristic culture, 3, 10, 16, 41, 51–52, 132, 138, 143–45, 147, 173
consumption, 2–3, 5, 9, 14, 32, 36, 39, 41, 50, 60, 68, 70, 75–76, 84, 95–96, 100, 103, 108–11, 113, 131, 176
  conspicuous, 57–67
  ideology of, 51, 68
  insatiable, 2, 65–66, 70, 72, 75–76, 97
  modern, 77–78, 80–84, 86
  norm, 59–60, 65–66, 87, 114
  vicarious, 62, 64, 66, 90
convention, social. *See* social convention
conviction of sin, 15, 174
corporation, 69, 71–75, 95, 140–41, 145
correlation, 132–33, 168–70
covetousness, 50–51
culture, 12, 59, 63, 83, 93, 135–36, 138–39, 154, 162, 177
  Christian, 17, 167
  consensus, 40, 97, 139
  consumer. *See* consumeristic culture
  of solidarity, 53
  of waste, 53
  pluralistic, 155, 160–61
  postmodern, 83
  theology. *See* theology of culture
  Western, 17–18, 96, 138–41, 143–44, 157, 172, 174, 176
Cushman, Philip, 140, 143–44

Dawson, Scott, 6
debt, 56, 66, 102–9, 129
decision, unconscious. *See* unconscious decision
Derrida, Jacques, 44
Diamond, Jared, 3, 18, 24
diminishing marginal utility, 70, 91, 97, 102, 128–29
disposable personal income, 100–101
distinction, 64–65, 76, 144, 159
Dittmar, Helga, 141, 145, 148–49
division of labor, 60, 68

doubt, 134, 136–37, 166–67, 170, 175
Douglas, Mary, 148
Duesenberry, James, 72–73
Dunlap, Thomas, 21, 36–37

Eagleton, Terry, 49, 55–56
Easterlin, Richard, 112, 114
ecological design, 142–43
economic theory, 14, 49, 73, 97, 114
   neoclassical, 68, 70
economy, 8, 23–25, 36–37, 44
   capitalist. *See* capitalism
   global, 8, 26, 29, 38, 41
   industrial, 69
   information, 36
   material, 114, 116
   network, 26–27, 29, 34, 41–45
   positional, 114, 116
education, 66, 70, 73, 87, 89–91, 116
   as positional good, 14, 47, 88–90, 115–16, 119
egoism, 84, 146, 168–69, 172
Emerson, Ralph Waldo, 37
employment, 27–28, 30, 65, 97–99
   full-time, 30, 98–99
   women's, 30, 100
emulation, 58–62, 68, 72, 110, 119
Enlightenment, 3, 18, 68, 74, 79
entertainment industry, 74
environmental sustainability, 4, 8–9, 21, 66, 172
environmentalism, 20, 36–38, 174
epistemology, 93
esteem, social. *See* social esteem
ethics, 94
   theological. *See* theological ethics
evolution, 59–60, 63, 95
existential
   anxiety, 30, 37, 134, 137, 146, 148, 154–55, 158, 161–62, 166–67, 170
   courage, 134, 145, 166
   decision, 11

defense, 137, 146, 148, 155, 158, 163
despair, 39, 132, 134, 137, 139, 154, 161–62, 164, 170–71
estrangement, 134, 158, 160–65, 167–70
failure, 10, 164, 171
faith, 4, 12, 133, 161, 163–71, 174–77
form of life, 3–4, 11, 34, 138–39, 146, 157–58, 165, 170, 173, 175
fragmentation, 170
predicament, 19, 159, 161
meaning, 9–10, 12, 41, 54, 133–34, 143–44, 146–47, 151–52, 155, 158, 160–61, 163–66, 168–71, 173, 176
motivation. *See* motivation, existential
problem of meaning, 4, 15, 20, 63, 132–33, 146, 151, 161, 168–70, 173–74, 176
risk, 137, 167
strategy, 14–16, 28, 32–33, 38, 132–33, 135–39, 144–46, 148, 151–59, 161, 163–65, 167–74, 176–77
validation, 32, 36, 42, 134–36, 147, 151
existentialism, 19, 43–44
   Christian, 44
   philosophical, 43–44, 46, 161, 169

faith, 4, 12, 133, 159, 165
   conversion to, 11, 159, 161–62, 164, 170–71, 174–75, 177
   existential. *See* existential faith
fashion, 64, 80
finitude, 45, 134–35, 137, 155, 159, 161, 167, 176
   self-sufficient, 19
Firat, A. Fuat, 141

Index

framing, 122
Frank, Robert, xi, 114–15, 117, 150
freedom, 51–52, 59, 76, 90, 92,
    159–60, 166–68
  and destiny, 135–36, 158, 160–61
  finite, 161
Fromm, Erich, 146, 168

Galbraith, John Kenneth, 14, 48,
    67–75, 82, 89, 95, 109, 119,
    124–25
Gilkey, Langdon, 23
globalization, 8, 19, 22, 24–26, 29
Goffman, Erving, 149, 152
grace, 11, 162, 164–65, 171, 175
Great Recession, 1, 96
greed, 47, 49–57, 61, 68, 77, 109,
    111, 113, 119, 124, 130–31,
    157
Greenberg, Jeff, 139, 155
Griffen, Dale, 118
Gustafson, James, 93, 95

Habermas, Jürgen, 5
habit, 58–59, 124
habituation, 122
happiness, 5–7, 14–15, 42, 52, 72,
    111–14, 131, 158
hedonism, 51, 53, 55–56, 73, 76,
    80–81, 84, 114, 173
  imaginative. *See* imaginative
    hedonism
Hemenway, David, 119
heteronomy, 33, 160–61
  religious. *See* religion,
    heteronomous
Hirsch, Fred, 114–15, 150
historical validation. *See* validation,
    historical
Horkheimer, Max, 67–68, 74–75
housing, 14–15, 87, 89–91, 108,
    126–31, 179–89
  as positional good, 14, 47, 88–91,
    115–16, 119–20

Hunt, James, 145
hypocrisy, 175

identity, 22, 25, 27, 40–41, 75, 77,
    79, 84, 134, 143–44, 147, 153,
    160
  aspirational, 86
  categorical. *See* identity, social
  Christian, 163
  consumeristic, 145, 147
  fragmented, 4, 22, 42, 44
  imaginary, 47–48, 84–85, 87
  individual, 19, 22, 32–34, 39, 42,
    44, 64, 86, 144, 148–50, 160
  social, 56, 65, 76, 86, 145, 147,
    149–50, 160–61, 164, 166
  subjective, 55, 75, 77, 80–81, 84,
    86
ideology, 93
idolatry, 9, 51, 55, 84, 86, 174–76
imaginative hedonism, 47, 64,
    75–87, 109–11, 113, 119, 124,
    131, 157
income, 6, 14, 32, 65–66, 73, 96–97,
    99–101, 105–6, 110, 113,
    117–18, 127–30
  disposable. *See* disposable personal income
  effect, 102
  inequality. *See* inequality,
    economic
individualism, 53–54
Industrial Revolution, 78
industrialization, 61, 68–69
inequality, economic, 5, 31–32,
    101–2, 113, 116
insatiability. *See* consumption,
    insatiable
insecurity, 29
instinct, 55–56, 58–59, 76
institution
  commercial. *See* corporation
  noncommercial, 140
  social. *See* social institution

Index

intentionality, 135
invidious comparison, 58–59, 61, 63, 65, 67, 73, 110
Isherwood, Baron, 148

Jhally, Sut, 140–42, 148
John Paul II, 2, 14, 48–57, 59, 77, 89, 95, 109
Johnston, Lucy, 122
justice, 4–5, 8, 172
justification, 15, 162, 169–70

Kahneman, Daniel, 121
Kant, Immanuel, 5, 172
Kasser, Tim, 5–8, 139, 145, 147–48
Kawakami, Kerry, 122
Kernan, Jerome, 145
Keynes, John Maynard, 23
Kierkegaard, Søren, 134, 137, 156, 165–66, 175
Kline, Stephen, 140–42, 148

labor force participation, 98–99
   women's, 100, 113
language, 138
Lash, Scott, 147–48
Leiss, William, 140–42, 148
leisure, 73, 78, 96–97, 99, 109, 116
   class, 60–62, 64, 70
   conspicuous, 61–62, 67
   vicarious, 62
Levitt, Theodore, 143–44, 159
Levy, Sidney, 149
liberalization, economic, 113
lifestyle, 18, 36, 38, 40–42, 52, 65, 68
   affinity group, 65
Luther, Martin, 11, 168–69
Luttmer, Erzo, 117–19
luxury, 54–55, 60, 68, 70, 78

Malthus, Thomas, 23
manipulation, 47, 57, 67–77, 86, 109–11, 119, 124–25, 131, 157, 159

Marcuse, Herbert, 67, 75
market segmentation, 63
marketing, 45, 68, 71–72, 75, 110, 131, 140, 143
marriage, 7, 30, 126–27, 179–83
Marxism, 20, 33–35, 37–39, 46, 51
mass media, 63, 68, 72, 74–76, 82, 110, 139–41, 143–44, 158
mass society, 64
materialism, 6–9, 50–51, 55–56
McCracken, Grant, 139, 141, 145, 147–48
meaning, 11, 41, 54, 135, 138–41
   assertion, 65, 77, 134–35, 146–47, 149–50, 152–53, 155, 157–60, 164, 168, 173
   existential. *See* existential meaning
   existential problem of. *See* existential problem of meaning
   ground of, 43–44, 94, 132, 134, 136, 138, 156, 159–60, 162–63, 165, 167–68
   individual. *See* existential meaning
   of goods, 63, 66, 68, 77, 81, 131, 140–42, 144–45
   personal. *See* existential meaning
   positional, 144, 150
   social transmission, 145–46
   strategy. *See* existential strategy
   subjective, 80–81, 153, 168
   system, 12, 94, 134–38, 140–41, 144–46, 151–58, 160, 163–64, 168, 171, 174–77
   ultimate, 11–12, 56, 160, 164
   validation, 134–35, 140, 147, 150–52
meaningful individual life. *See* existential meaning
meaninglessness, 37, 44–45, 52, 133–34, 137, 139, 146, 148, 150, 155–56, 158, 160–62, 165–67, 170–71

Index

Meethan, Kevin, 144
mere exposure, 142
metanoia, 162, 171
metaphor, 142
metaphysical validation. *See* validation, metaphysical
metaphysics, 94
metonymy, 142
Mick, David Glen, 6, 141, 143, 148
Miles, Steven, 144
Miller, Vincent, 48
mimicry, unconscious. *See* unconscious mimicry
Mitchell, Deborah, 145
moral pluralism, 172
morality, 34, 42, 63, 76, 79–80, 83, 85, 134, 162, 167, 170–71
motivation, 1, 14, 47–48, 58, 91
    existential, 132, 134–36, 146, 158–59
    moral, 4, 144, 166, 168–71
    of consumerism. *See* consumerism, motivation
    unconscious. *See* unconscious motivation

narcissism. *See* egoism.
nationalism, 19, 33–34, 37, 39, 45
natural selection, 59
nature, 9, 37, 79, 83
necessity, 49, 87, 89–90, 110, 158, 160–61, 164
Nelson, Robert, xi, 18, 21, 23, 35
New Being, 161–64, 166–67, 170–71
Nord, Walter, 142
North, Adrian, 122
novelty, 77, 80–84, 86

Ogden, Charles, 135, 138–39
ontology, 135, 138, 158
Oppenheimer, Paul, 77, 85–86
original sin, 35, 168–69

parental concern, 14, 47, 87–91, 119–20, 124, 126–27, 131, 157
Pauline-Augustinian-Lutheran tradition, 133, 162, 164, 168
Peirce, Charles Sanders, 141, 152
perception-behavior link, 121–22
Peter, J. Paul, 142
polytheism
    psychological, 42
    situational, 177
positional
    competition, 65, 89–91, 115–20, 131, 158–59
    economy. *See* economy, positional
    good, 57, 65, 88, 114–17, 119, 147, 150, 158–59
    meaning. *See* meaning, positional
positionality, 117–19, 149
postmodernism, 43–46, 86
Postrel, Virginia, 77, 86–87
post-structuralism, 44
poverty, 15, 22, 30, 42, 53, 97, 110, 176
progress
    idea of, 19, 21, 23, 33–34, 83
    ideology of, 75, 84
property, 60–61, 148
Puritanism, 78
Putnam, Robert, 8, 22, 29–31, 34, 100, 140
Pyszczynski, Thomas, 139, 155

Rank, Otto, 151, 154, 160
Rawls, John, 5
recognition
    categorical, 149–50, 158, 173
    individual, 149–50, 158, 162
    intra-group, 149–50
    mutual, 152–53, 164, 173
    social, 3, 42, 76, 135, 147, 149, 152–53, 159, 165–66
reference group, 66, 115–16, 118

Index

reflexivity, 92–93, 134–35, 138, 144, 166–67
relativism, 52, 55
religion, 11, 33, 54, 93, 139, 143, 162, 170, 173–74, 177
   conventional, 165–66, 168, 174–77
   heteronomous, 39–40, 45, 174
   institutional, 39–43
   private, 151
   therapeutic, 42–43
religious
   basic experience, 9–10
   fragmentation. *See* existential fragmentation
   meaning. *See* existential meaning
   pluralism, 34, 155–56, 161, 167
   sphere of culture, 20, 39, 46, 174
Religious Socialism, 19
repentance, 174–75
responsibility, 5, 134
revealed preference, 97
revelation, 11
Richards, Ivor, 135, 138–39
Richins, Marsha, 6
risk, 27, 29, 89, 105–7, 109, 136
   existential. *See* existential risk
Romanticism, 78–81, 83, 95
   consumption ethic, 78, 82–83
Rothenberg, Jerome, 71–72

Saussure, Ferdinand de, 143
savings, 15, 66, 89, 96–97, 102, 109, 116
   rate, 1, 14, 100–102
scapegoating, 155, 176
scarcity, 68, 71, 114, 148–50
Schor, Juliet, 57, 66–67
science, 19–21, 93, 157
   social. *See* social science
Sciotovsky, Tibor, 71–72
secularism, 17–18
secularization, 20, 40, 174
Sedgwick, Peter, 48

self, 134–35, 137–38, 143, 147–50, 153–54, 156, 160, 165–68
   actualization, 5, 7, 162
   affirmation, spiritual, 43, 133–34
   awareness, 4, 6, 154–55, 176–77
   centered, 162, 167
   contradiction, 161, 170
   critique, 176–77
   deception, 6, 154–55, 171, 176
   destruction, 11, 161–62, 164, 167, 170
   differentiation, 64
   esteem, 60, 139, 146, 154–56, 164
   meaningful, 146, 150, 152–53, 158, 164, 173
   reflexive, 135, 148
   symbolic, 147
   transcendence, 156, 162, 164
semiotic
   pluralism, 66–67, 77
   system, 65, 76–77, 138–39, 141, 143, 146–50, 152–53, 158–59, 164, 166
Sen, Amartya, 115
Sennett, Richard, 27–28
sign, 141
   goods as, 3, 37, 56–57, 60, 65–66, 75–77, 86, 141–42, 144, 146–50, 152–53, 158–59, 164, 173
   system. *See* semiotic system
significance. *See* meaning
Simmel, Georg, 57, 64
Simon, Julian, 125
simul justus et peccator, 170, 175
sin, 52, 170, 174
   noetic effect of, 15, 169
   original. *See* original sin
situation
   cultural, 58–59
   religious, 12–13, 17–18, 39, 157
social
   consensus. *See* culture, consensus
   convention, 58–60, 80, 82, 148, 165

Index

social (cont.)
   enforcement, 68, 76, 145
   esteem, 60, 73
   institution, 58–59, 63, 124, 138, 173
   science, 92–95
   trust, 31, 40
   validation. *See* validation, social
socialization, 57, 59, 139, 144–45
Soetevent, Adriaan, 115
solidarity, 53
solipsism, 86
Solnick, Sara, 119
Solomon, Sheldon, 139, 155
Sombart, Werner, 49, 54–56
Stanovich, Keith, 121
status, 57, 60, 66–68, 76, 90–91, 110, 115, 149–50, 158–59
   defense, 65–67, 73
   identity, 76
   seeking, 65–67
   signaling, 47, 57–68, 77, 86, 109–10, 115, 119–20, 124, 131, 149, 157
stereotyping, 122
Stevenson, Betsy, 112–3
stewardship, 53
Stiglitz, Joseph, 24, 26
Stone, G. P., 149
subjectivism, 55, 84–85
substance, 11, 16, 133, 139, 143, 160–61, 174, 177
substitution effect, 102–3
suburbanization, 22, 88
sufficiency, economic, 2–3, 8, 15, 90, 97
symbol, 6, 17, 21, 33, 37, 56, 74, 76, 138, 144, 165
syncretism, 20, 41–43, 174, 176–77
System 1, 121–24
System 2, 121

taste, 65, 147
Taylor, Mark C., 25, 44

technocracy, 69–71
technology, 19–21
Tellis, Gerard, 124–25
theological ethics, 12, 15, 49, 92–95, 157, 177
theological use of the law, 11, 15
theology, 13, 159–60, 162–63, 168, 170, 176
   material norm of, 161
   of culture, 11–13, 139, 143, 170, 177
Tillich, Paul, 2, 4, 9–13, 17, 19–24, 27, 33–35, 39, 43, 92–94, 132–38, 143, 146, 153, 155, 159–62, 164–70, 177
Tversky, Amos, 118
Tyagi, Amelia Warren, 14, 48, 87–91, 95, 109, 115, 120, 126–28, 130–31

ultimate concern, 16, 132–33, 136, 144, 160–61, 174
unconscious
   decision, 120, 131
   evaluation, 123
   goal-oriented activity, 123, 140
   meaning association, 140, 142
   meaning system, 144, 153–56, 158, 169–70
   mimicry, 122
   motivation, 57, 59, 66, 68, 120, 131, 158–59, 169–70, 173
unemployment, 22, 89, 96, 113
Urry, John, 147–48
utility, 73, 88, 91, 116
   absolute, 58, 75, 88, 114, 118
   diminishing marginal. *See* diminishing marginal utility
   function, 114
   material. *See* utility, absolute
   social, 15, 65, 68, 114, 118, 158–59, 173

Vakratsas, Demetrios, 124

validation
    categorical. *See* recognition, categorical
    empirical, 14–15, 82–83, 91–92, 95–96, 119, 130, 132, 157–59, 173
    existential. *See* existential validation
    historical, 135–36, 151, 160, 162, 169
    individual. *See* recognition, individual
    metaphysical, 136, 151, 169, 176
    social, 79–80, 135–37, 147, 150–53, 155–56, 158, 160, 162–64, 168–70, 173, 175–76
Veblen, Thorstein, 2, 14, 48, 57–68, 70, 72–73, 76–78, 82, 90, 95, 109, 115–16, 119–20, 124
vicarious learning, 142–43

Waide, John, 145
Warren, Elizabeth, 14, 48, 87–91, 95, 109, 115, 120, 126–28, 130–31
waste, 61
Weber, Max, 27–28, 78
Weiss, Doyle, 124
West, Richard, 121
Whybrow, Peter, 49, 56–57
will
    bound. *See* bondage of the will
    free, 4
Wolfers, Justin, 112–13
world, 12, 138–39, 161
Wuthnow, Robert, 29, 40–42, 147, 175, 177

www.ingramcontent.com/pod-product-compliance
Lightning Source LLC
Chambersburg PA
CBHW031358230426
43670CB00006B/582